From Zero to AI Hero

How Language Models Are Changing the World

Index

Foreword

In the rapidly evolving field of Artificial Intelligence (AI), large language models have captured the attention of researchers, entrepreneurs, and students alike. Their capacity for human-like text generation and nuanced understanding of language reflects a milestone in computational progress—one that has profound implications for scholarship, industry, and everyday life. Such advancements emerge from an intricate tapestry of discoveries in natural language processing, machine learning, and cognitive science, each contributing to our expanding horizons.

This book, *From Zero to AI Hero: How Language Models Are Changing the World*, aspires to guide readers through a landscape that has evolved at a breathtaking pace. By presenting technical foundations alongside practical insights, we aim to satisfy the intellectual rigor expected at leading institutions such as Harvard or Stanford, while remaining accessible to those new to the field. Each chapter builds on the last, offering an in-depth exploration of the concepts, ethics, and applications that collectively define modern AI.

As you embark on this journey, you will encounter historical breakthroughs, the theoretical underpinnings of machine learning, and the real-world deployments that shape global industries. Whether you are a student charting your academic path, a professional seeking to diversify your skill set, or a policy-maker grappling with regulatory questions, this book offers a balanced perspective on what language models can do—and what they ought to do—for society.

We invite you to join us in this exploration of AI's most transformative corner. May this text serve not only as a comprehensive resource but also as an inspiration to think critically, innovate responsibly, and contribute to the future of human-computer interaction.

Chapter 1: The AI Boom—Why Now?

1.1. The AI Renaissance

1.1.1. A Brief History of AI

Origins and Foundational Concepts

The historical roots of Artificial Intelligence (AI) stretch further back than many realize, with conceptual underpinnings dating to ancient philosophies about mechanized reasoning and automata. However, the field formally began to take shape in the mid-20th century. One pivotal moment was Alan Turing's seminal 1950 paper, *"Computing Machinery and Intelligence"*, which posed the famous question: *"Can machines think?"* (Turing, 1950). While Turing's "Imitation Game" is often referenced in popular culture, it also introduced crucial ideas about symbolic manipulation and the possibility of a machine achieving human-level intelligence.

During this early era, optimism ran high. John McCarthy coined the term "Artificial Intelligence" in 1956 at the Dartmouth Conference, a gathering often considered the official birth of AI as a distinct research area (Nilsson, 2010). The participants, including influential minds such as Marvin Minsky and Claude Shannon, speculated that replicating aspects of human intelligence could be a matter of a few decades' concerted work. Their ambitions, ranging from language understanding to problem-solving in complex domains, set the stage for the next few decades of research.

Symbolic AI and Early Enthusiasm

From the late 1950s through the 1970s, AI research was dominated by symbolic methods—an approach sometimes referred to as "Good Old-Fashioned AI" (GOFAI). Symbolic AI relies on rules, logic, and knowledge bases to solve problems or reason about the world (Russell and Norvig, 2021). Notable projects, such as the Logic Theorist (considered the first AI program), and the General Problem Solver (GPS), sought to model human problem-solving strategies through symbolic manipulation.

Despite initial successes, these early systems lacked the ability to handle real-world complexity. They performed well on constrained problems—like proving geometric theorems or solving puzzles—but struggled with ambiguity, noise, and the huge variety of contexts in which real human intelligence operates (Mitchell, 1997). This shortcoming became apparent as researchers tried to scale up symbolic AI to more nuanced tasks, leading to growing skepticism about whether such methods could ever truly replicate or exceed human-level intelligence.

AI Winters

By the mid-1970s and again in the late 1980s, AI faced prolonged periods referred to as "AI winters." These were characterized by reduced funding, diminished public interest, and a collective sense of disappointment in the technology's inability to meet its lofty promises (Nilsson, 2010). Factors such as the "combinatorial explosion," where the number of logical possibilities grows exponentially, contributed to the stagnation of symbolic methods. Additionally, computational constraints made it difficult to process large amounts of data or run complex algorithms.

It was during these winters, however, that foundational research in areas like machine learning, neural networks, and computational neuroscience quietly continued. The seeds of the next revolution were being planted—researchers like Geoffrey Hinton, Yann LeCun, and Jürgen Schmidhuber explored neural network architectures at a time when enthusiasm for such approaches was far from mainstream (LeCun, Bengio and Hinton, 2015). Their work, although niche, paved the way for the deep learning renaissance that would come decades later.

Bridge **to** **the** **Modern** **Era**
Despite setbacks, the field of AI never truly ceased to progress. Incremental advances in hardware—transitioning from mainframes to personal computers to specialized graphics processing units (GPUs)—kept the hope alive. Simultaneously, developments in statistics and probability theory began to merge with computer science, forming the bedrock of modern machine learning (Jordan and Mitchell, 2015). By the early 2000s, improved algorithms, combined with the exponential increase in data from the internet, established the conditions for AI's next great leap forward.

Key **Takeaway**
The history of AI is marked by cycles of hype and disappointment, but underlying progress in computing hardware, theoretical research, and data availability laid the groundwork for today's powerful systems. Understanding this evolution helps us appreciate the complexity of AI's journey—and the significance of the modern resurgence.

1.1.2. The Data Explosion

The **Rise** **of** **Big** **Data**
One of the crucial factors in AI's modern renaissance is the vast increase in data generation. The term "Big Data" emerged in the early 2000s to describe datasets so large and complex that traditional data-processing software could not effectively handle them (Gandomi and Haider, 2015). The confluence of smartphones, social media platforms, e-commerce, and sensor technologies (from IoT devices) has led to exponential growth in digital data. Estimates suggest that by the mid-2020s, the global datasphere will reach hundreds of zettabytes—numbers so large that they defy conventional imagination.

Data is the lifeblood of machine learning. Algorithms, particularly deep neural networks, often improve as the size and variety of training data increase. This phenomenon is sometimes referred to as the "unreasonable effectiveness of data," alluding to how simpler models trained on massive datasets can outperform more sophisticated models trained on limited data (Halevy, Norvig and Pereira, 2009).

Quality   vs.   Quantity

While the surge in available data has undoubtedly propelled AI research, it also raises the question of quality. Not all data is created equal: noisy, incomplete, or biased data can lead to unreliable models. For instance, a natural language processing (NLP) system trained primarily on text from one demographic group may fail to generalize well for others, perpetuating biases in applications like hiring or loan approvals (Barocas, Hardt and Narayanan, 2018).

Efforts to address these issues include curated datasets, better data cleaning methodologies, and the introduction of fairness and bias detection tools. These tools not only examine a model's outputs for disparities across demographic groups but also scrutinize the data sources themselves for structural imbalances. Techniques like oversampling underrepresented categories or employing domain adaptation can help mitigate some risks, but the most robust solutions often require interdisciplinary collaboration among statisticians, sociologists, ethicists, and computer scientists.

Data   Governance   and   Regulation

As data's value has soared, so too has concern about its ethical and legal implications. The European Union's General Data Protection Regulation (GDPR) marked a watershed moment for data governance, setting precedents for consent, data portability, and the "right to be forgotten" (European Commission, 2021). Similar regulations in other regions, such as the California Consumer Privacy Act (CCPA), underscore a global movement toward greater data protection and user rights.

For AI researchers and practitioners, these regulations add layers of complexity and responsibility. Secure data handling, anonymization techniques, and transparent data usage policies are now essential for compliance. Furthermore, the concept of "data sovereignty" has gained traction, wherein nations seek to keep data generated within their borders under local regulatory frameworks, influencing how multinational corporations structure their AI projects.

Implications   for   AI   Progress

Abundant data is a double-edged sword: it enables remarkable capabilities but also mandates ethical vigilance, legal compliance, and careful curation. Large-scale datasets—such as those used to train large language models—have propelled new frontiers in NLP, image recognition, and even robotics. At the same time, the complexities around data privacy and governance remind us that technological progress cannot be divorced from societal norms and legal constraints.

Key   Takeaway

The data explosion has been instrumental in AI's ascent, especially for data-intensive algorithms like deep learning. Yet, it introduces critical challenges around bias, ethics, and regulation. Navigating this terrain requires a holistic view of data's role—both as an asset and a responsibility.

1.1.3. The Perfect Storm: Computing Power + Algorithms

Hardware   **Acceleration**

Concurrent with the surge in data, improvements in hardware have helped transform AI from a research curiosity into a practical powerhouse. Graphics Processing Units (GPUs), originally designed for rendering video game graphics, turn out to be highly efficient at the linear algebra operations fundamental to training neural networks (Goodfellow, Bengio and Courville, 2016). Companies like NVIDIA capitalized on this trend, producing GPUs tailored for deep learning tasks. More recently, Google introduced Tensor Processing Units (TPUs), and other hardware vendors followed suit with specialized AI chips, field-programmable gate arrays (FPGAs), and application-specific integrated circuits (ASICs).

This hardware acceleration was pivotal for training models containing billions, or even trillions, of parameters (Brown et al., 2020). Without it, deep learning's computational demands would require impractically long training times, rendering breakthroughs like GPT (Generative Pre-trained Transformer) family models or advanced vision systems unfeasible.

Transformative   **Algorithms**

The other half of this "perfect storm" lies in algorithmic innovation. While neural networks trace their lineage back to the 1940s (McCulloch and Pitts, 1943), the modern surge in interest owes much to "deep learning," which stacks multiple layers of processing units (neurons) to learn hierarchical representations. This enables the model to capture increasingly abstract features at deeper layers—such as edges turning into shapes, which then become object parts, culminating in entire objects at the highest layers of a convolutional neural network for image recognition (LeCun, Bengio and Hinton, 2015).

Among the most groundbreaking developments in recent years is the **transformer architecture**, introduced by Vaswani et al. (2017). By relying on a mechanism called *self-attention*, transformers can process entire sequences of data (e.g., words in a sentence) in parallel, significantly improving speed and performance on NLP tasks. The transformer's design eschewed recurrent or convolutional layers in favor of attention-based mechanisms, enabling models like BERT, GPT, and T5 to achieve state-of-the-art results in tasks ranging from machine translation to question answering.

Synergy   **and**   **Scale**

The synergy between high-powered hardware and advanced algorithms has dramatically shortened training cycles. Models that once would have taken months to train on CPUs can now be trained in days (or even hours) on clusters of GPUs or TPUs. This shift not only accelerates the pace of research but also lowers the barrier to entry—small teams and startups can now train relatively sophisticated models, provided they have access to cloud computing resources.

Scaling these models, however, is not without challenges. Training large language models requires massive energy consumption, raising concerns about environmental impact (Strubell, Ganesh and McCallum, 2019). Researchers are exploring more efficient architectures, better parallelization strategies, and techniques like model distillation to reduce computational footprint without sacrificing performance.

Looking   **Ahead**

As hardware continues to advance—through more powerful GPUs, specialized AI chips, and possibly even quantum computing—algorithmic innovation is expected to follow suit. Some researchers speculate about the emergence of new paradigms beyond deep learning, integrating ideas from areas such as neuroscience, probabilistic programming, or symbolic reasoning in hybrid architectures. The exact path of AI's next leaps remains uncertain, but history suggests that breakthroughs often arise from the interplay between new hardware capabilities and creative algorithmic solutions.

Key   **Takeaway**

AI's modern boom is driven by a convergence of computing power and transformative algorithms. GPUs and TPUs, combined with deep learning and attention-based architectures, have unlocked capabilities that were once theoretical. This confluence underscores the interdisciplinary nature of AI, where progress in one domain catalyzes leaps in another.

1.2. AI's Real-World Impact

1.2.1. Everyday AI: Voice Assistants, Recommendations & More

Voice   **Interfaces**   **and**   **Personal**   **Assistants**

Today, voice assistants like Siri, Google Assistant, and Alexa are so commonplace that one can forget just how complex they are under the hood. These systems employ advanced NLP techniques to convert spoken language into textual queries (speech recognition), analyze and interpret meaning (natural language understanding), and generate appropriate responses (natural language generation) (Hoy, 2018). The result is a seemingly intuitive interface that can answer trivia questions, set reminders, or even control smart home devices.

But beyond convenience, voice interfaces highlight a broader shift in how humans interact with technology. Rather than requiring specialized skills or knowledge, such as typing commands into a terminal, conversational AI allows novices and experts alike to engage seamlessly with digital systems. As speech-to-text and text-to-speech algorithms improve, the potential for truly hands-free computing expands—whether in vehicles, healthcare settings, or industrial control rooms.

Recommendation   **Systems**

Another ubiquitous yet often "behind-the-scenes" AI technology is the recommendation engine. Platforms like Netflix, YouTube, and Amazon rely on machine learning models to suggest what users might want to watch, read, or buy next (Gomez-Uribe and Hunt, 2015). These systems employ a combination of collaborative filtering—identifying patterns among similar users—and content-based methods that analyze item characteristics (e.g., genre, topic, style) to make tailored suggestions.

The business implications are massive: personalized recommendations can significantly increase user engagement and sales. Yet, these models also raise questions about the "filter bubble," where users encounter only content aligning with their existing preferences or beliefs (Pariser, 2011). Balancing personalization with diversity of content remains an area of active research, as platforms grapple with the ethical and societal implications of high-impact recommendation systems.

Translation and Real-Time Communication

Another area where AI visibly touches everyday life is language translation. Services like Google Translate use neural machine translation (NMT) models to convert text or speech from one language to another in near real-time. These transformations rely on large bilingual or multilingual corpora to learn mappings between words, phrases, and syntactic structures in different languages (Wu et al., 2016). The result is not perfect, but it is good enough to enable travelers, businesses, and educators to cross linguistic barriers effortlessly.

Real-time language translation holds promise for bridging cultural and linguistic gaps. It can facilitate international collaborations, global customer support, and access to knowledge resources in multiple languages. However, these advances also underscore the digital divide: while major languages are well-supported, "low-resource" languages still lack sufficient training data, perpetuating inequalities in who benefits most from AI-driven translation tools.

Invisible AI in the Background

Beyond these high-profile applications, countless smaller AI systems operate behind the scenes—filtering spam emails, detecting credit card fraud, optimizing supply chains, or routing internet traffic. Their invisibility can be both a blessing and a curse. While it spares end-users from complexity, it also makes it harder for the public to understand AI's pervasiveness and potential risks.

Key Takeaway

From speaking to our devices to receiving curated product suggestions, AI permeates daily life in both obvious and subtle ways. Awareness of these systems fosters better-informed choices about privacy, personalization, and how we wish to engage with technology.

1.2.2. Industries Disrupted: Finance, Healthcare, Retail

Finance: Automated Trading, Risk Assessment, and Fraud Detection
Few sectors have embraced AI as enthusiastically as finance. Automated trading systems—sometimes called "algorithmic trading" or "high-frequency trading"—execute buy and sell orders in milliseconds based on machine learning-driven analysis of market signals. These algorithms often combine historical price data, real-time news analysis, and even social media sentiment to predict short-term price movements (Fawcett and Provost, 2013). While highly profitable, such systems can exacerbate market volatility, leading regulators to question how best to oversee AI-driven market activities.

Risk assessment and fraud detection also benefit from AI. Machine learning models excel at identifying anomalous patterns in vast amounts of transactional data. By learning what "normal" behavior looks like, models can flag potentially fraudulent activities with far greater accuracy than rule-based systems. This reduces financial losses for institutions and can enhance consumer trust—though concerns about false positives and fair access to credit persist, especially when models rely on opaque features or proxies that may inadvertently correlate with protected attributes (Barocas, Hardt and Narayanan, 2018).

Healthcare: Diagnostics, Personalized Medicine, and Beyond
In healthcare, AI promises to streamline diagnostics, personalize treatment plans, and optimize resource allocation. Deep learning models can analyze medical images—X-rays, MRIs, CT scans—with accuracy that sometimes rivals trained radiologists (Esteva et al., 2017). By highlighting suspicious areas in images, these systems serve as a second pair of eyes, potentially catching early signs of diseases like cancer or neurological disorders.

Additionally, AI-driven predictive models can identify patients at high risk for conditions like sepsis or readmission, enabling preemptive interventions. In personalized medicine, genomic data analysis allows for treatments that are tailored to an individual's unique genetic makeup. This approach aligns with the growing field of precision medicine, where machine learning helps parse vast genetic and clinical datasets to find correlations that might inform therapy options.

However, data privacy in healthcare is paramount. Regulations like HIPAA in the United States and the GDPR in Europe place stringent requirements on data handling and patient consent. Moreover, the lack of transparency in certain AI models (so-called "black box" algorithms) complicates doctors' ability to explain diagnoses and treatments to patients, leading to calls for more interpretable and accountable AI in clinical settings.

Retail: Inventory Management, Supply Chain Optimization, and Customer Engagement
Retailers leverage AI to manage everything from inventory levels to personalized marketing campaigns. Machine learning models can anticipate spikes in demand, reducing instances of overstocking or stockouts. This not only cuts costs but also

improves the customer experience. Some large retailers deploy AI-enabled robots in warehouses to move and sort products, enhancing efficiency and safety.

In brick-and-mortar settings, "smart shelves" and computer vision systems can track product placement and foot traffic, while loyalty programs use AI to predict buying patterns and tailor promotions. Online, personalized recommendations and dynamic pricing—where prices fluctuate based on real-time supply, demand, and consumer behavior—are increasingly sophisticated. While effective in boosting sales and customer satisfaction, these practices again raise ethical questions about price discrimination and consumer privacy.

Cross-Industry   **Implications**

These examples illustrate AI's transformative effect across diverse sectors. Common threads include the automation of complex tasks, predictive analytics to anticipate future scenarios, and personalization to meet individual needs or preferences. Such disruptions can lead to job realignments, requiring workers to shift from routine tasks to more value-added roles, such as overseeing AI systems or leveraging AI insights to make strategic decisions.

Key   **Takeaway**

AI's disruptive power reshapes industries by automating tasks, enhancing decision-making, and enabling highly personalized services. While this transformation offers efficiencies and new opportunities, it also invites scrutiny regarding regulation, ethics, and workforce impact.

1.2.3. Society's Shift: Jobs, Ethics, and the Future of Work

Workforce   **Displacement**   **and**   **Augmentation**

One of the most debated aspects of AI is its influence on employment. Skeptics argue that automation and AI-driven processes will lead to widespread job losses, particularly in roles involving repetitive or predictable tasks—such as basic data entry or assembly-line work (Brynjolfsson and Mitchell, 2017). Others suggest that while some jobs will indeed vanish, new roles will emerge that leverage uniquely human capabilities like creativity, emotional intelligence, and complex problem-solving (Autor, 2015).

In practice, AI often augments rather than outright replaces human labor. For instance, in customer support, chatbots can handle routine queries, freeing human agents to address more complex or sensitive issues. In fields like healthcare, AI tools can handle preliminary image analysis or triage, but doctors and nurses ultimately oversee patient care. The net outcome for employment likely hinges on factors such as re-skilling, education, and policy interventions designed to support workforce transitions.

Ethical   **Questions**   **and**   **Regulatory**   **Responses**

Beyond job disruption, AI raises a host of ethical dilemmas. Biased decision-making, invasion of privacy, and potential misuse of surveillance technology are among the most pressing concerns (Floridi et al., 2018). High-profile incidents—ranging from facial recognition systems that misidentify individuals of certain ethnicities to discriminatory lending algorithms—have prompted calls for industry-wide standards and government oversight.

Regulatory frameworks such as the *EU Artificial Intelligence Act* (European Commission, 2021) aim to classify AI systems by risk level, imposing stricter requirements on "high-risk" applications like healthcare, law enforcement, or transportation. These policies emphasize transparency, accountability, and fairness, seeking to balance innovation with public interest. For companies and researchers, navigating this legal landscape adds complexity but also underscores a commitment to responsible AI development.

Beyond Automation: AI as a Collaborative Partner
An emerging perspective views AI not merely as an automation tool but as a collaborator that can amplify human capabilities. Examples include "human-in-the-loop" systems that merge machine efficiency with human judgment. These collaborations can thrive in creative fields—such as music composition or storytelling—where AI-generated content serves as inspiration or a rough draft, leaving final aesthetic decisions to human creators.

Such synergies challenge the classical narrative of AI as a competitor to human intelligence. Instead, they posit that AI is most powerful when integrated seamlessly into workflows that value both machine precision and human nuance. This approach may reduce resistance to AI adoption by demonstrating tangible benefits while maintaining human oversight.

Long-Term Outlook
Speculations about superintelligent AI, singularities, or fully automated societies often surface in public discourse (Kurzweil, 2005). While such scenarios capture the imagination, most experts agree that these possibilities lie far in the future if they occur at all. The immediate issues revolve around practical deployments, ensuring models serve society ethically, and preparing the workforce for inevitable changes. As research continues to push boundaries, the interplay between technology, policy, and ethics will shape AI's legacy in the coming decades.

Key Takeaway
AI's societal impact transcends technology, affecting jobs, ethics, and our collective vision for the future of work. The choices made today—regarding regulation, workforce development, and collaborative AI design—will determine whether AI evolves as a tool of empowerment or a catalyst for inequality.

1.3. Common Misconceptions

1.3.1. AI vs. Automation: Where Is the Line?

Defining AI and Automation

At the outset, it can be challenging to draw a clear boundary between AI and automation. Automation typically refers to the use of machines or software to carry out repetitive tasks based on predefined rules or instructions (Brynjolfsson and McAfee, 2014). AI, however, involves learning from data, adapting to new information, and making decisions in complex scenarios—capabilities that extend beyond rigid rule-based paradigms (Russell and Norvig, 2021).

In a warehouse context, a traditional conveyor belt setup that sorts packages by weight or size based on fixed criteria exemplifies automation. Conversely, an AI-driven system might analyze historical shipment data, predict seasonal peaks, and dynamically reconfigure itself to optimize throughput. The difference lies in adaptability: AI systems attempt to replicate aspects of cognitive functions, such as pattern recognition and decision-making, while automation systems follow explicit, predetermined workflows.

Overlap in Real-World Systems

In practice, organizations often blend AI with automation to create hybrid solutions. Consider a customer service chatbot: it may rely on a rule-based engine for standard greetings and frequently asked questions, but use a machine learning model to handle more nuanced queries or sentiment detection. This synergy can yield faster response times, improved accuracy, and better user experiences.

However, conflating the two can lead to inflated expectations. Companies might label simple automations as "AI solutions" for marketing purposes, contributing to the hype cycle. Understanding whether an application truly leverages machine learning or advanced cognitive techniques is critical for accurately assessing its capabilities and limitations.

Implications for Strategy and Investment

Distinguishing between automation and AI is crucial for strategic planning. Purely rule-based automations can deliver quick wins for well-defined, repetitive tasks—often with relatively low risk and cost. AI deployments, on the other hand, may require significant data resources, specialized expertise, and iterative experimentation. Although they can potentially yield greater long-term benefits by adapting to unforeseen changes, the initial investment is typically higher.

From an educational standpoint, the difference also shapes how individuals prepare for future job roles. Mastering process automation tools might be sufficient for certain roles, whereas harnessing AI's predictive and adaptive capabilities demands deeper mathematical, statistical, and programming knowledge.

Key   **Takeaway**

While automation and AI are interlinked, they are not interchangeable. Recognizing their differences helps stakeholders set realistic goals, allocate resources effectively, and measure success appropriately.

1.3.2. AI Hype vs. Reality: Separating Fact from Fiction

Overpromising   **and**   **Under-Delivering**

AI has been subject to bursts of hype since its inception, with each "boom" followed by a period of disillusionment when lofty promises failed to materialize. Today, media headlines about AI achieving human-like cognition can stoke misperceptions. Some marketing efforts further blur the line by labeling automated or rule-based systems as "AI," leading to inflated expectations.

These misconceptions can harm the field in several ways. First, they may lead investors or decision-makers to allocate funds imprudently, backing projects without a clear roadmap to feasibility. Second, high-profile failures or ethical oversights can erode public trust, making it harder for genuinely innovative AI solutions to gain acceptance (Marcus and Davis, 2019).

Technical   **Limitations**

Despite remarkable advances, current AI systems remain constrained in significant ways. They often excel in narrow tasks but lack the broad contextual understanding characteristic of human intelligence (Lake, Ullman and Tenenbaum, 2017). For instance, a language model may generate grammatically correct text but can struggle with logical consistency or factual accuracy if not carefully fine-tuned or provided with real-time information.

Additionally, AI models can be brittle when faced with edge cases, adversarial inputs, or new environments. A neural network trained to recognize certain dog breeds in images might be easily fooled by slight pixel perturbations or changes in lighting conditions. This brittleness stems from the models' statistical nature: they learn correlations in training data rather than acquiring a deep, causal understanding of the world.

Human-Centric   **Intelligence**

Many tasks that humans perform effortlessly—such as common-sense reasoning or understanding nuanced social cues—remain elusive for AI. While large language models might mimic conversation, they do not "understand" in the way humans do; rather, they predict the most likely sequence of tokens (words) based on patterns learned from vast datasets (Bender and Koller, 2020). This distinction underscores the gap between functional performance and true comprehension or sentience.

For fields like education, mental health, or complex decision-making, purely algorithmic approaches risk oversimplification. A system might flag anomalies or provide predictions, but it cannot replicate the emotional intelligence, moral judgment, or empathetic communication that human professionals bring to the table. Recognizing these boundaries helps maintain realistic expectations and ensures humans remain in the loop for critical decisions.

Striking **a** **Balance**
A measured approach to AI involves celebrating genuine innovations—like improved language translation or medical image analysis—while acknowledging limitations. This balance fosters sustainable progress, as researchers and practitioners focus on tangible goals, and public trust is earned through transparent reporting of capabilities and risks. By dispelling myths, we can better direct collective efforts toward meaningful, ethical, and robust AI applications.

Key **Takeaway**
AI is powerful, but it is not magic. Understanding its limitations and common pitfalls—especially the tendency for hype to outpace reality—is crucial for responsible deployment and continued advancement.

1.3.3. Fear and Fascination: Public Perception of AI

Historical **Context** **of** **AI** **Fears**
Public perception of AI has oscillated between utopian visions of intelligent machines solving humanity's greatest challenges and dystopian nightmares of autonomous robots usurping human jobs or freedoms. Fiction—from Mary Shelley's *Frankenstein* to Isaac Asimov's *I, Robot*—has long explored the tensions around artificial beings with minds of their own. These stories, while imaginative, often contribute to the cultural lens through which real-world AI developments are interpreted (Fast and Horvitz, 2017).

Sensational news headlines about AI beating humans at complex games (e.g., IBM's Deep Blue beating Garry Kasparov in chess, or DeepMind's AlphaGo defeating Go champion Lee Sedol) further fuel both awe and anxiety. These milestones highlight AI's potential but can also spark fears of a looming "singularity" where machine intelligence surpasses human control (Kurzweil, 2005).

Contemporary **Concerns**
Modern discussions often focus on job displacement, privacy, and the ethical use of AI. High-profile examples, such as facial recognition systems misidentifying individuals of color, underscore the technology's fallibility and potential societal harm (Buolamwini and Gebru, 2018). The public's concerns range from immediate issues (like losing employment opportunities) to existential risks (AI developing goals misaligned with human values).

Additionally, the widespread collection of personal data for AI training raises fears about surveillance and erosion of civil liberties. Governments and corporations have unprecedented visibility into daily life, often without transparent guidelines or user awareness.

Educational   Efforts   and   Advocacy
Various institutions and thought leaders advocate for improved public understanding of AI. Open-source platforms (e.g., TensorFlow, PyTorch) and educational initiatives (like online AI courses) enable a broader community to explore AI's mechanisms, reducing the mystique. Some nonprofit organizations, such as the Partnership on AI and AI Now Institute, focus on research and policy recommendations to ensure AI development aligns with human well-being.

Public workshops, media coverage that includes expert perspectives, and the integration of AI topics into school curricula can demystify AI. This fosters a more nuanced public discourse, moving beyond sensationalism to informed engagement with the real challenges and opportunities AI presents.

Shaping   AI's   Public   Narrative
How AI is portrayed in mainstream media, entertainment, and policy debates has tangible effects on its adoption and regulation. Balanced reporting that highlights AI's capabilities and pitfalls, along with transparent disclosure of research findings, can bolster public trust. By engaging with communities, educators, journalists, and policymakers, AI practitioners can help create a narrative that acknowledges both the promise and the limitations of the technology.

Key   Takeaway
Public perception of AI is shaped by cultural narratives, media representation, and real-world controversies. Enhancing public understanding through education and transparent communication can temper unfounded fears while also addressing legitimate concerns about bias, privacy, and societal impact.

1.4. Framing the Future

1.4.1. Exponential Growth or Steady Evolution?

Two   Visions   of   Progress
Experts often diverge in their forecasts of AI's trajectory. Some adopt a singularity-style outlook, positing that AI will continue growing exponentially due to self-improving algorithms and ever-faster hardware (Kurzweil, 2005). They point to the rapid progress from rule-based systems to neural networks to transformers, suggesting that each breakthrough builds on the last at an accelerating pace.

Others advocate for a more measured viewpoint, arguing that AI will advance in fits and starts, driven by incremental improvements rather than radical leaps (Agrawal, Gans and Goldfarb, 2019). According to this perspective, each new method or architecture often addresses specific limitations of its predecessor, implying a pattern of slow but steady refinements.

Factors   Influencing   Growth

Several variables will shape which path AI takes:

1. **Hardware Limits**: Moore's Law, once a reliable predictor of transistor scaling, has shown signs of slowing. While specialized hardware like GPUs and TPUs can compensate, physical constraints may eventually bottleneck raw computational growth.

2. **Data Availability**: The quantity and quality of data power AI models. Should privacy regulations or data scarcity limit access to training data, progress might plateau.

3. **Research Breakthroughs**: Transformative developments, akin to the discovery of backpropagation or attention mechanisms, can trigger leaps in AI capabilities. The frequency and impact of such breakthroughs are difficult to predict.

4. **Socioeconomic and Policy Factors**: Public and governmental support for AI research, funding levels, and international collaboration or competition can either accelerate or temper the field's momentum.

Practical   Implications

Whether AI progresses exponentially or in a more linear fashion has implications for talent development, investment, and policy. If exponential growth holds, the pace of disruption in various industries could intensify, requiring rapid re-skilling and more agile regulatory frameworks. A slower, more evolutionary trajectory might allow for a smoother integration of AI into society, with ample time for ethical guardrails and robust testing.

For researchers and practitioners, understanding the nuances of these growth models can guide strategic decisions—whether to focus on incremental optimization of existing techniques or to pursue moonshots that might lead to paradigm-shifting advances.

Key   Takeaway

While AI's future path is uncertain, both exponential leaps and incremental improvements are possible. Keeping an open yet critical mindset helps stakeholders prepare for multiple scenarios, ensuring that rapid progress remains sustainable and ethically guided.

1.4.2. AI's Place in Modern Technology Stacks

AI   as   an   Enabling   Layer

The integration of AI into standard technology stacks underscores its evolving role as a foundational component rather than a niche add-on. Software engineers, data scientists, and product managers increasingly treat AI modules—such as recommendation engines, image classifiers, or chatbots—as essential services within an application's architecture.

Cloud providers (e.g., AWS, Azure, Google Cloud) offer pre-trained models and automated machine learning (AutoML) tools, lowering the barrier for adoption.

Microservices architecture further facilitates this integration. Instead of embedding AI functionalities as monolithic blocks, organizations can deploy them as containerized services that communicate through APIs. This modularity fosters scalability, fault tolerance, and ease of updates. If a better model becomes available or user demand spikes, the AI service can be swapped or scaled independently.

DevOps   and   MLOps
With AI increasingly woven into production systems, the discipline of **MLOps** (Machine Learning Operations) has emerged to bridge the gap between data science experimentation and reliable software deployment. MLOps adapts DevOps principles—continuous integration and delivery, automated testing, version control—to AI workflows, accounting for complexities like evolving datasets and model drift. This evolution reflects the reality that AI models are not static artifacts; they need periodic retraining and performance monitoring to remain accurate and relevant (Sculley et al., 2015).

For developers and data scientists, familiarity with MLOps practices is becoming essential. Tools like Kubeflow, MLflow, and Airflow facilitate model training pipelines, experiment tracking, and deployment orchestration. These platforms streamline collaboration between different teams—data engineers, ML researchers, and operations—ensuring that AI solutions can be robustly managed throughout their lifecycle.

From   Edge   to   Cloud
While much AI training still occurs in the cloud, where resources are plentiful, inference—the stage where trained models make predictions—can happen on the edge (e.g., on smartphones or embedded devices) for latency or privacy reasons. Frameworks like TensorFlow Lite or ONNX Runtime enable developers to compress and deploy models on constrained hardware, making AI-driven features available even in environments with limited connectivity (Lane et al., 2015).

This transition to edge AI is particularly important for time-sensitive applications like autonomous vehicles or industrial control systems. Rather than sending sensor data to a remote server for analysis, devices can perform real-time inferencing locally, reducing response times and bandwidth requirements. However, edge deployments require careful optimization to fit model parameters into smaller footprints, a challenge that has spurred research into techniques like network pruning, quantization, and distillation.

Challenges   and   Opportunities
As AI becomes more deeply embedded in technology stacks, questions arise about interoperability, standardization, and vendor lock-in. Proprietary cloud AI services can create dependency, while open-source solutions offer flexibility but may demand more

maintenance. Security is another concern, as adversaries can attack AI pipelines by injecting poisoned data or reverse-engineering models to reveal sensitive information.

Despite these hurdles, the trend is clear: AI is no longer a futuristic addon—it is a core component of modern software ecosystems. Continued innovation in MLOps, edge deployment, and standardization efforts promises to make AI both more powerful and more accessible.

Key   **Takeaway**

AI's embedding in mainstream technology stacks signals its maturation from a specialized research domain to a foundational layer. This shift demands robust operational practices (MLOps), new hardware strategies, and thoughtful attention to security and ethics.

1.4.3. The Road Ahead for AI Enthusiasts

Academic   **and**   **Research**   **Opportunities**

For students and researchers, AI presents a wealth of opportunities for intellectual exploration. Interdisciplinary programs that combine computer science, statistics, mathematics, and domain-specific knowledge (e.g., biology, linguistics, finance) are increasingly common. Top institutions, such as Harvard or Stanford, offer specialized courses and lab opportunities that delve into cutting-edge topics like reinforcement learning, generative models, and neurosymbolic AI.

Graduate students and postdoctoral researchers may find fertile ground in emerging subfields—federated learning, causal inference in AI, or human-centered AI, for instance. Competitive grants and fellowship programs often prioritize AI research with clear societal benefits, reflecting a collective push toward ethical, impactful innovation.

Career   **Paths**   **and**   **Industry**   **Demand**

Outside academia, industry demand for AI talent remains high. Roles like machine learning engineer, data scientist, and AI product manager are in demand across sectors—technology giants, startups, healthcare organizations, financial institutions, and more. Many companies invest heavily in in-house AI research labs, offering opportunities for scientists to publish papers while working on real-world problems.

For those inclined toward entrepreneurship, AI's rapidly evolving landscape presents myriad avenues to create or join startups focusing on niche applications—whether it's AI in mental health, renewable energy, agriculture, or robotics. Access to open-source tools and cloud-based computing resources levels the playing field, allowing small teams to prototype and launch complex solutions with relative speed.

Ethical   **and**   **Responsible**   **Innovation**

Increasingly, AI careers demand not only technical prowess but also ethical literacy. Professionals are expected to grapple with questions of bias, fairness, and accountability, especially in areas like hiring algorithms, facial recognition, and automated decision systems in critical domains (education, finance, policing). Engaging with frameworks for responsible AI design—attending workshops, collaborating with ethicists, or obtaining certifications—can position enthusiasts as leaders who drive positive societal impact.

Continuous Learning and Community Engagement

The velocity of AI research makes continuous learning essential. Online platforms, conferences, and open-source communities allow practitioners to stay abreast of innovations. Tools like arXiv, GitHub, and specialized forums (e.g., Hugging Face for NLP models) provide real-time updates and collaborative opportunities.

Many AI professionals also commit to mentorship, knowledge-sharing, and fostering inclusive communities, recognizing that diversity fuels creativity and resilience. Participating in local AI meetups, hackathons, or open-source projects can help build networks and accelerate skill development.

Key Takeaway

For AI enthusiasts, the future holds diverse paths—academic research, industry roles, entrepreneurship—each demanding a blend of technical expertise, ethical awareness, and adaptability. As AI continues its rapid evolution, those committed to continuous learning and responsible innovation will help steer the field toward meaningful progress.

References

- Agrawal, A., Gans, J. and Goldfarb, A. (2019) *Artificial Intelligence: The Ambiguous Labor Market Impact of Automating Prediction*. Cambridge, MA: National Bureau of Economic Research.

- Autor, D. (2015) 'Why Are There Still So Many Jobs? The History and Future of Workplace Automation', *Journal of Economic Perspectives*, 29(3), pp. 3–30.

- Barocas, S., Hardt, M. and Narayanan, A. (2018) *Fairness and Machine Learning*. [Preprint]. Available at: http://fairmlbook.org (Accessed: 10 February 2025).

- Bender, E.M. and Koller, A. (2020) 'Climbing towards NLU: On Meaning, Form, and Understanding in the Age of Data', in *Proceedings of the 58th Annual Meeting of the Association for Computational Linguistics*. Stroudsburg, PA: ACL, pp. 5185–5198.

- Brown, T. et al. (2020) 'Language Models are Few-Shot Learners', in *Advances in Neural Information Processing Systems* (NeurIPS). Red Hook, NY: Curran Associates. Available at: https://proceedings.neurips.cc/ (Accessed: 10 February 2025).

- Brynjolfsson, E. and McAfee, A. (2014) *The Second Machine Age: Work, Progress, and Prosperity in a Time of Brilliant Technologies*. New York: W.W. Norton & Company.

- Brynjolfsson, E. and Mitchell, T. (2017) 'What Can Machine Learning Do? Workforce Implications', *Science*, 358(6370), pp. 1530–1534.

- Buolamwini, J. and Gebru, T. (2018) 'Gender Shades: Intersectional Accuracy Disparities in Commercial Gender Classification', in *Proceedings of Machine Learning Research* (FAT* 2018). New York: PMLR, pp. 77–91.

- European Commission (2021) *Proposal for a Regulation Laying Down Harmonised Rules on Artificial Intelligence (Artificial Intelligence Act)*. Available at: https://digital-strategy.ec.europa.eu (Accessed: 10 February 2025).

- Esteva, A. et al. (2017) 'Dermatologist-Level Classification of Skin Cancer with Deep Neural Networks', *Nature*, 542(7639), pp. 115–118.

- Fast, E. and Horvitz, E. (2017) 'Long-Term Trends in the Public Perception of Artificial Intelligence', in *Proceedings of the AAAI Conference on Human Computation and Crowdsourcing*. Palo Alto, CA: AAAI Press.

- Fawcett, T. and Provost, F. (2013) 'Data Science and its Relationship to Big Data and Data-Driven Decision Making', *Big Data*, 1(1), pp. 51–59.

- Floridi, L. et al. (2018) 'AI4People—An Ethical Framework for a Good AI Society: Opportunities, Risks, Principles, and Recommendations', *Minds and Machines*, 28(4), pp. 689–707.

- Gandomi, A. and Haider, M. (2015) 'Beyond the Hype: Big Data Concepts, Methods, and Analytics', *International Journal of Information Management*, 35(2), pp. 137–144.

- Gomez-Uribe, C.A. and Hunt, N. (2015) 'The Netflix Recommender System: Algorithms, Business Value, and Innovation', *ACM Transactions on Management Information Systems*, 6(4), Article 13.

- Goodfellow, I., Bengio, Y. and Courville, A. (2016) *Deep Learning*. Cambridge, MA: MIT Press.

- Halevy, A., Norvig, P. and Pereira, F. (2009) 'The Unreasonable Effectiveness of Data', *IEEE Intelligent Systems*, 24(2), pp. 8–12.

- Hoy, M. (2018) 'Alexa, Siri, Cortana, and More: An Introduction to Voice Assistants', *Medical Reference Services Quarterly*, 37(1), pp. 81–88.

- Jordan, M.I. and Mitchell, T.M. (2015) 'Machine Learning: Trends, Perspectives, and Prospects', *Science*, 349(6245), pp. 255–260.

- Kurzweil, R. (2005) *The Singularity is Near: When Humans Transcend Biology*. New York: Viking.

- Lake, B.M., Ullman, T.D. and Tenenbaum, J.B. (2017) 'Building Machines that Learn and Think Like People', *Behavioral and Brain Sciences*, 40, e253.

- Lane, N.D. et al. (2015) 'DeepX: A Software Accelerator for Low-Power Deep Learning Inference on Mobile Devices', in *Proceedings of the 14th International Conference on Information Processing in Sensor Networks* (IPSN). New York: ACM, pp. 1–12.

- LeCun, Y., Bengio, Y. and Hinton, G. (2015) 'Deep Learning', *Nature*, 521(7553), pp. 436–444.

- Marcus, G. and Davis, E. (2019) *Rebooting AI: Building Artificial Intelligence We Can Trust*. New York: Pantheon Books.

- McCulloch, W.S. and Pitts, W.H. (1943) 'A Logical Calculus of Ideas Immanent in Nervous Activity', *The Bulletin of Mathematical Biophysics*, 5(4), pp. 115–133.

- Mitchell, T. (1997) *Machine Learning*. New York: McGraw-Hill.

- Nilsson, N. (2010) *The Quest for Artificial Intelligence*. Cambridge: Cambridge University Press.

- Pariser, E. (2011) *The Filter Bubble: What the Internet Is Hiding from You*. New York: Penguin Press.

- Russell, S. and Norvig, P. (2021) *Artificial Intelligence: A Modern Approach*. 4th edn. Hoboken, NJ: Pearson.

- Sculley, D. et al. (2015) 'Hidden Technical Debt in Machine Learning Systems', in *Advances in Neural Information Processing Systems* (NeurIPS). Red Hook, NY: Curran Associates.

- Strubell, E., Ganesh, A. and McCallum, A. (2019) 'Energy and Policy Considerations for Deep Learning in NLP', in *Proceedings of the 57th Annual Meeting of the Association for Computational Linguistics*. Florence, Italy: ACL, pp. 3645–3650.

- Turing, A. (1950) 'Computing Machinery and Intelligence', *Mind*, 59(236), pp. 433–460.

- Vaswani, A. et al. (2017) 'Attention Is All You Need', in *Advances in Neural Information Processing Systems* (NeurIPS). Red Hook, NY: Curran Associates.

- Wu, Y. et al. (2016) 'Google's Neural Machine Translation System: Bridging the Gap between Human and Machine Translation', *arXiv preprint* arXiv:1609.08144.

Chapter 2: Fundamentals of Machine Learning

2.1. Key ML Concepts

2.1.1. Supervised, Unsupervised, and Reinforcement Learning

Overview of Learning Paradigms

Machine learning (ML) is often described as the process by which computers improve performance on a task through experience, rather than by being explicitly programmed (Mitchell, 1997). Within this field, there are three principal paradigms: **supervised**, **unsupervised**, and **reinforcement** learning. Each paradigm has distinct objectives, methods, and real-world applicability.

- **Supervised Learning**: In supervised learning, the training process relies on labeled examples. That is, each data point is paired with the "correct" answer—often termed a label, target, or ground truth. The model's goal is to map inputs (e.g., features) to outputs (e.g., classes or continuous values) with high accuracy. Tasks such as image classification, spam detection, and housing price prediction typically fall under supervised learning (Russell and Norvig, 2021).

- **Unsupervised Learning**: By contrast, unsupervised learning has no labels. The model must detect patterns, groupings, or latent structures in the data on its own. Common techniques include clustering (e.g., k-means) and dimensionality reduction (e.g., principal component analysis). These methods can reveal hidden insights—such as customer segmentation or outlier detection—without predefined categories (Hastie, Tibshirani and Friedman, 2009).

- **Reinforcement Learning (RL)**: Inspired by behavioral psychology, RL involves an agent making sequential decisions in an environment to maximize cumulative reward (Sutton and Barto, 2018). Instead of labeled examples, the agent receives feedback in the form of rewards (positive) or penalties (negative) based on its actions. Applications range from game-playing AI (e.g., AlphaGo) to real-time bidding in online advertising and robotic control.

Why These Paradigms Matter

Each learning paradigm addresses different types of problems. Supervised learning excels in well-defined tasks where historical data includes correct labels—typical in predictive analytics for business or in standard computer vision tasks. Unsupervised learning is crucial for exploratory data analysis and discovering previously unknown patterns. Reinforcement learning shines in dynamic environments requiring complex, sequential decision-making.

Hybrid Approaches

Real-world applications often demand hybrid or semi-supervised approaches. For instance, **semi-supervised learning** leverages a small set of labeled data alongside a larger pool of unlabeled data—beneficial when labeling is expensive or time-consuming

(Chapelle, Schölkopf and Zien, 2006). **Self-supervised learning** has also risen in prominence, especially in natural language processing, where large neural networks learn by predicting parts of the input (Devlin et al., 2019).

Key Challenges

- **Data Quantity and Quality**: Supervised methods typically require extensive labeled datasets, which may be expensive to produce.

- **Scalability and Compute**: Reinforcement learning can demand high computational resources, especially for tasks that simulate complex environments.

- **Interpretability**: Many advanced algorithms operate as "black boxes," making it difficult to interpret or explain outcomes.

Practical   **Tip**
When starting an ML project, carefully match the learning paradigm to the problem context. Is your data labeled? Is the task exploratory? Is there a clear reward signal for sequential actions? The answers guide you toward the right choice of algorithms.

2.1.2. Data Collection and Preparation

The   **Role**   **of**   **Data**   **in**   **ML**
Data is the fuel that drives machine learning. Regardless of the chosen algorithm, the success of an ML project hinges critically on the quality, relevance, and volume of available data (Goodfellow, Bengio and Courville, 2016). Even the most sophisticated models cannot compensate for flawed or insufficient datasets.

Data   **Sources**   **and**   **Acquisition**
Common data sources include:

- **Databases & Data Warehouses**: Transactional data from enterprise systems, web analytics logs, or customer relationship management (CRM) platforms.

- **Public Datasets**: Research communities often publish open-source datasets (e.g., ImageNet, Common Crawl for text).

- **Web Scraping**: Tools like Scrapy or Beautiful Soup allow organizations to compile specialized datasets from websites.

- **APIs and Sensors**: Social media APIs, IoT devices, and third-party data providers can supply real-time data streams.

Acquiring data often entails legal and ethical considerations. Regulations like the GDPR in the European Union demand explicit user consent and strict guidelines for data handling (European Commission, 2021). Failures to comply can result in significant fines and reputational damage. Additionally, data that is illegally or unethically sourced can embed biases or reflect problematic social structures, compromising downstream analytics (Barocas, Hardt and Narayanan, 2018).

Cleaning and Preprocessing

Before feeding data into a model, practitioners generally undertake:

1. **De-duplication**: Removing duplicate rows or records that might distort training or inflate performance metrics.

2. **Handling Missing Values**: Strategies range from simple imputation (mean, median) to more advanced techniques like k-nearest neighbors or model-based imputation.

3. **Outlier Detection**: Outliers can skew training. Sometimes they are genuine rare cases to be flagged, other times they are errors needing correction.

4. **Normalization or Standardization**: Scaling numeric features to a common range or distribution (e.g., z-score standardization).

5. **Categorical Encoding**: Converting text categories into numeric form using methods like one-hot encoding, label encoding, or embeddings.

6. **Tokenization (for NLP)**: Splitting text into words or subwords, and cleaning punctuation or special characters.

Feature Engineering

Feature engineering transforms raw data into informative attributes that models can better understand. In the past, manual feature crafting (e.g., combining multiple columns or creating domain-specific attributes) was critical to achieving high accuracy (Domingos, 2012). Modern deep learning architectures automate some of this process, especially in fields like image recognition or NLP, where convolutional or transformer layers learn hierarchical feature representations (LeCun, Bengio and Hinton, 2015). Still, domain knowledge remains invaluable for structuring data effectively.

Data Augmentation

When data is scarce, augmentation can artificially inflate the size of a dataset, particularly in computer vision or speech recognition. For images, transformations like rotation, flipping, and color jitter simulate varied capture conditions. In NLP, synonym replacement or back-translation can diversify text samples (Shorten and Khoshgoftaar, 2019). This approach helps models generalize better and reduces the risk of overfitting.

Practical Tip

Invest substantial effort in data preparation. A well-prepared dataset not only improves model performance but also expedites iterative cycles of experimentation—crucial for building robust machine learning solutions.

2.1.3. Model Training and Evaluation

Defining **Model** **Objectives**

Effective machine learning begins with clearly defined objectives. Are you predicting a probability, labeling an image, or generating text? The primary performance metric—accuracy, F1 score, mean squared error—depends on the nature of the problem (Fawcett and Provost, 2013). Selecting appropriate metrics at the outset is crucial for guiding both model development and evaluation.

Splitting **the** **Dataset**

A common practice is to partition data into **training**, **validation**, and **test** sets:

- **Training Set**: Used to adjust the parameters of the model.

- **Validation Set**: Assists in hyperparameter tuning and model selection.

- **Test Set**: Serves as a final, unbiased measure of model performance.

In some cases, practitioners use **cross-validation**, dividing the dataset into k folds and cycling through each fold as a test set, to obtain a more robust estimate of generalization performance (Hastie, Tibshirani and Friedman, 2009).

Loss **Functions** **and** **Optimization**

Model training usually revolves around minimizing a loss function that quantifies the discrepancy between predictions and ground truth. For classification tasks, **cross-entropy loss** is common; for regression, **mean squared error** or **mean absolute error** might be employed (Goodfellow, Bengio and Courville, 2016). Optimization techniques like **stochastic gradient descent (SGD)** or its variants (e.g., Adam, RMSProp) iteratively adjust the model's parameters to reduce the chosen loss.

Hyperparameter **Tuning**

While parameters (weights) are learned during training, **hyperparameters** (e.g., learning rate, number of layers, or regularization strength) remain fixed unless deliberately adjusted. Approaches like **grid search**, **random search**, or **Bayesian optimization** systematically explore hyperparameter settings to identify configurations that yield optimal performance (Bergstra and Bengio, 2012). This tuning process can be computationally expensive, prompting the use of distributed training or specialized hardware (GPUs, TPUs).

Monitoring **Training** **Dynamics**

Practitioners frequently track metrics such as training loss, validation accuracy, or F1 score per epoch (training cycle). Visual tools (e.g., TensorBoard) provide real-time plots, assisting in diagnosing issues like exploding gradients or overfitting. Early stopping—a technique where training halts if validation performance stops improving—further guards against overfitting and reduces computation time.

Practical **Tip**

Be systematic about evaluation. Document hyperparameter choices and keep a consistent experimental setup. This discipline aids reproducibility—a hallmark of quality scientific work in both academia and industry.

2.1.4. Overfitting, Underfitting, and Generalization

Defining Overfitting and Underfitting

- **Overfitting** occurs when a model fits the training data too closely, capturing noise or random fluctuations rather than the underlying patterns. While it may achieve near-perfect performance on training examples, it performs poorly on unseen test data (Hawkins, 2004).

- **Underfitting** indicates the model has not adequately captured the data's complexity. This typically manifests in low training accuracy or high error, suggesting the model is too simple or training is insufficient.

The **Bias-Variance** **Trade-Off**

These concepts are often framed via the **bias-variance trade-off**:

- **Bias**: The systematic error introduced by a model's assumptions. High-bias models (e.g., linear regression with few parameters) risk underfitting because they cannot capture complex relationships.

- **Variance**: The sensitivity of a model's predictions to small fluctuations in the training data. High-variance models (e.g., very deep neural networks with minimal regularization) risk overfitting, as they adapt too precisely to the training set's idiosyncrasies.

Successful machine learning strives to balance these two forces, achieving a low overall error.

Regularization **Techniques**

Regularization is key to combat overfitting (Ng, 2004). Common techniques include:

1. **L2 (Ridge) Regularization**: Adds a penalty proportional to the sum of squared weights, discouraging large weights.

2. **L1 (Lasso) Regularization**: Uses the absolute values of weights, encouraging sparsity.

3. **Dropout** (in neural networks): Randomly "dropping" neurons during training to prevent co-adaptation (Srivastava et al., 2014).

4. **Data Augmentation**: Expanding the dataset so the model sees varied examples, reducing the chance of memorizing noise.

Cross-Validation for **Robustness**

A robust way to spot overfitting is through cross-validation (Kohavi, 1995). If performance on the training set is excellent but plummets during validation folds, overfitting is likely. Conversely, consistently low performance across both training and validation sets may point to underfitting.

Generalization and **Model** **Complexity**

Generalization—how well a model performs on unseen data—is often the ultimate measure of machine learning success. While complex models (e.g., very deep networks) can capture intricate relationships, they also risk high variance. Simplifying the architecture, introducing regularization, or gathering more data are standard remedies.

Practical **Tip**

Always monitor validation and test set performance. If the gap between training and validation accuracy widens significantly, consider employing regularization or collecting additional data. Strive for simplicity; the best models are often those that achieve high performance with minimal complexity.

2.2. Deep Learning Essentials

2.2.1. Neural Networks Explained

From **Perceptrons** to **Deep** **Networks**

Neural networks, loosely inspired by the neuronal structures of the brain, have been central to machine learning since the 1950s. The **perceptron**, introduced by Rosenblatt (1958), was a simple linear classifier that updated weights based on misclassifications (Nilsson, 2010). Despite early enthusiasm, perceptrons had notable limitations—such as inability to learn the XOR function—and the field briefly lost momentum during the first "AI winter."

A renaissance occurred in the 1980s with the popularization of **backpropagation**, a method to systematically compute gradients for multi-layer networks (Rumelhart, Hinton and Williams, 1986). This paved the way for deeper architectures—multiple stacked layers of neurons—and eventually catalyzed the deep learning revolution in the 2000s.

Core Components of a Neural Network

1. **Layers**: Composed of interconnected nodes (neurons). Each neuron computes a weighted sum of inputs followed by an activation function.

2. **Weights and Biases**: Learned parameters that the training process iteratively adjusts.

3. **Activation Functions**: Nonlinear transformations (e.g., ReLU, sigmoid, tanh) enabling networks to approximate complex functions.

4. **Loss Function**: Quantifies the error between predictions and targets.

5. **Optimizer**: Algorithm (e.g., SGD, Adam) that updates weights based on gradients.

Depth   and   Representation

"Depth" refers to the number of layers in the network. Deeper networks can capture more complex features, but are harder to train due to issues like vanishing or exploding gradients (Glorot and Bengio, 2010). Innovations such as **batch normalization**, **residual connections**, and better initializations have mitigated these challenges, enabling networks with hundreds or even thousands of layers (He et al., 2016).

Universal   Approximation

A fundamental theorem states that a sufficiently large feedforward network with even a single hidden layer can approximate any continuous function on a compact set, under mild assumptions (Hornik, Stinchcombe and White, 1989). This theoretical result bolsters confidence in neural networks' expressive power. However, practical performance depends on architecture, data quality, and hyperparameter tuning.

Practical   Tip

Start experimenting with simpler, shallow networks before scaling to deeper architectures. Monitor training curves diligently to diagnose vanishing gradients or other training instabilities early in the process.

2.2.2. Convolutional vs. Recurrent Architectures

Convolutional   Neural   Networks   (CNNs)

CNNs revolutionized computer vision by exploiting local spatial correlations in images (LeCun et al., 1989). A convolutional layer slides learnable filters (kernels) across the input, capturing spatial features like edges, textures, and shapes. Stacking multiple convolutional layers uncovers increasingly abstract representations. Pooling layers reduce spatial dimensions, making computations more efficient.

Key CNN breakthroughs include:

- **AlexNet (2012)**: Demonstrated the power of CNNs on ImageNet classification, sparking widespread adoption in vision tasks (Krizhevsky, Sutskever and Hinton, 2012).

- **VGGNet**: Showed that smaller filters (3×3) stacked deep could improve performance.

- **ResNet**: Introduced **skip connections** or **residual blocks**, mitigating vanishing gradients in very deep architectures (He et al., 2016).

CNNs are not limited to images; they also apply to 1D signals (audio waveforms, time series) and 3D data (volumetric scans, video frames) (Maturana and Scherer, 2015).

Recurrent Neural Networks (RNNs)

Where CNNs excel at spatial data, RNNs specialize in **sequential** data. Traditional RNNs incorporate feedback loops, maintaining a hidden state that evolves over time (Rumelhart, Hinton and Williams, 1986). However, they suffer from vanishing or exploding gradients when sequences are long (Bengio, Simard and Frasconi, 1994).

To address these challenges, advanced RNN variants like **Long Short-Term Memory (LSTM)** (Hochreiter and Schmidhuber, 1997) and **Gated Recurrent Units (GRU)** (Cho et al., 2014) introduced gating mechanisms. These gates control the flow of information, enabling the model to maintain or discard hidden state information across many time steps. RNNs and their variants have historically excelled in language modeling, speech recognition, and time-series forecasting (Goodfellow, Bengio and Courville, 2016).

Transformer Disruption

While CNNs and RNNs remain influential, the **transformer** architecture (discussed in Chapter 4) has displaced RNNs in many NLP tasks. By leveraging *attention* mechanisms that weigh the relevance of different parts of the input, transformers avoid the pitfalls of sequential processing. However, CNNs still dominate many vision tasks, although some research explores attention-based networks for images as well (Dosovitskiy et al., 2021).

Choosing the Right Architecture

The choice between CNN, RNN, or a hybrid approach depends on the problem domain. Vision tasks typically favor CNNs, sequential tasks often rely on RNNs or transformers, and tasks involving both spatial and temporal data (e.g., video processing) might combine convolutional layers for spatial features with recurrent or attention mechanisms for temporal dynamics.

Practical Tip

Match the architecture to your data's structure. For purely sequential data (e.g., time series), consider LSTM/GRU or transformers. For images, start with CNNs. Hybrid approaches can address more complex scenarios like video classification or multimodal learning (image + text).

2.2.3. Activation Functions and Regularization

Activation Functions

Activation functions introduce nonlinearity into neural networks—a requirement for approximating complex functions. Common functions include:

- **Sigmoid**: Maps inputs to (0, 1). Historically popular, now less common due to saturation and slow convergence.

- **Tanh**: Similar to sigmoid but outputs in (-1, 1). Often performs better in practice, yet can still saturate.

- **ReLU (Rectified Linear Unit)**: Defined as max(0, x). Simple and efficient, it mitigates saturation for positive inputs (Nair and Hinton, 2010). However, "dying ReLU" can occur when inputs are frequently negative, leading neurons to output zeros persistently.

- **Leaky ReLU/ELU**: Variants that allow slight negative outputs, reducing the risk of neuron "death" (Maas, Hannun and Ng, 2013).

The choice of activation can significantly influence training dynamics. ReLU-based functions generally speed up convergence, particularly in deep architectures, but one might switch to other functions if encountering dead neurons or certain specialized tasks.

Regularization Strategies

Deep networks risk overfitting due to large parameter counts. Beyond L1/L2 regularization, several techniques aim to enhance generalization:

1. **Dropout**: Randomly sets a fraction of activations to zero during training, preventing co-adaptation (Srivastava et al., 2014).

2. **Batch Normalization**: Normalizes layer inputs, stabilizing training and allowing higher learning rates (Ioffe and Szegedy, 2015).

3. **Data Augmentation**: Mentioned in Section 2.1.2, artificially increases data diversity.

4. **Weight Decay**: A form of L2 regularization, particularly common in large-scale training to discourage overly large weights (Krogh and Hertz, 1992).

5. **Early Stopping**: Terminates training once validation performance plateaus, preventing further memorization of training data.

Choosing Appropriate Techniques

Selecting the right combination of activation and regularization can drastically influence model outcomes. CNNs often use ReLU or ReLU variants coupled with batch normalization and dropout. LSTMs have gating mechanisms inherently, so dropout remains a primary method of regularization. Transformers incorporate specialized normalization layers and rely heavily on large datasets plus attention-based architectures for generalization (Vaswani et al., 2017).

Practical Tip

Start with ReLU and batch normalization for deep networks. If you notice training instabilities, try alternative activations or tweak your normalization strategy. For models that still overfit, gradually add more regularization (dropout, weight decay) rather than piling on everything at once.

2.2.4. Transfer Learning: Pre-Trained Models and Fine-Tuning

Rationale for Transfer Learning

Training deep neural networks from scratch requires massive datasets and substantial computational resources. **Transfer learning** addresses these challenges by leveraging a model pre-trained on a large dataset (e.g., ImageNet for vision, massive text corpora for NLP) and then reusing its learned representations for a new, often related task (Yosinski et al., 2014). This approach:

- Reduces the need for large labeled datasets.

- Accelerates model convergence.

- Potentially improves performance on specialized tasks.

Common Approaches

1. **Feature Extraction**: Freeze most layers of the pre-trained model and use the final representations as features. Only the last classifier layer is retrained on the target dataset.

2. **Fine-Tuning**: Unfreeze some (or all) layers and continue training with a lower learning rate, allowing the model to adapt further without destroying the valuable initial weights (Howard and Ruder, 2018).

3. **Prompt Engineering** (in NLP): For large language models, design input prompts or task-specific "heads" that guide the model's generation or classification without fully retraining.

Applications

- **Computer Vision**: Models like VGG, ResNet, or EfficientNet pre-trained on ImageNet are widely adopted for tasks like medical image classification or object detection in specialized domains (Tan and Le, 2019).

- **Natural Language Processing**: BERT, GPT, and other transformer-based models can be fine-tuned for tasks like sentiment analysis, question answering, or named entity recognition (Devlin et al., 2019).

- **Speech Recognition**: Pre-trained acoustic models can be adapted to different dialects or noise conditions.

- **Tabular Data**: While less common, methods that generate robust embeddings from large tabular datasets or autoencoders can sometimes be transferred across related tasks.

Best Practices and Caveats

Choosing how many layers to unfreeze depends on domain similarity and dataset size. Large domain shifts (e.g., from everyday images to specialized scientific images) may require more layers to be trainable, whereas minor shifts (e.g., from dogs vs. cats to birds vs. fish) can often succeed with only the final layers retrained. Practitioners must also be cautious of **catastrophic forgetting**, where the fine-tuning process disrupts earlier learned weights excessively.

Practical   **Tip**

Assess domain similarity. The closer your target task to the pre-trained domain, the fewer layers you may need to unfreeze. Always monitor performance metrics to ensure you're not overfitting or catastrophically forgetting valuable representations.

2.3. Practical Tools and Frameworks

2.3.1. Popular ML Libraries (TensorFlow, PyTorch, Scikit-Learn)

TensorFlow

Developed by Google, **TensorFlow** is a widely adopted open-source platform for end-to-end machine learning. Its computational graph approach (in versions up to TF1.x) offered robust deployment options but came with a steeper learning curve. TensorFlow 2 introduced **eager execution** by default, simplifying debugging and iterative model development (Abadi et al., 2016). The ecosystem includes:

- **Keras**: A high-level API that allows rapid prototyping of neural networks.

- **TensorFlow Extended (TFX)**: Tools for model deployment and pipeline management.

PyTorch

Created by Facebook's AI Research lab, **PyTorch** emphasizes an imperative programming style that is more "Pythonic," making it popular among researchers (Paszke et al., 2019). Its dynamic computation graph allows flexible debugging. With the introduction of **TorchScript** and improvements to distributed training, PyTorch has expanded from research prototyping to production environments.

Scikit-Learn

For classical machine learning—linear/logistic regression, decision trees, random forests—**scikit-learn** (Pedregosa et al., 2011) remains a staple in Python. It offers a clean, consistent API for tasks ranging from feature extraction to model selection. While less suited for large-scale deep learning, scikit-learn is excellent for smaller or more traditional ML workflows.

Other Notable Libraries

- **XGBoost, LightGBM**: Gradient boosting libraries for structured data (Chen and Guestrin, 2016).

- **Fast.ai**: High-level wrappers around PyTorch, facilitating quick experimentation with advanced techniques.

- **Hugging Face Transformers**: Specializes in large-scale NLP models, simplifying fine-tuning for tasks like text classification or question answering (Wolf et al., 2020).

Choosing   the   Right   Tool
The "best" library depends on the problem type, dataset size, and developer preference. TensorFlow and PyTorch dominate deep learning, with Keras providing a user-friendly layer on top of TensorFlow. For non-deep learning tasks or quick prototypes, scikit-learn's simpler approach often suffices.

Practical   Tip
Beginners might start with scikit-learn for classical algorithms or Keras for deep learning. As projects scale in complexity, exploring lower-level frameworks like TensorFlow or PyTorch can provide finer control.

2.3.2. Hardware Acceleration (GPUs, TPUs, Cloud Solutions)

Why   Hardware   Matters
Machine learning tasks, especially deep neural networks, are computationally intensive. **Central Processing Units (CPUs)** handle control-intensive tasks well but struggle with the parallel arithmetic operations at ML's core. **Graphics Processing Units (GPUs)** excel at parallel computations, making them ideal for large matrix multiplications in neural network training (Goodfellow, Bengio and Courville, 2016).

GPUs
Initially designed for gaming, GPUs like NVIDIA's GeForce or Tesla series are now standard in ML workflows. They can accelerate training by factors of 10 to 100 compared to CPUs. However, GPUs require specialized libraries (e.g., CUDA, cuDNN) and are most effective when batch sizes and data structures are optimized for parallelization.

TPUs   (Tensor   Processing   Units)
Google developed **TPUs** to optimize TensorFlow workloads in their data centers, focusing on both training and inference. TPUs feature **systolic arrays** tailored to matrix multiplications required by deep learning. Cloud platforms (e.g., Google Cloud) offer TPU instances for rent, enabling large-scale training tasks without extensive local hardware investment (Jouppi et al., 2017).

Cloud   Solutions
Major cloud providers (AWS, Azure, Google Cloud) offer on-demand GPU or TPU instances, removing the need for on-premise hardware procurement. This elasticity is valuable for businesses that see spikes in workload. Additionally, managed AI services

provide auto-scaling, ML pipelines, and integrated development environments—though they can be costlier over time compared to local setups for consistently high workloads.

Edge and Mobile Deployment

While training typically demands powerful GPUs or TPUs, **inference** can occur on smaller devices. Frameworks like TensorFlow Lite, PyTorch Mobile, and ONNX Runtime facilitate model deployment on smartphones or edge devices (Lane et al., 2015). However, the model often needs optimization—quantization, pruning—to fit hardware constraints.

Practical Tip

Evaluate your project's scale. If you're training large models with big data, cloud-based GPU/TPU instances can accelerate development. For smaller tasks or tight budgets, local GPUs may suffice. Always factor in the cost of data transfer, security, and compliance when choosing cloud resources.

2.3.3. Working with Big Data Ecosystems

Defining Big Data

"Big Data" typically denotes datasets so large, varied, or fast-moving that traditional software struggles to manage them (Gandomi and Haider, 2015). Machine learning with big data can lead to improved accuracy but requires specialized infrastructure for storage, processing, and analysis.

Distributed Storage and Processing

- **Hadoop Distributed File System (HDFS)**: Stores large files across multiple nodes, enabling parallel access.

- **Spark**: A versatile cluster-computing framework supporting batch and streaming data. Spark's MLlib library provides scalable implementations of common ML algorithms (Zaharia et al., 2016).

- **Data Lakes**: Central repositories like Amazon S3 or Azure Data Lake, which handle structured and unstructured data at scale.

Scalable ML Workflows

Distributed training frameworks allow models to be trained on multiple GPUs or machines simultaneously:

1. **Horovod**: Developed by Uber for distributed deep learning across TensorFlow, PyTorch, and MXNet (Sergeev and Del Balso, 2018).

2. **PyTorch Distributed**: Built-in functionality for multi-GPU or multi-node setups.

3. **TensorFlow's MirroredStrategy**: Simplifies data parallel training across multiple GPUs on a single machine.

For iterative data processing, **Spark MLlib** or **Ray** can distribute tasks across nodes. This approach is beneficial when working with massive datasets that exceed the memory capacity of a single machine.

Challenges and Best Practices

- **Data Shuffling and Communication Overheads**: Large-scale training often becomes bottlenecked by network transfer rather than compute speed.

- **Fault Tolerance**: Nodes can fail mid-training. Frameworks must checkpoint progress and resume seamlessly.

- **Hyperparameter Tuning**: Larger datasets may require more complex search strategies or distributed hyperparameter optimization tools (e.g., Ray Tune).

Practical   **Tip**
Start with smaller subsets of data to prototype your pipeline. Only scale to full cluster resources once your code is stable and well-tested. This minimizes wasted compute time and costs in large-scale deployments.

2.3.4. Experiment Tracking and Version Control

The   **Need**   **for**   **Rigorous**   **Experimentation**
Machine learning experimentation involves rapidly iterating on datasets, model architectures, and hyperparameters. Without careful tracking, it becomes nearly impossible to reproduce past results or understand performance changes.

Tools for Experiment Tracking

- **TensorBoard**: Native to TensorFlow, offering real-time visualizations of metrics, histograms, and embeddings (Abadi et al., 2016).

- **Weights & Biases (wandb)**, **Neptune.ai**, **Comet.ml**: Hosted solutions that track experiments, hyperparameters, metrics, and logs with minimal setup.

- **MLflow**: An open-source platform covering experiment tracking, model packaging, and deployment (Zaharia et al., 2018).

These tools create a structured record of each run, capturing code versions, library dependencies, parameter choices, and results. Visual comparison dashboards help identify the best-performing models and the hyperparameters that led to those results.

Data   **and**   **Model**   **Versioning**
Beyond code version control (e.g., Git), data and model checkpoints also require versioning. Tools like **DVC (Data Version Control)** or **Git LFS (Large File Storage)** can store dataset snapshots and model binaries. This ensures that any experiment can be

recreated by retrieving the exact data and model states used originally (Dunne et al., 2021).

Collaboration and Reproducibility

In academia, reproducibility is vital for scientific integrity. In industry, it ensures robust product development. By systematically tracking experiments, teams can collaborate without confusion, hand off models seamlessly, and roll back to stable configurations if new changes degrade performance.

Practical Tip

Establish a consistent naming convention for experiments. For instance, embed timestamps, brief descriptors, or commit hashes. Regularly back up logs and model checkpoints to ensure you can revisit or share successful outcomes.

2.4. Building an ML Mindset

2.4.1. Problem Scoping and Feasibility

Defining the Business or Research Question

Effective machine learning starts with **clear objectives**. Whether it's predicting sales, classifying medical images, or reducing churn, the first step is articulating a research or business question with measurable success criteria. Vague goals, such as "use AI to transform our business," usually lead to scope creep and subpar results (Domingos, 2012).

Data Availability and Constraints

Assess the feasibility of your ML project by evaluating data:

- **Quantity**: Is there enough labeled data for a supervised approach?

- **Quality**: Are there systemic biases, missing values, or other flaws?

- **Freshness**: Do you need real-time data? If so, is the pipeline prepared for streaming ingestion?

- **Regulatory**: Does compliance with GDPR or HIPAA limit what can be collected or shared (European Commission, 2021)?

Resource and Stakeholder Alignment

Machine learning projects rarely exist in a vacuum. Collaborate with domain experts to define relevant features and interpret results. Engage stakeholders from legal, finance, and IT to understand constraints around budgeting, infrastructure, and risk tolerance.

Success Metrics

Beyond typical accuracy or F1 scores, consider business-level metrics—like revenue uplift, cost savings, or user satisfaction—that reflect genuine impact. Detailed metrics guide iteration and communicate progress clearly to non-technical stakeholders.

Practical **Tip**

Draft a short **Project Charter** summarizing objectives, stakeholders, data sources, constraints, and metrics. This ensures alignment before investing time and resources in model development.

2.4.2. Evaluating Data Quality and Bias

Data **Quality** **Dimensions**

Data quality directly influences model performance and fairness. Key dimensions include:

- **Completeness**: Are all necessary fields present?

- **Consistency**: Are data formats and types uniform across sources?

- **Accuracy**: Does the dataset faithfully represent ground truth?

- **Timeliness**: How up-to-date is the data?

Low-quality data can introduce spurious correlations or degrade model reliability. Exploratory data analysis—visualizing distributions, checking outliers—helps uncover issues early.

Sources **of** **Bias**

Bias can stem from:

1. **Sampling**: Over-representation of certain demographics or under-representation of others.

2. **Measurement**: Instruments or processes that systematically skew data collection.

3. **Historical**: Structural biases embedded in real-world decision-making processes (e.g., redlining in loan data).

These biases can perpetuate discrimination when models automate decisions in sensitive domains (e.g., hiring, lending, healthcare) (O'Neil, 2016).

Mitigation Strategies

- **Balanced Sampling**: Oversampling minority classes or undersampling majority classes to achieve equitable representation.

- **Algorithmic Fairness Tools**: Various open-source libraries (e.g., IBM's AI Fairness 360, Microsoft's Fairlearn) assess metrics like disparate impact or equalized odds (Barocas, Hardt and Narayanan, 2018).

- **Regular Auditing**: Continuously monitor predictions across demographic groups to detect drift or emergent biases.

Ethical **Responsibilities**

Regulatory frameworks increasingly mandate fairness assessments. Beyond compliance, organizations that proactively address bias build trust with customers and stakeholders. Ethical data usage is not only a moral imperative but also a strategic advantage in a world where data-driven decisions influence everything from credit scores to parole recommendations.

Practical **Tip**

Start with a small **bias audit** on your dataset—examine key demographic variables if available. Look for statistically significant disparities in performance or data representation. Address these findings before proceeding to full-scale model training.

2.4.3. Iteration, Tuning, and Patience

The **Iterative** **Nature** **of** **ML**

Machine learning is seldom a linear process. It often involves multiple feedback loops:

1. **Model Building**: Train an initial model on available data.

2. **Evaluation**: Compare metrics against benchmarks or baselines.

3. **Refinement**: Adjust hyperparameters, collect more data, or engineer better features.

4. **Reassessment**: Evaluate again on validation or test sets.

This cycle may repeat several times before performance stabilizes, and each iteration yields insights into data quality, model assumptions, and hyperparameter sensitivities (Shah et al., 2020).

Hyperparameter **Tuning** **and** **Model** **Selection**

Given the myriad of hyperparameters—learning rates, number of layers, regularization coefficients—systematic approaches are key (Bergstra and Bengio, 2012). Begin with coarse-grained searches or domain knowledge to narrow ranges, then adopt more fine-grained methods like Bayesian optimization. Meanwhile, track each experiment's configuration meticulously (see Section 2.3.4).

Managing **Expectations**

Organizations and novice practitioners sometimes expect instant "plug-and-play" solutions. In reality, building robust ML systems can take weeks or months of iteration. Rushed deployments often fail to generalize or overlook hidden biases. Setting realistic timelines aligns stakeholders and fosters a culture that values thoroughness over superficial results (Domingos, 2012).

When **to** **Stop**

Despite iterative improvements, diminishing returns inevitably set in. If performance plateaus despite repeated architectural changes or data augmentation, it might be time to:

- Shift focus to interpretability or user experience.

- Revisit the problem definition to see if a simpler approach suffices.

- Investigate alternative models or paradigms (e.g., from supervised to semi-supervised or active learning).

Practical **Tip**

Embrace experimentation. Treat each training run—successful or not—as data to inform the next step. Document your findings and resist pressure to skip rigorous evaluation just to meet deadlines or hype.

2.4.4. The ML Lifecycle in Practice

End-to-End **Pipeline**

A typical end-to-end ML lifecycle involves:

1. **Data Ingestion**: Pulling raw data from sources.

2. **Preprocessing**: Cleaning, normalization, feature engineering.

3. **Model Training**: Iterative process with hyperparameter tuning.

4. **Validation**: Checking performance on hold-out sets.

5. **Deployment**: Integrating model into production systems.

6. **Monitoring**: Tracking real-world performance and retraining if drift occurs.

Modern tools—MLflow, Kubeflow, TFX—can orchestrate these steps, ensuring reproducibility and automated workflow management (Zaharia et al., 2018).

DevOps **vs.** **MLOps**

While DevOps focuses on continuous integration/continuous delivery (CI/CD) of software, **MLOps** extends these principles to handle the complexities of data versioning, model tracking, and performance monitoring. Implementing MLOps can significantly reduce friction in maintaining, updating, and scaling ML models (Lwakatare et al., 2020).

Post-Deployment **Considerations**

Once in production, models can degrade due to:

- **Concept Drift**: Changes in data distribution over time (e.g., consumer behavior shifts).

- **Data Quality Issues**: Upstream changes to data pipelines that introduce new errors or formats.

- **User Feedback**: Errors or dissatisfaction from end-users.

Monitoring systems track input distributions and prediction metrics in real-time, issuing alerts when anomalies occur. This prompts retraining or reevaluation, closing the loop in the ML lifecycle.

Building   a   Resilient   ML   Culture
A resilient ML culture emphasizes **continuous learning, collaboration, and ethical considerations**. Team members understand not just the technical details but also the broader social impact of their models. This integrated approach fosters responsible innovation and sustained success in an AI-driven world.

Practical   Tip
Structure your ML lifecycle around "pipelines." Automating data ingestion, training, and deployment ensures reliability, especially as your organization scales its AI initiatives.

References (Harvard Style)

- Abadi, M. et al. (2016) 'TensorFlow: A System for Large-Scale Machine Learning', in *12th USENIX Symposium on Operating Systems Design and Implementation (OSDI 16)*, pp. 265–283.

- Barocas, S., Hardt, M. and Narayanan, A. (2018) *Fairness and Machine Learning*. [Preprint]. Available at: http://fairmlbook.org (Accessed: 10 February 2025).

- Bengio, Y., Simard, P. and Frasconi, P. (1994) 'Learning Long-Term Dependencies with Gradient Descent Is Difficult', *IEEE Transactions on Neural Networks*, 5(2), pp. 157–166.

- Bergstra, J. and Bengio, Y. (2012) 'Random Search for Hyper-Parameter Optimization', *Journal of Machine Learning Research*, 13(Feb), pp. 281–305.

- Chapelle, O., Schölkopf, B. and Zien, A. (2006) *Semi-Supervised Learning*. Cambridge, MA: MIT Press.

- Chen, T. and Guestrin, C. (2016) 'XGBoost: A Scalable Tree Boosting System', in *Proceedings of the 22nd ACM SIGKDD International Conference on Knowledge Discovery and Data Mining*, pp. 785–794.

- Cho, K. et al. (2014) 'Learning Phrase Representations using RNN Encoder–Decoder for Statistical Machine Translation', in *Proceedings of the 2014 Conference on Empirical Methods in Natural Language Processing (EMNLP)*. Stroudsburg, PA: ACL, pp. 1724–1734.

- Devlin, J. et al. (2019) 'BERT: Pre-Training of Deep Bidirectional Transformers for Language Understanding', in *Proceedings of the 2019 Conference of the North American Chapter of the ACL (NAACL)*, pp. 4171–4186.

- Domingos, P. (2012) 'A Few Useful Things to Know about Machine Learning', *Communications of the ACM*, 55(10), pp. 78–87.

- Dosovitskiy, A. et al. (2021) 'An Image is Worth 16x16 Words: Transformers for Image Recognition at Scale', in *International Conference on Learning Representations* (ICLR). Available at: https://openreview.net (Accessed: 10 February 2025).

- Dunne, C. et al. (2021) 'Git LFS and DVC: Strategies for Large File Versioning in Collaborative ML Projects', *Journal of Open Source Software*, 6(58), p. 3125.

- European Commission (2021) *Proposal for a Regulation Laying Down Harmonised Rules on Artificial Intelligence (Artificial Intelligence Act)*. Available at: https://digital-strategy.ec.europa.eu (Accessed: 10 February 2025).

- Fawcett, T. and Provost, F. (2013) 'Data Science and its Relationship to Big Data and Data-Driven Decision Making', *Big Data*, 1(1), pp. 51–59.

- Gandomi, A. and Haider, M. (2015) 'Beyond the Hype: Big Data Concepts, Methods, and Analytics', *International Journal of Information Management*, 35(2), pp. 137–144.

- Glorot, X. and Bengio, Y. (2010) 'Understanding the Difficulty of Training Deep Feedforward Neural Networks', in *Proceedings of the 13th International Conference on Artificial Intelligence and Statistics (AISTATS)*, pp. 249–256.

- Goodfellow, I., Bengio, Y. and Courville, A. (2016) *Deep Learning*. Cambridge, MA: MIT Press.

- Hastie, T., Tibshirani, R. and Friedman, J. (2009) *The Elements of Statistical Learning: Data Mining, Inference, and Prediction*. 2nd edn. New York: Springer.

- Hawkins, D.M. (2004) 'The Problem of Overfitting', *Journal of Chemical Information and Computer Sciences*, 44(1), pp. 1–12.

- He, K. et al. (2016) 'Deep Residual Learning for Image Recognition', in *Proceedings of the IEEE Conference on Computer Vision and Pattern Recognition (CVPR)*, pp. 770–778.

- Hochreiter, S. and Schmidhuber, J. (1997) 'Long Short-Term Memory', *Neural Computation*, 9(8), pp. 1735–1780.

- Hornik, K., Stinchcombe, M. and White, H. (1989) 'Multilayer Feedforward Networks are Universal Approximators', *Neural Networks*, 2(5), pp. 359–366.

- Howard, J. and Ruder, S. (2018) 'Universal Language Model Fine-tuning for Text Classification', in *Proceedings of the 56th Annual Meeting of the Association for Computational Linguistics (ACL)*. Stroudsburg, PA: ACL, pp. 328–339.

- Ioffe, S. and Szegedy, C. (2015) 'Batch Normalization: Accelerating Deep Network Training by Reducing Internal Covariate Shift', in *Proceedings of the 32nd International Conference on Machine Learning (ICML)*, pp. 448–456.

- Jouppi, N.P. et al. (2017) 'In-Datacenter Performance Analysis of a Tensor Processing Unit', in *Proceedings of the 44th Annual International Symposium on Computer Architecture (ISCA)*, pp. 1–12.

- Kohavi, R. (1995) 'A Study of Cross-Validation and Bootstrap for Accuracy Estimation and Model Selection', in *Proceedings of the 14th International Joint Conference on Artificial Intelligence (IJCAI)*, pp. 1137–1145.

- Krizhevsky, A., Sutskever, I. and Hinton, G.E. (2012) 'ImageNet Classification with Deep Convolutional Neural Networks', *Communications of the ACM*, 60(6), pp. 84–90.

- Krogh, A. and Hertz, J.A. (1992) 'A Simple Weight Decay Can Improve Generalization', in *Advances in Neural Information Processing Systems 4*. San Francisco, CA: Morgan Kaufmann, pp. 950–957.

- Lane, N.D. et al. (2015) 'DeepX: A Software Accelerator for Low-Power Deep Learning Inference on Mobile Devices', in *Proceedings of the 14th International Conference on Information Processing in Sensor Networks (IPSN)*. New York: ACM, pp. 1–12.

- LeCun, Y. et al. (1989) 'Backpropagation Applied to Handwritten Zip Code Recognition', *Neural Computation*, 1(4), pp. 541–551.

- LeCun, Y., Bengio, Y. and Hinton, G. (2015) 'Deep Learning', *Nature*, 521(7553), pp. 436–444.

- Lwakatare, L.E. et al. (2020) 'DevOps and MLOps in Practice: A Case Study on Software Development for Machine Learning', in *International Conference on Product-Focused Software Process Improvement*. Cham: Springer, pp. 422–437.

- Maas, A.L., Hannun, A.Y. and Ng, A.Y. (2013) 'Rectifier Nonlinearities Improve Neural Network Acoustic Models', in *Proceedings of the 30th International Conference on Machine Learning (ICML) Workshop on Deep Learning for Audio, Speech, and Language Processing*. Atlanta, GA: JMLR.org.

- Marcus, G. and Davis, E. (2019) *Rebooting AI: Building Artificial Intelligence We Can Trust*. New York: Pantheon Books.

- Maturana, D. and Scherer, S. (2015) 'VoxNet: A 3D Convolutional Neural Network for Real-Time Object Recognition', in *IEEE/RSJ International Conference on Intelligent Robots and Systems (IROS)*, pp. 922–928.

- Mitchell, T. (1997) *Machine Learning*. New York: McGraw-Hill.

- Nair, V. and Hinton, G.E. (2010) 'Rectified Linear Units Improve Restricted Boltzmann Machines', in *Proceedings of the 27th International Conference on Machine Learning (ICML)*, pp. 807–814.

- Ng, A. (2004) 'Feature Selection, L1 vs. L2 Regularization, and Rotational Invariance', in *Proceedings of the Twenty-first International Conference on Machine Learning (ICML)*, p. 78.

- Nilsson, N. (2010) *The Quest for Artificial Intelligence*. Cambridge: Cambridge University Press.

- O'Neil, C. (2016) *Weapons of Math Destruction: How Big Data Increases Inequality and Threatens Democracy*. New York: Crown.

- Paszke, A. et al. (2019) 'PyTorch: An Imperative Style, High-Performance Deep Learning Library', in *Advances in Neural Information Processing Systems* (NeurIPS), pp. 8024–8035.

- Pedregosa, F. et al. (2011) 'Scikit-learn: Machine Learning in Python', *Journal of Machine Learning Research*, 12, pp. 2825–2830.

- Rosenblatt, F. (1958) 'The Perceptron: A Probabilistic Model for Information Storage and Organization in the Brain', *Psychological Review*, 65(6), pp. 386–408.

- Rumelhart, D.E., Hinton, G.E. and Williams, R.J. (1986) 'Learning Representations by Back-Propagating Errors', *Nature*, 323(6088), pp. 533–536.

- Russell, S. and Norvig, P. (2021) *Artificial Intelligence: A Modern Approach*. 4th edn. Hoboken, NJ: Pearson.

- Sergeev, A. and Del Balso, M. (2018) 'Horovod: Fast and Easy Distributed Deep Learning in TensorFlow', *arXiv preprint* arXiv:1802.05799.

- Shah, S.A.A. et al. (2020) 'Predictable, Reliable and Resource-Efficient Deep Learning via Small-Batch SGD', in *International Conference on Learning Representations (ICLR)*. Available at: https://openreview.net (Accessed: 10 February 2025).

- Shorten, C. and Khoshgoftaar, T.M. (2019) 'A Survey on Image Data Augmentation for Deep Learning', *Journal of Big Data*, 6(1), p. 60.

- Srivastava, N. et al. (2014) 'Dropout: A Simple Way to Prevent Neural Networks from Overfitting', *Journal of Machine Learning Research*, 15(1), pp. 1929–1958.

- Sutton, R.S. and Barto, A.G. (2018) *Reinforcement Learning: An Introduction*. 2nd edn. Cambridge, MA: MIT Press.

- Tan, M. and Le, Q. (2019) 'EfficientNet: Rethinking Model Scaling for Convolutional Neural Networks', in *International Conference on Machine Learning (ICML)*, pp. 6105–6114.

- Vaswani, A. et al. (2017) 'Attention Is All You Need', in *Advances in Neural Information Processing Systems*(NeurIPS). Red Hook, NY: Curran Associates.

- Wolf, T. et al. (2020) 'Transformers: State-of-the-Art Natural Language Processing', in *Proceedings of the 2020 Conference on Empirical Methods in Natural Language Processing: System Demonstrations*. Stroudsburg, PA: ACL, pp. 38–45.

- Yosinski, J. et al. (2014) 'How Transferable are Features in Deep Neural Networks?', in *Advances in Neural Information Processing Systems* (NeurIPS). Red Hook, NY: Curran Associates, pp. 3320–3328.

- Zaharia, M. et al. (2016) 'Apache Spark: A Unified Engine for Big Data Processing', *Communications of the ACM*, 59(11), pp. 56–65.

- Zaharia, M. et al. (2018) 'Accelerating the Machine Learning Lifecycle with MLflow', *Data-Driven Intelligence Workshop at NeurIPS*. Montréal, Canada: NeurIPS.

Chapter 3: Introduction to Language Models

3.1. What Is NLP?

3.1.1. The Evolution of NLP

From Rule-Based Systems to Statistical Approaches
Natural Language Processing (NLP) is a multidisciplinary field at the intersection of linguistics, computer science, and artificial intelligence, focused on enabling computers to understand, interpret, and generate human language (Jurafsky and Martin, 2023). Early efforts in NLP date back to the 1950s, with attempts at machine translation often relying on direct word substitutions and extensive, manually crafted rules (Hutchins, 2005). These "rule-based" systems dominated until the late 1980s but struggled with the vast ambiguity and variability present in natural language.

By the early 1990s, the **statistical revolution** ushered in a paradigm shift. Researchers began leveraging probabilistic models—such as Hidden Markov Models (HMMs) and N-gram language models—to handle tasks like part-of-speech tagging, speech recognition, and translation (Manning and Schütze, 1999). These models didn't require exhaustive rule databases; instead, they learned from annotated corpora how likely certain word sequences or tags were, thus improving robustness and scalability.

Deep Learning Comes to NLP
While statistical methods performed well, they often depended on complex feature engineering and domain expertise. The advent of **deep learning** in the late 2000s changed this dynamic. Neural network architectures—ranging from recurrent networks (RNNs) to convolutional networks—enabled data-driven feature extraction, obviating some of the need for meticulous feature crafting (Goldberg, 2017). However, it was the development of the **transformer architecture**(Vaswani et al., 2017) that sparked the modern wave of large language models (LLMs), significantly advancing NLP capabilities in tasks like translation, summarization, and question answering.

NLP's Expanding Influence
Today, NLP techniques underpin a wide array of applications: from voice assistants (e.g., Alexa, Siri) and chatbots, to automated content moderation on social media, to advanced search engines like Google and Bing. The field's success draws on progress in **computational linguistics**, **machine learning**, and **high-performance computing**, reflecting how interdisciplinary collaboration fuels innovation.

Historical Milestones

- **1950s–1960s**: Early machine translation experiments; rule-based morphological analysis.

- **1970s–1980s**: Focus on knowledge representation (semantic networks, logic-based systems); limited domain-specific success (e.g., SHRDLU for block-world dialogues).

- **1990s–Early 2000s**: Statistical revolution—HMMs, maximum entropy models, and SVMs gain traction for NLP tasks.

- **2010s–Present**: Neural networks and transformers dominate, enabling unprecedented breakthroughs in language understanding and generation.

Key   Insight
Understanding NLP's evolution—from hand-crafted rules to probabilistic methods to deep learning—reveals how the field continually adapts to the growing complexity of language tasks and the availability of computational resources.

3.1.2. Syntax, Semantics & Pragmatics

Syntax: The   Structural   Layer
Syntax concerns the grammatical arrangement of words within sentences. Syntactic analysis aims to parse sentences into phrases, clauses, and parts of speech, providing a scaffold for higher-level understanding (Chomsky, 1957). Traditional syntactic parsing methods often involve context-free grammars or dependency grammars, while modern approaches employ **neural parsers** that directly learn syntactic structure from labeled treebanks (Kiperwasser and Goldberg, 2016). Even for large language models, an implicit grasp of syntax emerges through exposure to vast text corpora, but explicit syntactic annotations still help in linguistic research or specialized applications.

Semantics: Meaning   and   Interpretation
Semantics delves into the meaning behind words and sentences. Tasks like **word sense disambiguation** illustrate the complexity of mapping word forms to concepts (Navigli, 2009). For instance, the word "bank" can refer to a financial institution or the side of a river, and semantic models must discern context to choose the correct interpretation. Traditional semantics used lexical databases like WordNet (Fellbaum, 1998) or semantic role labeling frameworks. Neural models, however, often capture semantic nuances through contextual embeddings, as seen in BERT or GPT-based architectures (Devlin et al., 2019).

Pragmatics: Context   and   Usage
Pragmatics extends beyond literal meaning to consider the speaker's intent, context, and the relationship between interlocutors (Levinson, 1983). For instance, "Could you open the window?" is syntactically a question but pragmatically a request. In dialogue systems, capturing pragmatic cues can be vital for producing coherent, contextually appropriate responses. Consider how chatbots might need to recognize sarcasm, politeness levels,

or rhetorical questions—factors heavily influenced by situational context, cultural norms, and conversation history.

Balancing   All   Three

Real-world NLP solutions must integrate syntax, semantics, and pragmatics. For example:

- A machine translation system cannot merely translate words (semantics) without preserving grammatical structure (syntax) or context (pragmatics).

- Sentiment analysis goes beyond dictionary-based approaches by incorporating domain-specific usage (e.g., sarcasm or irony).

Modern large language models implicitly learn these layers through deep contextual embeddings, though they still face challenges—particularly in nuanced pragmatic contexts or ambiguous semantic territory. Researchers continue striving for more explicit models that integrate linguistic theories, potentially leading to systems with deeper "understanding."

Key   Insight

Syntax, semantics, and pragmatics provide a layered understanding of language, guiding how NLP systems parse structure, interpret meaning, and adapt to context. Mastery of these layers is fundamental for designing sophisticated language models.

3.1.3. Role of Data in NLP

Corpora   and   Language   Resources

NLP thrives on large **corpora**—collections of text or speech that reflect natural language usage. Famous examples include the **British National Corpus**, **Common Crawl**, or domain-specific sets (e.g., legal, medical texts). These corpora act as training grounds where models learn word distributions, syntactic patterns, and semantic relationships (Manning and Schütze, 1999).

- **Monolingual Data**: Typically used for language modeling, sentiment analysis, or topic classification.

- **Parallel Data**: Aligned text in two (or more) languages, essential for machine translation.

- **Annotated Data**: Labeled for tasks like part-of-speech tagging, named entity recognition (NER), or sentiment classification, crucial for supervised learning.

Data   Quality   and   Diversity

Quality matters. Biased or unrepresentative datasets can skew model performance, rendering them less effective or even discriminatory (Bender and Friedman, 2018). For instance, a sentiment analysis model trained primarily on social media data from English-speaking teenagers may poorly handle text from older or non-English-speaking populations. Similarly, large language models like GPT or BERT can inadvertently learn and perpetuate harmful biases present in their training corpora (Bommasani et al., 2021).

Linguistic   Complexity   and   Low-Resource   Languages
Many NLP breakthroughs center on English, which enjoys abundant data resources. However, the majority of the world's 7,000+ languages are **low-resource**—lacking large corpora or standardized writing systems. Researchers employ techniques like **transfer learning, multilingual embeddings**, and **data augmentation** to extend language model capabilities to underrepresented languages (Conneau et al., 2020). This area remains a critical challenge, as equitable NLP advancements require bridging linguistic divides.

Ethical   Considerations
Collecting language data at scale often intersects with privacy and consent issues. Regulatory frameworks like the **EU General Data Protection Regulation (GDPR)** restrict data usage, especially sensitive content such as health information or personal identifiers (European Commission, 2021). Maintaining transparency about data collection and respecting opt-out rights is essential for responsible NLP development.

Key   Insight
Data is the bedrock of NLP. Its volume, diversity, and quality directly influence model robustness and fairness. Researchers and practitioners must carefully select, preprocess, and document datasets to ensure ethical, inclusive, and high-performing language technologies.

3.2. Statistical vs. Neural NLP

3.2.1. N-grams & Probabilistic Models

Foundations   of   Statistical   NLP
Before neural networks rose to prominence, **statistical NLP** dominated the field. The most iconic representation of this era is the **N-gram model**, which estimates the probability of a word given the preceding $n-1n-1$ words (Jurafsky and Martin, 2023). An N-gram model for trigram ($n=3n=3$) might compute:

$$P(word_t | word_{t-1}, word_{t-2}) P(word_t | word_{t-1}, word_{t-2})$$

These probabilities are typically derived from relative frequencies in a large corpus. For example, "New York City" might appear frequently, yielding a high probability for "City" following "New York," while "New York Latte" would have a lower probability.

Strengths   and   Weaknesses
N-gram models excel in simplicity and interpretability. They are easy to implement, and their predictions can be understood by looking at simple frequency counts. However, they suffer from:

1. **Data Sparsity:** As nn grows, the likelihood of seeing exact sequences plummets, making it challenging to estimate probabilities accurately.

2. **Context Limitations:** N-gram models only capture local context, ignoring long-distance dependencies.

3. **Vocabulary Explosion:** Handling large vocabularies can be problematic, often requiring smoothing techniques (e.g., Kneser-Ney smoothing) to avoid zero probabilities (Chen and Goodman, 1999).

Hidden   Markov   Models   (HMMs)
Another statistical approach is **Hidden Markov Models**, used extensively in part-of-speech tagging, speech recognition, and named entity recognition (Rabiner, 1989). In HMMs, states represent hidden linguistic properties (e.g., tags or phonemes), and observed symbols represent words or acoustic features. Viterbi decoding is applied to find the most likely sequence of hidden states.

While HMMs and N-gram models were groundbreaking, they still share limitations: reliance on Markov assumptions and inability to capture more complex language structures without exponentially increasing complexity.

Continued   Relevance
Despite their age, N-gram and HMM-based methods remain relevant in resource-constrained environments (e.g., embedded systems) or as baselines for research comparisons. They also provide foundational knowledge for understanding how modern methods address the same linguistic challenges more comprehensively.

Key   Insight
Statistical models like N-grams and HMMs laid the groundwork for NLP, showing the power of data-driven approaches. They introduced essential concepts—such as language modeling and probabilistic inference—that neural methods build upon today.

3.2.2. The Neural Network Advantage

From   Representation   to   End-to-End   Learning
Neural networks revolutionized NLP by shifting away from hand-crafted features toward **learned representations**. This approach reduces reliance on domain-specific rules or labor-intensive feature engineering (Goldberg, 2017). Through hidden layers and distributed representations, neural networks can encode subtle linguistic patterns, such as word analogies or syntactic roles.

Word   Embeddings
A critical innovation in neural NLP was the introduction of **word embeddings**—dense, low-dimensional vectors representing semantic and syntactic properties of words. Early methods like **word2vec** (Mikolov et al., 2013) or **GloVe**(Pennington, Socher and Manning,

2014) learned embeddings by predicting word co-occurrences. The result was a vector space where synonyms or related concepts appear close together (e.g., "king" near "queen," "Italy" near "Rome"). Word embeddings provided a robust foundation for downstream tasks like text classification or named entity recognition, outperforming sparse, one-hot representations.

Contextual Embeddings and Transformers

While static embeddings improved model performance, they could not capture how a word's meaning changes with context. For example, the word "play" has different senses in "play a game," "play a role," or "play the violin." **Contextual embedding** models like ELMo (Peters et al., 2018) and BERT (Devlin et al., 2019) dynamically generate word vectors depending on the surrounding text. These developments culminated in the **transformer architecture**, which uses self-attention to model relationships across words in a sentence more efficiently than RNNs (Vaswani et al., 2017).

Advantages Over Statistical Methods

Neural approaches offer several benefits:

1. **Longer Context**: Recurrent networks and transformers can, in theory, process or attend to tokens from entire sentences or documents, surpassing the local scope of N-gram models.

2. **Representation Learning**: Instead of manual feature crafting, neural networks learn relevant linguistic features automatically.

3. **Scalability**: With sufficient computational resources and data, neural networks can scale to tasks of immense complexity—e.g., GPT models with billions of parameters.

Challenges

Neural models require significant data, powerful hardware (GPUs, TPUs), and careful hyperparameter tuning. They can also be **opaque**: explaining why a neural model outputs a certain prediction remains non-trivial (Belinkov and Glass, 2019). Researchers balance performance gains with interpretability, employing techniques like attention visualization, gradient-based saliency methods, or model distillation.

Key Insight

Neural networks brought about a paradigm shift in NLP, enabling models to learn features and context from raw text. Their capacity to scale and capture nuanced linguistic phenomena has led to state-of-the-art performance in numerous tasks.

3.2.3. Common Benchmarks & Datasets

Benchmarking in NLP

Benchmarks are crucial for measuring progress and comparing models under consistent conditions (Bowman et al., 2015). Well-curated datasets and standard evaluation metrics (accuracy, BLEU, ROUGE, F1, etc.) allow researchers to gauge advances and identify weaknesses. They also help reveal overfitting if models begin to "memorize" well-known benchmarks without truly generalizing.

Popular NLP Benchmarks

1. **GLUE and SuperGLUE**: General Language Understanding Evaluation (GLUE) includes tasks like sentiment analysis (SST-2), natural language inference (MNLI), and question answering (QNLI). SuperGLUE raises the difficulty with tasks emphasizing deeper reasoning, e.g., Winograd Schema Challenge (Wang et al., 2019).

2. **SQuAD (Stanford Question Answering Dataset)**: Focuses on reading comprehension by asking questions about paragraphs from Wikipedia (Rajpurkar et al., 2016).

3. **CNN/Daily Mail and XSum**: Used for text summarization, featuring news articles and corresponding summaries (Hermann et al., 2015; Narayan, Cohen and Lapata, 2018).

4. **WMT (Workshop on Machine Translation)**: Offers parallel corpora in multiple language pairs, with annual competitions that spur innovation in translation algorithms.

Beyond English-Centric Benchmarks

While most benchmarks center on English, **multilingual** benchmarks like **XTREME** (Hu et al., 2020) assess how well models handle diverse languages. Such initiatives push the field to move beyond English, highlighting low-resource languages and evaluating cross-lingual transfer.

Limitations of Benchmarks

- **Test Set Leakage**: Over-reliance on known benchmarks can yield inflated performance if the model indirectly memorizes test examples.

- **Shallow Understanding**: High scores may mask superficial pattern matching rather than deep language comprehension (Marcus and Davis, 2019).

- **Context & World Knowledge**: Many tasks require real-world or domain-specific knowledge beyond the text. Models that excel on standard benchmarks may fail in more specialized or context-heavy scenarios.

Dataset Curation & Ethical Best Practices

Constructing robust benchmarks demands careful annotation and rigorous quality control. It also requires ethical diligence: some datasets inadvertently contain private information, hate speech, or other harmful content. Researchers and practitioners must respect data licensing, anonymize personal identifiers, and consider the dataset's potential social impacts (Bender and Friedman, 2018).

Key   **Insight**

Benchmarks drive progress in NLP by standardizing evaluation and fostering community-wide comparisons. Yet, caution is needed to avoid overfitting on benchmarks or ignoring real-world complexities and ethical considerations.

3.3. Key Tasks in NLP

3.3.1. Text Classification & Sentiment Analysis

Text   **Classification**   **Overview**

Text classification encompasses a wide range of tasks where the objective is to assign labels to textual inputs. Common examples include:

- **Topic Classification**: Grouping documents by subject matter (e.g., sports, politics).

- **Spam Detection**: Identifying unwanted or harmful emails.

- **Toxicity Detection**: Screening for hate speech or harassment on social media.

Traditional approaches often involved bag-of-words or TF-IDF representations fed into classifiers like Naive Bayes or SVMs. Today, neural methods use embeddings (static or contextual) and feed into architectures such as CNNs or transformers for end-to-end learning (Kim, 2014; Devlin et al., 2019).

Sentiment   **Analysis**

Sentiment analysis is a specialized form of text classification that gauges the emotional or subjective tone in text—often categorized as positive, negative, or neutral (Liu, 2012). This task is ubiquitous in social media monitoring, customer feedback analysis, and market research. Modern large language models can capture nuanced sentiment, though sarcasm, irony, and cultural references remain challenging (Van Hee, Lefever and Hoste, 2018).

Challenges and Context

1. **Domain Adaptation**: A model trained on movie reviews may falter when analyzing financial reports. Domain-specific language can require specialized fine-tuning.

2. **Class Imbalance**: Real-world data often skews heavily, e.g., minimal negative reviews compared to neutral or positive. Imbalance can undermine accuracy if not addressed (Chawla, 2009).

3. **Multilingual Settings**: Sentiment vocabulary varies across languages; a direct translation of "happy" might not exactly match the sentiment strength in another language.

Advanced   **Techniques**

State-of-the-art text classification pipelines often involve:

- **Contextual Embeddings** (BERT, RoBERTa, or multilingual variants).

- **Fine-Tuning** on domain-labeled datasets.

- **Ensemble Methods** for improved robustness.

Practical Applications

- **Social Listening**: Track brand sentiment in real-time to inform marketing strategies.

- **Healthcare**: Monitor patient feedback for adverse effects or satisfaction in telemedicine portals (McCoy, Cagan and Nembhard, 2020).

- **News Categorization**: Filter incoming feeds by topic or political stance.

Key   **Insight**

Text classification and sentiment analysis exemplify how NLP can distill large volumes of text into actionable insights. Despite breakthroughs from large language models, success depends on domain-relevant training data and careful attention to linguistic context.

3.3.2. Named Entity Recognition & Information Extraction

Named   **Entity**   **Recognition**   **(NER)**

NER involves identifying and classifying named entities— like **persons, organizations, locations**, or **dates**—within text (Tjong Kim Sang and De Meulder, 2003). Historically tackled via feature-based methods (Conditional Random Fields, HMMs), NER has seen major improvements using **BiLSTM-CRF** architectures and, more recently, transformer-based models (Lample et al., 2016; Devlin et al., 2019). Accurate NER is foundational for many downstream tasks:

- **Knowledge Graph Construction**: Extracting structured information from unstructured text.

- **Question Answering**: Pinpointing entities that relate to user queries.

- **Event Detection**: Identifying critical actors, places, and times in news streams.

Relation   **Extraction**

While NER identifies entity mentions, **relation extraction** determines how these entities connect (e.g., "Barack Obama" *is the 44th President of* "the United States"). Techniques often include supervised learning over annotated sentences or distant supervision using knowledge bases (Mintz et al., 2009). Neural models encode sentences with RNNs or transformers, then classify the relation type among identified entities (Zeng et al., 2015).

Event Extraction and Beyond

Information extraction can go deeper, identifying **events** (e.g., natural disasters, product launches), **temporal expressions**, and the causal or rhetorical structure of texts (Ji and Grishman, 2008). A typical pipeline might involve:

1. **Trigger Detection**: Finding words or phrases that signal an event.

2. **Argument Classification**: Linking entities to the event.

3. **Role Labeling**: Identifying who did what to whom, when, and where.

Domain Adaptation and Low-Resource Settings

Generic NER or relation extraction models trained on news corpora may struggle with specialized vocabularies in biomedical, legal, or financial texts (Zhang et al., 2020). Fine-tuning or domain-specific pre-training helps adapt the model's knowledge. In low-resource languages or domains, semi-supervised approaches and data augmentation can bridge data scarcity.

Challenges

- **Ambiguity**: Entities can appear in varied forms (nicknames, abbreviations).

- **Context Dependence**: Words like "Apple" might refer to a fruit or a tech company.

- **Overlapping Relations**: Text segments may imply multiple events or relationships simultaneously.

Applications

- **Contract Analysis**: Legal professionals use NER to identify clauses, parties, and obligations in lengthy documents.

- **Business Intelligence**: Automated extraction of key events or competitor activities from news feeds.

- **Healthcare**: Identifying drug mentions, dosages, or adverse effects from clinical reports.

Key Insight

NER and information extraction transform raw text into structured data, powering sophisticated knowledge systems. Advanced neural models can capture nuanced entity and relation patterns, but domain adaptation and context handling remain ongoing challenges.

3.3.3. Machine Translation & Summarization

Machine **Translation** **(MT)**

Machine translation aims to automatically convert text from one language to another, bridging linguistic barriers. Early rule-based systems struggled with idiomatic expressions and cultural nuances, leading to often comical mistranslations. **Statistical MT** (SMT), exemplified by phrase-based models, improved quality by learning translation probabilities from parallel corpora (Koehn, 2010). However, it was the advent of **neural machine translation (NMT)**—especially sequence-to-sequence (Seq2Seq) models with attention—that enabled breakthrough accuracy (Bahdanau, Cho and Bengio, 2015).

Modern NMT systems use **transformer architectures**, sidestepping some limitations of recurrent models (Vaswani et al., 2017). Key features include:

- **Self-Attention**: Captures long-range dependencies within sentences.
- **Positional Encoding**: Retains sequence order without explicit recurrence.
- **Massive Parallelism**: Speeds up training on large, multilingual datasets.

Despite major advances, true human-level translation remains elusive, especially for low-resource languages or culturally laden content. Yet commercial systems (e.g., Google Translate, Microsoft Translator) deliver near-human performance on many language pairs.

Text **Summarization**

Summarization condenses a longer text into a shorter version while retaining key information. Two major paradigms exist:

1. **Extractive Summarization**: Selects important sentences or phrases from the source text (Nallapati et al., 2017).
2. **Abstractive Summarization**: Generates novel sentences, rephrasing or synthesizing content (Rush, Chopra and Weston, 2015).

Abstractive methods often leverage Seq2Seq or transformer-based models that learn to paraphrase while preserving core meanings. Challenges include preventing factual inconsistencies, handling domain-specific jargon, and summarizing multiple document sources coherently.

Evaluation
Common metrics:

- **BLEU**: Compares machine outputs to reference translations or summaries based on overlapping n-grams (Papineni et al., 2002).
- **ROUGE**: Focuses on recall of key n-grams or sequences (Lin, 2004).
- **METEOR, CIDEr**: Variants tailored to translation or image captioning.

Human evaluations remain the gold standard, as metrics can overlook fluency, coherence, or factual correctness. Increasing attention goes toward **factual consistency** metrics for summarization, ensuring that generated text does not fabricate details (Maynez et al., 2020).

Real-World Applications

- **Global Communication**: Instant translation services in messaging apps or websites enable cross-cultural collaboration.

- **Information Overload**: Summaries for news articles, scientific papers, or legal documents help readers grasp essentials quickly.

- **Accessibility**: Summaries aid individuals with visual impairments or cognitive challenges by presenting core content more succinctly.

Key   **Insight**

MT and summarization exemplify the power of neural sequence-to-sequence learning. While performance has surged, ensuring faithfulness to source content—without errors or biases—remains a cornerstone of ongoing research.

References (Harvard Style)

- Bahdanau, D., Cho, K. and Bengio, Y. (2015) 'Neural Machine Translation by Jointly Learning to Align and Translate', in *3rd International Conference on Learning Representations (ICLR)*. San Diego, CA: ICLR.

- Belinkov, Y. and Glass, J. (2019) 'Analysis Methods in Neural Language Processing: A Survey', *Transactions of the Association for Computational Linguistics*, 7, pp. 49–72.

- Bender, E.M. and Friedman, B. (2018) 'Data Statements for NLP: Toward Mitigating System Bias and Enabling Better Science', *Transactions of the Association for Computational Linguistics*, 6, pp. 587–604.

- Bommasani, R. et al. (2021) 'On the Opportunities and Risks of Foundation Models', *arXiv preprint* arXiv:2108.07258.

- Bowman, S.R. et al. (2015) 'A Large Annotated Corpus for Learning Natural Language Inference', in *Proceedings of the 2015 Conference on Empirical Methods in Natural Language Processing (EMNLP)*. Stroudsburg, PA: ACL, pp. 632–642.

- Chawla, N.V. (2009) 'Data Mining for Imbalanced Datasets: An Overview', in *Data Mining and Knowledge Discovery Handbook*. 2nd edn. Boston, MA: Springer, pp. 875–886.

- Chen, S.F. and Goodman, J. (1999) 'An Empirical Study of Smoothing Techniques for Language Modeling', *Computer Speech & Language*, 13(4), pp. 359–394.

- Chomsky, N. (1957) *Syntactic Structures*. The Hague: Mouton.

- Conneau, A. et al. (2020) 'Unsupervised Cross-lingual Representation Learning at Scale', in *Proceedings of the 58th Annual Meeting of the Association for Computational Linguistics (ACL)*. Stroudsburg, PA: ACL, pp. 8440–8451.

- Devlin, J. et al. (2019) 'BERT: Pre-training of Deep Bidirectional Transformers for Language Understanding', in *Proceedings of the 2019 Conference of the North American Chapter of the ACL (NAACL)*, pp. 4171–4186.

- Fellbaum, C. (ed.) (1998) *WordNet: An Electronic Lexical Database*. Cambridge, MA: MIT Press.

- Goldberg, Y. (2017) *Neural Network Methods for Natural Language Processing*. San Rafael, CA: Morgan & Claypool.

- Hutchins, J. (2005) 'Current Commercial MT Systems and Computer-Based Translation Tools: System Types and Their Uses', *International Journal of Translation*, 17(1–2), pp. 5–38.

- Hu, J. et al. (2020) 'XTREME: A Massively Multilingual Multi-task Benchmark for Evaluating Cross-lingual Generalization', in *Proceedings of the 37th International Conference on Machine Learning (ICML)*, pp. 4411–4421.

- Ji, H. and Grishman, R. (2008) 'Refining Event Extraction through Cross-Document Inference', in *Proceedings of ACL-08: HLT*. Stroudsburg, PA: ACL, pp. 254–262.

- Jurafsky, D. and Martin, J.H. (2023) *Speech and Language Processing*. 3rd edn. Global Edition: Prentice Hall.

- Kim, Y. (2014) 'Convolutional Neural Networks for Sentence Classification', in *Proceedings of the 2014 Conference on Empirical Methods in Natural Language Processing (EMNLP)*. Stroudsburg, PA: ACL, pp. 1746–1751.

- Kiperwasser, E. and Goldberg, Y. (2016) 'Simple and Accurate Dependency Parsing Using Bidirectional LSTM Feature Representations', *Transactions of the Association for Computational Linguistics*, 4, pp. 313–327.

- Koehn, P. (2010) *Statistical Machine Translation*. Cambridge: Cambridge University Press.

- Lample, G. et al. (2016) 'Neural Architectures for Named Entity Recognition', in *Proceedings of the 2016 Conference of the North American Chapter of the ACL (NAACL)*. Stroudsburg, PA: ACL, pp. 260–270.

- Levinson, S.C. (1983) *Pragmatics*. Cambridge: Cambridge University Press.

- Lin, C.-Y. (2004) 'ROUGE: A Package for Automatic Evaluation of Summaries', in *Text Summarization Branches Out: Proceedings of the ACL-04 Workshop.* Stroudsburg, PA: ACL, pp. 74–81.

- Liu, B. (2012) *Sentiment Analysis and Opinion Mining.* San Rafael, CA: Morgan & Claypool.

- Manning, C.D. and Schütze, H. (1999) *Foundations of Statistical Natural Language Processing.* Cambridge, MA: MIT Press.

- Marcus, G. and Davis, E. (2019) *Rebooting AI: Building Artificial Intelligence We Can Trust.* New York: Pantheon Books.

- Maynez, J. et al. (2020) 'On Faithfulness and Factuality in Abstractive Summarization', in *Proceedings of the 58th Annual Meeting of the Association for Computational Linguistics (ACL).* Stroudsburg, PA: ACL, pp. 1906–1919.

- McCoy, A., Cagan, R. and Nembhard, H.B. (2020) 'Measuring Health Care System Responses to Patient Experience: A Systematic Review of System-Level Instruments', *American Journal of Medical Quality*, 35(3), pp. 231–239.

- Mikolov, T. et al. (2013) 'Distributed Representations of Words and Phrases and Their Compositionality', in *Advances in Neural Information Processing Systems* (NeurIPS). Red Hook, NY: Curran Associates, pp. 3111–3119.

- Mintz, M. et al. (2009) 'Distant Supervision for Relation Extraction without Labeled Data', in *Proceedings of the Joint Conference of the 47th Annual Meeting of the ACL and the 4th International Joint Conference on Natural Language Processing.* Stroudsburg, PA: ACL, pp. 1003–1011.

- Nallapati, R. et al. (2017) 'Summarunner: A Recurrent Neural Network Based Sequence Model for Extractive Summarization of Documents', in *AAAI Conference on Artificial Intelligence (AAAI).* Palo Alto, CA: AAAI Press, pp. 3075–3081.

- Narayan, S., Cohen, S.B. and Lapata, M. (2018) 'Don't Give Me the Details, Just the Summary! Topic-Aware Convolutional Neural Networks for Extreme Summarization', in *Proceedings of the 2018 Conference on Empirical Methods in Natural Language Processing (EMNLP).* Stroudsburg, PA: ACL, pp. 1797–1807.

- Navigli, R. (2009) 'Word Sense Disambiguation: A Survey', *ACM Computing Surveys*, 41(2), pp. 1–69.

- Papineni, K. et al. (2002) 'BLEU: A Method for Automatic Evaluation of Machine Translation', in *Proceedings of the 40th Annual Meeting of the Association for Computational Linguistics (ACL).* Stroudsburg, PA: ACL, pp. 311–318.

- Pennington, J., Socher, R. and Manning, C.D. (2014) 'Glove: Global Vectors for Word Representation', in *Proceedings of the 2014 Conference on Empirical*

Methods in Natural Language Processing (EMNLP). Stroudsburg, PA: ACL, pp. 1532–1543.

- Peters, M.E. et al. (2018) 'Deep Contextualized Word Representations', in *Proceedings of the 2018 Conference of the North American Chapter of the ACL (NAACL)*. Stroudsburg, PA: ACL, pp. 2227–2237.

- Rabiner, L. (1989) 'A Tutorial on Hidden Markov Models and Selected Applications in Speech Recognition', *Proceedings of the IEEE*, 77(2), pp. 257–286.

- Rajpurkar, P. et al. (2016) 'SQuAD: 100,000+ Questions for Machine Comprehension of Text', in *Proceedings of the 2016 Conference on Empirical Methods in Natural Language Processing (EMNLP)*. Stroudsburg, PA: ACL, pp. 2383–2392.

- Rush, A.M., Chopra, S. and Weston, J. (2015) 'A Neural Attention Model for Abstractive Sentence Summarization', in *Proceedings of the 2015 Conference on Empirical Methods in Natural Language Processing (EMNLP)*. Stroudsburg, PA: ACL, pp. 379–389.

- Tjong Kim Sang, E.F. and De Meulder, F. (2003) 'Introduction to the CoNLL-2003 Shared Task: Language-Independent Named Entity Recognition', in *Proceedings of the Seventh Conference on Natural Language Learning at HLT-NAACL 2003*. Stroudsburg, PA: ACL, pp. 142–147.

- Van Hee, C., Lefever, E. and Hoste, V. (2018) 'Exploring the Real-time Detection of Cyberbullying in Social Media', *ACL Special Interest Group on Social Media (SocialNLP)*, pp. 52–60.

- Vaswani, A. et al. (2017) 'Attention Is All You Need', in *Advances in Neural Information Processing Systems* (NeurIPS). Red Hook, NY: Curran Associates, pp. 5998–6008.

- Wang, A. et al. (2019) 'SuperGLUE: A Stickier Benchmark for General-Purpose Language Understanding Systems', in *Advances in Neural Information Processing Systems* (NeurIPS). Red Hook, NY: Curran Associates, pp. 3266–3280.

- Zeng, D. et al. (2015) 'Distant Supervision for Relation Extraction via Piecewise Convolutional Neural Networks', in *Proceedings of the 2015 Conference on Empirical Methods in Natural Language Processing (EMNLP)*. Stroudsburg, PA: ACL, pp. 1753–1762.

- Zhang, Y. et al. (2020) 'Biomedical and Clinical English Model Packages in Stanza', *Proceedings of the 28th International Conference on Computational Linguistics*, pp. 2136–2147.

Chapter 4: Transformers Unveiled

4.1. Self-Attention Mechanism

4.1.1. Why Attention?

From RNN Limitations to Attention

Historically, Recurrent Neural Networks (RNNs) dominated sequence processing in Natural Language Processing (NLP). Despite handling variable-length sequences token by token, RNNs struggle with **long-range dependencies**, often succumbing to vanishing or exploding gradients (Bengio, Simard and Frasconi, 1994). LSTM and GRU architectures (Hochreiter and Schmidhuber, 1997; Cho et al., 2014) introduced gating mechanisms that partially addressed these issues, yet sequential token processing remained a **bottleneck** for parallelization and efficiency.

The **attention mechanism** revolutionized this process (Bahdanau, Cho and Bengio, 2015). Instead of compressing all contextual information into a single hidden state, attention allows a model to "look back" at different tokens in the input sequence and assign relevance scores, enabling a richer context representation.

Key Intuition

Imagine reading a detailed paragraph: you often scan previous lines to recall relevant details. Attention emulates this behavior by computing weights (attention scores) for each token in the sequence, so the model can dynamically highlight the tokens most pertinent to the current task—without following a rigid left-to-right chain.

From Seq2Seq to Transformers

Initially, attention was integrated into Seq2Seq models (for tasks like machine translation). The **Transformer** (Vaswani et al., 2017) then **removed** recurrent connections entirely, offering a parallelizable architecture that captures **global** dependencies. This shift underpins the efficiency and scalability of modern large language models.

Key Insight

By shifting from strict recurrence to dynamic attention-based weighting, models can better learn complex, long-range interactions across entire input sequences—an essential component of the Transformer's success.

4.1.2. Scaled Dot-Product Attention

Defining the Computation

Vaswani et al. (2017) introduced **Scaled Dot-Product Attention**, where each token maps to three vectors: **Query (Q)**, **Key (K)**, and **Value (V)**. The attention output is computed as:

$$\text{Attention}(Q, K, V) = \text{softmax!}\left(\frac{Q\,K^\mathsf{T}}{\sqrt{d_k}}\right) V$$

- $Q\,K^\mathsf{T}$: Measures alignment between tokens (Query-Key similarity).

- $\sqrt{d_k}$: Scales dot products so the softmax does not skew excessively from large magnitudes.

- softmax($\cdot$): Produces normalized attention scores.

- V: Weighted Values form the final contextual representation.

Why   the   Scaling?
As dimension d_k grows, the raw dot products become large in magnitude, compressing the softmax distribution (Vaswani et al., 2017). Dividing by $\sqrt{d_k}$ keeps these values in a stable range, easing training (Shah et al., 2020).

Interpretability
One advantage of attention is partial transparency: by inspecting attention weights, researchers can see which tokens the model "focuses on" (Belinkov and Glass, 2019). While not a full explanation, it offers insight into which relationships a model captures.

Beyond   Text
Despite its origin in NLP, **Scaled Dot-Product Attention** is broadly applicable: image patches (Vision Transformers), speech frames, and even protein structures—wherever a set of elements interacts in a relational context (Dosovitskiy et al., 2021).

Key   Insight
Scaled dot-product attention looks simple—just a few matrix operations plus a softmax—but it enables efficient global context capture, outclassing older sequential methods by leveraging parallel self-attention.

4.1.3. Multi-Head Attention in Practice

Why   Multiple   Heads?
A single attention head can track only one kind of alignment at a time. **Multi-head attention** partitions the feature space into multiple "heads," each learning a distinct attention distribution (Vaswani et al., 2017). Results from all heads are concatenated and projected back to the full dimension:

- **Specialization**: One head may capture syntactic dependencies, another entity references, another pronoun coreference, etc.

- **Parallelism**: Each head processes attention in parallel, often leveraging GPU acceleration.

Implementation Details

For each attention head, the model learns separate linear projections to create Q, K, V, then applies scaled dot-product attention. The outputs are joined along the feature dimension and undergo a final linear transformation.

Head Specialization vs. Redundancy

Not all heads adopt unique roles; some overlap in their learned patterns (Voita et al., 2019). Redundancy can be beneficial for robustness. Empirically, multi-head attention consistently improves performance on tasks like WMT (machine translation) or GLUE (language understanding benchmarks).

Trade-Offs

- **Increased Parameters**: Each head has its own weight matrices.

- **Richer Representations**: Multiple heads let a single layer capture diverse context signals.

- **Empirical Dominance**: Multi-head attention is a mainstay in top-performing Transformer models, from BERT to GPT to T5.

Key Insight

Multi-head attention expands a Transformer's expressive capacity, yielding parallel "views" on the same input. This complexity pays off in more robust and nuanced learned relationships.

4.2. Transformer Architecture

4.2.1. Encoder-Decoder Stack

Separating Roles

The original Transformer architecture uses an **encoder** and a **decoder** (Vaswani et al., 2017). While BERT (encoder-only) and GPT (decoder-only) are common today, certain tasks—particularly sequence-to-sequence tasks like machine translation—rely on the full encoder-decoder structure:

1. **Encoder**: Consumes input (e.g., source text) to produce context-rich representations.

2. **Decoder**: Autoregressively produces the output (e.g., target text), attending to both the previously generated tokens and the encoder output.

Layer Arrangement

Typically, both the encoder and decoder contain multiple layers (6, 12, or more). The **encoder** layers each have:

- **Multi-head self-attention**

- **Feed-forward sub-layer**

- **LayerNorm + Residual connections**

The **decoder** layers mirror this, adding **masked self-attention** (to avoid seeing future tokens) and **encoder-decoder attention** (attending to encoder outputs).

When to Use Full Seq2Seq

- **Machine Translation**: Classic usage requiring both encoder and decoder.

- **Summarization**: Transformer-based summarizers generate compressed versions of source text.

- **Complex Sequenced Tasks**: Such as multi-turn QA or dialogue systems that transform an input sequence to a different structured output.

Variants
Apart from this canonical design, practical models often use one part or the other:

- **Encoder-Only**: BERT for classification or sequence labeling tasks.

- **Decoder-Only**: GPT for text generation.

- **Encoder-Decoder**: T5, focusing on a text-to-text framework (Raffel et al., 2020).

Key   **Insight**

The encoder-decoder blueprint remains highly relevant for tasks needing direct transformation of a source sequence to a target sequence. Other popular models often adapt just one side of the Transformer for specialized tasks.

4.2.2. Positional Encoding

Parallelism   **Without**   **Sequence**   **Ordering?**

Transformers handle sequences in **parallel**, losing the positional information that RNNs inherently encode via hidden states. Thus, **positional encoding** supplies the model with token order (Vaswani et al., 2017).

Sinusoidal   **Functions**

A widely known technique uses sine and cosine terms with different frequencies:

$$PE_{(pos,2i)} = \sin\left(\frac{pos}{10000^{\frac{2i}{d_{\text{model}}}}}\right), \quad PE_{(pos,2i+1)} = \cos\left(\frac{pos}{10000^{\frac{2i}{d_{\text{model}}}}}\right)$$

Where pos is the token index and i indexes even or odd dimensions in the embedding layer. These periodic patterns allow the model to generalize to longer sequences.

Fixed   **vs.**   **Learned**

While some Transformers (e.g., the original) use **fixed** sinusoidal encodings, others (e.g.,

BERT) adopt **learned** positional embeddings. Fixed encodings can extrapolate beyond training sequence lengths, while learned embeddings may yield slightly higher accuracy on in-domain lengths (Devlin et al., 2019).

Relative   **Positional**   **Embeddings**

Further research explores **relative** positions—focusing on how far apart tokens are rather than their absolute index (Shaw, Uszkoreit and Vaswani, 2018). This often benefits tasks with longer contexts or repeated patterns. Still, ignoring positional information altogether severely harms model performance.

Key   **Insight**

Positional encoding is essential for any parallel architecture. Whether using sinusoidal or learned embeddings, the Transformer must inject token-order knowledge to understand real-world language structure.

4.2.3. Layer Normalization & Residual Connections

Ensuring   **Training**   **Stability**

Deep networks can suffer from vanishing or exploding gradients. Transformers stack many layers, which intensifies the issue. They overcome this via **residual (skip) connections** and **layer normalization** (Ba, Kiros and Hinton, 2016; He et al., 2016).

Residual   **Connections**

A residual path adds the layer input back to its output:

$$\text{Output} = x + F(x)$$

This "shortcut" helps gradients propagate through numerous layers. In Transformers, each multi-head attention and feed-forward sub-layer has a residual connection.

Layer   **Normalization**

LayerNorm normalizes neurons **per example** rather than across the entire batch:

1. Compute mean and variance over the feature dimension (within a single training example).

2. Normalize each feature: $(z - \mu)/$.

3. Use learnable scale γ and $shift$ β.

Because it doesn't rely on batch statistics, LayerNorm is more stable under varying batch sizes and autoregressive decoding constraints.

Advantages

- **Stable Deep Networks**: Residuals and LayerNorm mitigate training pathologies.
- **Faster Convergence**: Normalization accelerates optimization.

- **Attention Compatibility**: Each attention sub-layer consistently receives normalized inputs.

Key   **Insight**

Layer normalization plus residual connections are fundamental to modern Transformer blocks. They address deep-network training challenges, making it feasible to train large Transformers without crippling gradient issues.

4.3. The Impact of Transformers

4.3.1. Speed, Parallelization & Training Efficiency

Parallelization   **vs.**   **Recurrence**

RNNs process tokens sequentially, whereas Transformers can handle entire sequences at once with self-attention (Vaswani et al., 2017). Although self-attention is $\mathcal{O}(n^2)$ for a sequence length n, in practice it outperforms the strictly sequential $\mathcal{O}(n)$ steps of RNNs—particularly when harnessing GPUs or TPUs for parallel matrix multiplications (Bahdanau, Cho and Bengio, 2015).

Scaling   **Laws**

Parallel training has enabled models to scale from millions to billions (and even trillions) of parameters (Brown et al., 2020). This expansion correlates with systematically better language modeling performance (Kaplan et al., 2020), though balancing dataset size and training length is crucial to avoid diminishing returns.

Distributed & Mixed-Precision Training

- **Data Parallelism**: The model is replicated across GPUs, each processing part of the mini-batch.

- **Model Parallelism**: Layers or parameters are split across multiple devices when a single GPU can't hold them (Shoeybi et al., 2019).

- **Mixed Precision**: Using half-precision or bfloat16 to reduce memory usage and boost speed (Micikevicius et al., 2018).

Frameworks like **Megatron-LM** and **DeepSpeed** optimize these methods, enabling efficient large-scale Transformer training.

Transformers   **Beyond**   **NLP**

Thanks to parallel self-attention, Transformers have spread beyond language:

- **Computer Vision**: Vision Transformer (ViT) processes image patches as tokens (Dosovitskiy et al., 2021).

- **Speech Recognition**: Conformer layers add convolution to attention for time-frequency representations (Gulati et al., 2020).

- **Reinforcement Learning**: Ongoing research explores Transformers for policy learning in sequential decision tasks (Chen et al., 2021).

Key   **Insight**

Transformers discard token-by-token recurrence in favor of global, parallel self-attention, unlocking immense speedups and scale. This approach underpins state-of-the-art performance in NLP and across broader AI domains.

4.3.2. Benchmark Breakthroughs: BLEU, GLUE & Beyond

Role   **of**   **Benchmarks**

NLP benchmarks spur competition and progress (Bowman et al., 2015). Before Transformers, Seq2Seq RNN/CNN models incrementally improved. The introduction of Transformers precipitated a quantum leap in many benchmark results.

Machine   **Translation:**   **BLEU**   **Score**

The **BLEU** metric measures overlap between system translations and reference translations (Papineni et al., 2002). Transformer-based models quickly dominated WMT tasks, surpassing older architectures (Vaswani et al., 2017; Chen et al., 2018). Despite ongoing challenges in nuanced contexts, numeric BLEU scores rose to near-human levels in certain language pairs.

Language Understanding: GLUE & SuperGLUE

- **GLUE**: Includes tasks like MNLI, QNLI, SST-2. Transformers (BERT, RoBERTa, GPT) rapidly overtook prior bests, sometimes matching human performance (Wang et al., 2018).

- **SuperGLUE**: Presents harder tasks, such as the Winograd Schema. T5, GPT-3, and others still advance but occasionally stumble on nuanced linguistic reasoning (Raffel et al., 2020).

Summarization   **&**   **Beyond**

For summarization datasets (CNN/Daily Mail, XSum), Transformers (e.g., BART, PEGASUS) greatly improved ROUGE scores (Lewis et al., 2020; Zhang et al., 2020). Though these metrics can't fully measure factual correctness or coherence, the jump in fluency has been remarkable.

Limitations of Benchmark-Focused Research

- **Overfitting**: Repeatedly tuning to a fixed test set can inflate scores without true generalization (Marcus and Davis, 2019).

- **Shallow vs. Deep Understanding**: A high benchmark score may reflect pattern matching.

- **Push for Novel Evaluations:** Initiatives like **BIG-bench** attempt to measure more creative and broad language abilities (Srivastava et al., 2022).

Key   **Insight**

Transformers set new records across major NLP benchmarks (MT, GLUE, summarization). However, focusing too heavily on benchmarks risks overlooking generalization gaps, requiring ongoing explorations into real-world linguistic competence.

4.3.3. Real-World Success Stories

Commercial   **Chatbots**   **&**   **Virtual**   **Assistants**

Many companies deploy Transformer-based models for chatbots and support systems. For instance, Microsoft's **DialoGPT** or OpenAI's GPT-based solutions yield more context-aware dialogues (Zhang et al., 2020). While they handle typical questions quickly, unusual or domain-specific issues may still need human intervention.

Content   **Moderation**   **&**   **Analysis**

Social platforms process vast text daily. Transformer classifiers excel at identifying hate speech, bullying, or extremist content, surpassing older rule-based filters (Georgakopoulos et al., 2020). This helps reduce toxicity but raises questions about potential bias, free speech, and trust in automated moderation.

Search   **&**   **Recommendation**

Leading search engines and e-commerce systems harness Transformers in retrieval and ranking algorithms. Google's integration of BERT (Nayak, 2019) improved the semantic matching of user queries and documents, enhancing result relevance. Similarly, product recommendations benefit from deeper text understanding, e.g., analyzing item descriptions and user reviews.

Industry-Specific Deployments

- **Healthcare:** Summarizing clinical notes, extracting medical entities (Huang et al., 2020).

- **Finance:** Parsing earnings reports for risk analysis, chatbots for customer service.

- **Legal:** Document analysis (contracts, case law), e-discovery for relevant clauses.

Societal   **Impact**   **&**   **Challenges**

Widespread success comes with new demands:

1. **Privacy:** Large-scale training may include sensitive data (European Commission, 2021).

2. **Bias & Fairness:** Models can perpetuate stereotypes if training corpora are skewed (Bender and Friedman, 2018).

3. **Interpretability**: High-stakes use cases (medical diagnoses, financial advice) need clarifications of outputs.

4. **Environmental Footprint**: Training large models consumes considerable energy (Strubell, Ganesh and McCallum, 2019).

Key **Insight**

The commercial impact of Transformers spans multiple domains—chatbots, moderation, retrieval—demonstrating tangible value. Yet the technology's scale magnifies ethical and ecological concerns, underscoring the need for responsible deployment strategies.

4.4. Practical Implementation

4.4.1. Setting Up a Transformer Model

Framework **Considerations**

Popular deep learning frameworks—**PyTorch, TensorFlow, JAX**—offer components for building Transformers. Libraries like **Hugging Face Transformers** simplify the process, packaging commonly used models and tokenizers (Wolf et al., 2020). Key setup steps include:

- **Architecture**: Encoder-only (BERT), decoder-only (GPT), or encoder-decoder (T5).

- **Vocabulary & Tokenization**: Typically subword-based (BPE, WordPiece, SentencePiece).

- **Model Size**: Balancing performance with training/inference cost.

Model Initialization

- **Pre-Trained Checkpoints**: Often used to skip the huge cost of training from scratch, e.g., BERT Base or GPT-2.

- **Random Initialization**: Rare, unless building a novel architecture or domain with no available checkpoint.

Tokenization **&** **Special** **Tokens**

Transformers use subword tokenization (e.g., Byte-Pair Encoding) to manage rare words (Sennrich, Haddow and Birch, 2016). **Special tokens** like [CLS], [SEP], <PAD> serve classification or separation roles. For sequence-to-sequence tasks, <BOS> (begin-of-sequence) and <EOS> (end-of-sequence) also appear.

Positional Encoding & Attention Masks

- **Positional Encoding**: Sinusoidal or learned embeddings for token order.

- **Attention Masks**: Hide padded tokens or restrict the model from seeing future tokens in auto-regressive decoders.

Implementing a Transformer demands selecting a model variant, tokenization, and whether to rely on pre-trained weights. High-level libraries make early experimentation straightforward, but deeper knowledge remains crucial for fine control or custom architectures.

4.4.2. Hyperparameter Tuning & Best Practices

Core Hyperparameters

1. **Learning Rate**: Often small (e.g., 2×10^{-5} to 5×10^{-5}) with a warm-up phase (Vaswani et al., 2017).

2. **Batch Size**: Larger batches can speed training but need more memory.

3. **Number of Layers/Heads**: More layers and heads increase expressivity but raise compute requirements.

4. **Embedding Dimensions**: Control feed-forward size (often $4 \times d_{\text{model}}$) and memory usage.

Regularization Methods

- **Dropout**: Usually around 0.1 in attention and feed-forward layers (Srivastava et al., 2014).

- **Weight Decay**: Typically 0.01, via AdamW (Loshchilov and Hutter, 2019).

- **Early Stopping**: Monitored using validation metrics (accuracy, perplexity, etc.).

Scheduling

- **Warm-Up**: Linear ramp-up of the learning rate over 5% _to_ 10% of steps.

- **Decay Schedules**: Cosine, polynomial, or inverse square root post-warm-up.

- **Gradient Clipping**: Bounding gradient norms to prevent exploding updates (Pascanu, Mikolov and Bengio, 2013).

$$\hat{g} = \frac{g}{\max !\left(1, \frac{|g|}{\text{clip}}\right)}$$

Documentation & Experiment Tracking

Tools like TensorBoard, Weights & Biases, or MLflow track training/validation losses, perplexity, or other metrics. Keeping rigorous notes is critical for reproducibility, especially when tuning many hyperparameters.

Key **Insight**

Tuning Transformers can be delicate. Small changes in learning rate, warm-up, or batch size can drastically affect stability and end performance. Iterative experimentation and thorough logging are essential.

4.4.3. Scaling & Distributed Training

Why **Go** **Big?**
Empirical evidence shows that increasing model size typically enhances performance (Brown et al., 2020). Nonetheless, bigger models demand distributed training on GPU or TPU clusters—and large curated datasets.

Data Parallelism & Model Parallelism

- **Data Parallelism**: Each GPU holds a copy of the model. The mini-batch is split, then gradients are averaged after each forward pass.

- **Model Parallelism**: The model's parameters are partitioned across GPUs if it is too large for a single device (Shoeybi et al., 2019). Pipeline parallelism is one strategy: consecutive layers run on different GPUs.

Memory & Compute Efficiency

- **Mixed Precision**: Halves memory usage and accelerates matrix ops (Micikevicius et al., 2018).

- **Gradient Checkpointing**: Recomputes some forward activations, saving memory at the cost of extra compute (Chen et al., 2016).

- **Sharded Optimizers**: Splits optimizer state across multiple devices (Rajbhandari et al., 2021).

$$\theta_{t+1} = \theta_t - \alpha \frac{1}{N} \sum_{i=1}^{N} \square \, \nabla_{\theta}^{(i)}$$

(where N is number of GPUs, $\nabla_{\theta}^{(i)}$ is the local gradient on GPU i, and α is the learning rate.)

Infrastructure
Cloud platforms (AWS, Azure, GCP) provide on-demand GPU/TPU clusters. On-premise HPC solutions (Kubernetes, Slurm) handle scheduling for large training jobs. Monitoring tools like Prometheus/Grafana track resource usage, ensuring stable multi-GPU operation.

Key **Insight**
Training Transformers at scale requires advanced parallel strategies, memory optimizations, and robust infrastructure orchestration. The payoff is stronger results, sometimes with emergent capabilities (e.g., zero-shot learning) smaller models cannot match.

References (Harvard Style)

- Bahdanau, D., Cho, K. and Bengio, Y. (2015) 'Neural Machine Translation by Jointly Learning to Align and Translate', in *3rd International Conference on Learning Representations (ICLR)*. San Diego, CA: ICLR.

- Ba, L.J., Kiros, J.R. and Hinton, G.E. (2016) 'Layer Normalization', *arXiv preprint* arXiv:1607.06450.

- Belinkov, Y. and Glass, J. (2019) 'Analysis Methods in Neural Language Processing: A Survey', *Transactions of the Association for Computational Linguistics*, 7, pp. 49–72.

- Bengio, Y., Simard, P. and Frasconi, P. (1994) 'Learning Long-Term Dependencies with Gradient Descent is Difficult', *IEEE Transactions on Neural Networks*, 5(2), pp. 157–166.

- Bowman, S.R. et al. (2015) 'A Large Annotated Corpus for Learning Natural Language Inference', in *Proceedings of the 2015 Conference on Empirical Methods in Natural Language Processing (EMNLP)*. Stroudsburg, PA: ACL, pp. 632–642.

- Brown, T. et al. (2020) 'Language Models Are Few-Shot Learners', in *Advances in Neural Information Processing Systems* (NeurIPS). Red Hook, NY: Curran Associates, pp. 1877–1901.

- Chen, J. et al. (2016) 'Training Deep Nets with Sublinear Memory Cost', *arXiv preprint* arXiv:1604.06174.

- Chen, M.X. et al. (2018) 'The Best of Both Worlds: Combining Recent Advances in Neural Machine Translation', in *Proceedings of the 56th Annual Meeting of the ACL (Volume 2: Short Papers)*. Stroudsburg, PA: ACL, pp. 76–81.

- Chen, X. et al. (2021) 'Decision Transformer: Reinforcement Learning via Sequence Modeling', in *Advances in Neural Information Processing Systems* (NeurIPS). Red Hook, NY: Curran Associates.

- Cho, K. et al. (2014) 'Learning Phrase Representations using RNN Encoder–Decoder for Statistical Machine Translation', in *Proceedings of the 2014 Conference on Empirical Methods in Natural Language Processing (EMNLP)*. Stroudsburg, PA: ACL, pp. 1724–1734.

- Devlin, J. et al. (2019) 'BERT: Pre-training of Deep Bidirectional Transformers for Language Understanding', in *Proceedings of the 2019 Conference of the North American Chapter of the ACL (NAACL)*. Stroudsburg, PA: ACL, pp. 4171–4186.

- Dosovitskiy, A. et al. (2021) 'An Image is Worth 16x16 Words: Transformers for Image Recognition at Scale', in *International Conference on Learning*

Representations (ICLR). Available at: https://openreview.net (Accessed: 10 February 2025).

- European Commission (2021) *Proposal for a Regulation Laying Down Harmonised Rules on Artificial Intelligence (Artificial Intelligence Act)*. Available at: https://digital-strategy.ec.europa.eu (Accessed: 10 February 2025).

- Georgakopoulos, S.V. et al. (2020) 'Hate Speech Detection: A Solved Problem? The Challenging Case of Long Tail on Twitter', *AI Communications*, 33(1), pp. 23–35.

- Gulati, A. et al. (2020) 'Conformer: Convolution-augmented Transformer for Speech Recognition', in *Interspeech 2020*. Shanghai, China: ISCA, pp. 5036–5040.

- He, K. et al. (2016) 'Deep Residual Learning for Image Recognition', in *Proceedings of the IEEE Conference on Computer Vision and Pattern Recognition (CVPR)*, pp. 770–778.

- Hochreiter, S. and Schmidhuber, J. (1997) 'Long Short-Term Memory', *Neural Computation*, 9(8), pp. 1735–1780.

- Kaplan, J. et al. (2020) 'Scaling Laws for Neural Language Models', *arXiv preprint* arXiv:2001.08361.

- Lewis, M. et al. (2020) 'BART: Denoising Sequence-to-Sequence Pre-training for Natural Language Generation, Translation, and Comprehension', in *Proceedings of the 58th Annual Meeting of the Association for Computational Linguistics (ACL)*. Stroudsburg, PA: ACL, pp. 7871–7880.

- Loshchilov, I. and Hutter, F. (2019) 'Decoupled Weight Decay Regularization', in *International Conference on Learning Representations (ICLR)*. Available at: https://openreview.net (Accessed: 10 February 2025).

- Marcus, G. and Davis, E. (2019) *Rebooting AI: Building Artificial Intelligence We Can Trust*. New York: Pantheon Books.

- Micikevicius, P. et al. (2018) 'Mixed Precision Training', in *International Conference on Learning Representations (ICLR)*. Available at: https://openreview.net (Accessed: 10 February 2025).

- Nayak, P. (2019) 'Understanding Searches Better than Ever Before', *Google AI Blog*. Available at: https://ai.googleblog.com (Accessed: 10 February 2025).

- Papineni, K. et al. (2002) 'BLEU: A Method for Automatic Evaluation of Machine Translation', in *Proceedings of the 40th Annual Meeting of the Association for Computational Linguistics (ACL)*. Stroudsburg, PA: ACL, pp. 311–318.

- Pascanu, R., Mikolov, T. and Bengio, Y. (2013) 'On the Difficulty of Training Recurrent Neural Networks', in *Proceedings of the 30th International Conference on Machine Learning (ICML)*. PMLR, pp. 1310–1318.

- Raffel, C. et al. (2020) 'Exploring the Limits of Transfer Learning with a Unified Text-to-Text Transformer', *Journal of Machine Learning Research*, 21(140), pp. 1–67.

- Shaw, P., Uszkoreit, J. and Vaswani, A. (2018) 'Self-Attention with Relative Position Representations', in *Proceedings of the 2018 Conference of the North American Chapter of the ACL (NAACL)*. Stroudsburg, PA: ACL, pp. 464–468.

- Shoeybi, M. et al. (2019) 'Megatron-LM: Training Multi-Billion Parameter Language Models Using Model Parallelism', *arXiv preprint* arXiv:1909.08053.

- Srivastava, A. et al. (2022) 'Beyond the Imitation Game: Quantifying and Extrapolating the Capabilities of Language Models', *arXiv preprint* arXiv:2206.04615.

- Srivastava, N. et al. (2014) 'Dropout: A Simple Way to Prevent Neural Networks from Overfitting', *Journal of Machine Learning Research*, 15(1), pp. 1929–1958.

- Strubell, E., Ganesh, A. and McCallum, A. (2019) 'Energy and Policy Considerations for Deep Learning in NLP', in *Proceedings of the 57th Annual Meeting of the Association for Computational Linguistics (ACL)*. Florence, Italy: ACL, pp. 3645–3650.

- Vaswani, A. et al. (2017) 'Attention Is All You Need', in *Advances in Neural Information Processing Systems*(NeurIPS). Red Hook, NY: Curran Associates, pp. 5998–6008.

- Voita, E. et al. (2019) 'Analyzing Multi-Head Self-Attention: Specialized Heads Do the Heavy Lifting, the Rest Can Be Pruned', in *Proceedings of the 57th Annual Meeting of the ACL (ACL)*. Stroudsburg, PA: ACL, pp. 5797–5808.

- Wang, A. et al. (2018) 'GLUE: A Multi-Task Benchmark and Analysis Platform for Natural Language Understanding', in *Proceedings of the 2018 EMNLP Workshop BlackboxNLP*. Stroudsburg, PA: ACL, pp. 353–355.

- Wolf, T. et al. (2020) 'Transformers: State-of-the-Art Natural Language Processing', in *Proceedings of the 2020 Conference on Empirical Methods in Natural Language Processing: System Demonstrations*. Stroudsburg, PA: ACL, pp. 38–45.

- Zhang, Y. et al. (2020) 'PEGASUS: Pre-training with Extracted Gap-sentences for Abstractive Summarization', in *International Conference on Machine Learning (ICML)*. PMLR, pp. 11328–11339.

- Zhang, J. et al. (2020) 'DIALOGPT: Large-Scale Generative Pre-training for Conversational Response Generation', in *Proceedings of the 58th Annual Meeting of the Association for Computational Linguistics (ACL): System Demonstrations*. Stroudsburg, PA: ACL, pp. 270–278.

Chapter 5: Popular Large Language Models

5.1. GPT Family

5.1.1. GPT-1 & GPT-2: Early Milestones

Origins of **GPT**

The **Generative Pre-trained Transformer (GPT)** series, introduced by OpenAI, emerged as a landmark in large language model (LLM) development. The initial version, **GPT-1**, was unveiled in 2018 and demonstrated how a transformer-based model, pre-trained on vast amounts of unlabeled text, could be fine-tuned for diverse downstream tasks with surprisingly strong performance (Radford et al., 2018). GPT-1's novelty lay in showing that large-scale unsupervised pre-training plus minimal task-specific supervision could surpass more complex, specialized architectures of the time.

Following GPT-1, OpenAI released **GPT-2** in early 2019 (Radford et al., 2019). Notable for its much larger parameter count (1.5 billion parameters vs. GPT-1's 117 million), GPT-2 became infamous when OpenAI initially withheld the full model release due to concerns about generating realistic misinformation. When eventually made public, GPT-2's performance on language generation tasks highlighted the scaling hypothesis—that increasing model size and data leads to qualitatively better text coherence and contextual understanding.

Model **Architecture**

Both GPT-1 and GPT-2 adopt a **decoder-only** transformer design:

- **Masked self-attention** ensures the model only sees tokens up to the current position during training, preserving an autoregressive property.

- **Pre-trained** on large corpora: BookCorpus for GPT-1 (~700M tokens) and a variety of web text for GPT-2 (~8M documents).

- **Fine-tuning** approach: A minimal amount of labeled data is used to adapt the pre-trained model to specific tasks (e.g., classification, question answering).

Contributions to NLP

1. **Few-Shot and Zero-Shot Learning**: GPT-2, in particular, showcased the capacity to adapt to new tasks with minimal to no labeled examples, a precursor to the massive leaps seen in later GPT models.

2. **Text Generation Quality**: GPT-2 significantly raised the bar for fluent, contextually relevant text generation, spurring new applications (and ethical debates) in content creation, chatbots, and more.

3. **Public Awareness**: The partial release controversy amplified discussions on the societal impact of advanced language models, including the balance between open research and responsible disclosure.

Limitations

- Despite improved text generation, GPT-2 still produced factual errors and lacked **grounded reasoning** (Marcus and Davis, 2019).

- It retained biases present in the training corpus, raising concerns about fairness and ethical usage (Bender and Friedman, 2018).

- Large memory and compute requirements made it harder for smaller research labs or organizations to replicate the results at scale.

Key   Insight

GPT-1 and GPT-2 laid the groundwork for a new generation of LLMs. They proved that scaling transformer-based autoregressive models on massive text corpora yields striking advances in language understanding and generation—while also raising ethical and societal questions.

5.1.2. GPT-3 & Beyond: Emergence of Few-Shot Learning

GPT-3's   Unprecedented   Scale

Released in 2020, **GPT-3** took the LLM world by storm with a staggering 175 billion parameters—over 100 times more than GPT-2 (Brown et al., 2020). Trained on diverse internet-scale corpora (Common Crawl, WebText, Books, Wikipedia), GPT-3 demonstrated capabilities in:

- **Few-Shot and Zero-Shot Learning**: Users provide minimal examples (or sometimes none) in a textual prompt, and GPT-3 performs tasks such as translation, summarization, or coding assistance with competitive accuracy.

- **Multi-Task Generalization**: GPT-3 tackled an array of tasks—arithmetic, text classification, question answering—without additional fine-tuning.

Prompt   Engineering

A crucial aspect of GPT-3's paradigm is **prompt engineering**: carefully crafting input text that guides the model to perform desired tasks. For instance, to classify sentiments, one might supply a few labeled examples and then a final "unlabeled" example for the model to process. GPT-3's large capacity allows it to "infer" task structure from these prompts.

API   Accessibility   and   Ecosystem

OpenAI introduced a commercial API for GPT-3, enabling developers to build applications (e.g., chatbots, coding assistants, text analysis tools) without hosting the massive model themselves. This spurred an explosion of prototypes and startups leveraging GPT-3 for tasks like content creation, language tutoring, or virtual customer service (Zhang et al., 2022). The "model-as-a-service" approach made advanced NLP capabilities more accessible, albeit at a cost and with potential vendor lock-in.

Advanced Behavior and Limitations

- **Emergent Abilities**: GPT-3 displayed surprising skills in code generation (e.g., basic websites), reasoning about short riddles, and even creativity in poetry (Chen et al., 2021).

- **Hallucinations and Errors**: Like predecessors, GPT-3 can confidently produce factually incorrect statements or "hallucinations." (Maynez et al., 2020).

- **Bias and Toxicity**: Large-scale web data inevitably includes biased or offensive content, which the model can reproduce. OpenAI and others introduced content filters and "instruction tuning" to mitigate these issues (Bender and Friedman, 2018).

GPT-3.5, GPT-4, and Beyond

Subsequent iterations—like GPT-3.5 and GPT-4—improved factual grounding, reasoning, and multi-modal inputs, though exact technical details often remain proprietary (OpenAI, 2023). GPT-4 especially focuses on safer deployment (reducing harmful outputs) and better reasoning over extended contexts. Researchers continue exploring how to further harness "in-context learning," alignment with human values, and domain specialization through model compression or fine-tuning.

Key   Insight

GPT-3's scale and flexibility propelled few-shot learning into the mainstream. Its successors refined these capabilities, striving for more reliable, less biased text generation. Nonetheless, balancing accessibility, cost, and ethical considerations remains a moving target in the GPT lineage.

5.1.3. Applications & Pitfalls

Applications Across Industries

1. **Content Generation**: GPT models can write marketing copy, short stories, or product descriptions, cutting down human effort.

2. **Customer Support**: Chatbot systems offer instant query resolution, although escalations to human agents may be needed for complex or sensitive issues.

3. **Software Development**: Models like GitHub Copilot (powered by GPT variants) suggest code snippets, unit tests, or documentation (Ziegler et al., 2021).

4. **Education and Tutoring**: GPT-based assistants can help students brainstorm essay topics, summarize lectures, or simulate language practice, albeit with caution around accuracy.

Pitfalls and Cautions

- **Reliability and Accuracy**: LLMs often present "authoritative" but incorrect statements, risking misinformation in high-stakes areas like healthcare or finance (Marcus and Davis, 2019).

- **Ethical Concerns**: The capacity to generate realistic text can facilitate spam, phishing, deepfake news, and other malicious uses if not carefully guarded (Solaiman et al., 2019).

- **Data Privacy**: Sensitive or personal data in training corpora may inadvertently appear in model outputs. Regulatory compliance and data anonymization thus become essential (European Commission, 2021).

- **Bias and Fairness**: Models can amplify societal biases (gender, race, religion) embedded in their training data (Bender and Friedman, 2018).

Mitigations

- **Human-in-the-Loop**: Combining GPT outputs with expert review to verify correctness or ethical compliance.

- **Content Moderation Pipelines**: Automatic and manual screening of generated text for toxicity or policy violations.

- **Fine-Tuning or Instruction Tuning**: Adjusting the model to follow guidelines or specialized domain knowledge, reducing the risk of inappropriate outputs (Ouyang et al., 2022).

Research   Directions

Scholars explore approaches like **chain-of-thought prompting**, **self-consistency decoding**, and **retrieval-augmented generation** to improve factual accuracy and interpretability. GPT's success catalyzed the broader field to investigate how to combine large-scale transformers with external knowledge sources, better alignment techniques, and domain-specific optimizations.

Key   Insight

GPT-powered solutions hold transformative potential but come with significant caveats. Ensuring reliability, minimizing harm, and respecting privacy are central to the responsible deployment of these powerful models.

5.1.4. Developer Ecosystem & API Access

OpenAI **API**

The release of GPT-3 spurred the creation of the **OpenAI API**, a cloud-based platform offering various GPT models. Developers can integrate the API into applications without hosting massive computational resources. Key features include:

- **Rate Limits**: Throttling usage to manage load and prevent abuse.

- **Content Filters**: Basic toxicity checks.

- **Fine-Tuning** (for older GPT versions): Customizing smaller GPT derivatives on proprietary datasets.

Other **Providers**

Competitors and open-source communities also provide large language models:

- **Cohere, AI21, Anthropic**: Commercial LLM APIs with focuses on enterprise integration or "constitutional AI" safety measures.

- **Hugging Face**: Hub hosting hundreds of open-source transformer models, including GPT-2, GPT-Neo, and GPT-J, allowing local deployment.

Deployment Considerations

- **Latency and Throughput**: Real-time applications must handle the sometimes high computational overhead of generating text. Server-side caching, stream-based generation, or distillation can reduce response times (Sajjad et al., 2022).

- **Cost**: API pricing can be substantial for large-scale deployments, prompting some organizations to weigh self-hosting open-source alternatives.

- **Scaling**: For high-demand scenarios, load balancing or dynamic scaling strategies ensure stable user experiences.

- **Security**: Models must be integrated with robust authentication, logging, and compliance frameworks, especially in regulated sectors (finance, healthcare).

Community **and** **Plugins**

A vibrant developer ecosystem has emerged, with **GUI-based prompt builders, no-code** integration templates, and specialized "prompt marketplaces." Plug-and-play solutions for e-commerce, content generation, or data analysis abound, democratizing GPT usage while also raising questions about intellectual property rights, training data ownership, and potential misuse.

Key **Insight**

GPT's widespread availability through APIs and open-source variants accelerated innovation but introduced new dependencies and ethical considerations. Balancing ease of use with responsible and secure deployment remains a central challenge for the GPT ecosystem.

5.2. BERT & Friends

5.2.1. BERT: The Bidirectional Breakthrough

Revisiting   Contextual   Embeddings

Before **BERT** (*Bidirectional Encoder Representations from Transformers*), contextual word embeddings were often derived from left-to-right (or right-to-left) language models (Peters et al., 2018). BERT innovated by training a **deep bidirectional** model that considers both left and right context simultaneously—dramatically improving tasks like question answering and named entity recognition (Devlin et al., 2019).

Masked   Language   Modeling

BERT's core pre-training objective is **Masked Language Modeling (MLM)**. Randomly selected tokens in the input are replaced with a [MASK] symbol, and the model attempts to predict the missing tokens. This forces BERT to learn bidirectional context rather than simply predicting the next word, as GPT does. A **Next Sentence Prediction (NSP)** task, later refined by other models, also helps BERT learn relationships between sentence pairs.

Architecture

- **Encoder-Only Transformer**: BERT is essentially a stack of transformer encoder layers (12 in BERT Base, 24 in BERT Large).

- **Token, Segment, and Position Embeddings**: Each token's representation includes identity, sentence segment (A or B), and positional information.

- **CLS Token**: A special classification token [CLS] is prepended to each sequence, enabling easy extraction of the entire sentence embedding for classification tasks.

Performance   Impact

BERT revolutionized a range of NLP benchmarks by providing a universal pre-trained encoder. Fine-tuning BERT on small labeled datasets (often just a few thousand examples) yielded state-of-the-art results for tasks as diverse as sentiment analysis, sentence classification, and NER. Industry adoption soared, as BERT-based solutions required less data labeling effort while improving accuracy or F1 scores significantly.

Challenges

- **Computational Intensity**: Training BERT from scratch demands massive compute resources. Even inference can be resource-heavy for real-time applications.

- **NSP Critiques**: Follow-up research questioned the utility of BERT's NSP objective; models like RoBERTa remove NSP entirely, using more robust training data and hyperparameters (Liu et al., 2019).

- **Context Length Limitations**: BERT typically handles up to 512 tokens, constraining tasks involving longer documents (Beltagy, Peters and Cohan, 2020).

Key   **Insight**

BERT's bidirectional encoding marked a watershed moment in NLP, emphasizing the value of rich contextual embeddings for downstream tasks. Its pre-training approach remains influential, inspiring myriad variants and adaptations.

5.2.2. RoBERTa & DistilBERT: Optimizations & Distillations

RoBERTa: **Refining**   **Training**   **Protocols**

Released by Facebook AI Research, **RoBERTa** (*Robustly Optimized BERT Approach*) demonstrated that by removing the Next Sentence Prediction task, using **more data**, larger batch sizes, and dynamic masking strategies, one could significantly boost BERT's performance on GLUE, RACE, and other benchmarks (Liu et al., 2019). RoBERTa underscored how careful hyperparameter tuning and extended training times could extract more from the same underlying architecture:

- **Longer Training with Bigger Batches**: Iterating over 160GB of text with batch sizes up to 8,000 examples.

- **Dynamic Masking**: Randomly generating masks each time a sequence is fed to the model, increasing data diversity.

- **Removal of NSP**: Found to be less critical for performance, enabling simpler training objectives.

DistilBERT: **Lightweight**   **Alternative**

While BERT and RoBERTa offered robust results, their size can hinder real-time inference on limited hardware (Sanh et al., 2020). **DistilBERT** employs **knowledge distillation**, training a smaller "student" model to mimic the full-scale "teacher" BERT's behavior. Key benefits:

- **Compact Architecture**: About 40% fewer parameters than BERT, with ~60% faster inference speeds.

- **Competitive Accuracy**: Retains 95–97% of BERT's performance across many NLP tasks.

- **Practical Use Cases**: Ideal for deployment on edge devices or latency-sensitive applications, such as mobile apps or real-time chatbots.

Trade-Offs

- **Performance vs. Efficiency**: DistilBERT is faster and smaller but may lose some nuance for complex tasks.

- **Hyperparameter Sensitivity**: Distillation can be tricky, requiring careful selection of teacher layers to match, temperature settings for soft targets, and training schedules.

- **Benchmarking**: While DistilBERT often matches or comes close to BERT Base, advanced tasks requiring large context windows or domain-specific knowledge might still benefit from full-scale BERT or RoBERTa.

Legacy and Community Adoption
The success of RoBERTa and DistilBERT catalyzed a wave of derivatives (e.g., TinyBERT, ALBERT, MobileBERT) aiming to optimize or compress transformer-based models. This ecosystem helps democratize advanced NLP capabilities, especially in production settings where compute or memory might be constrained (Zhang et al., 2020a).

Key Insight
RoBERTa illustrated the gains from thorough hyperparameter tuning and large-scale training, while DistilBERT opened the door to lightweight deployment. Both lines demonstrate how the BERT architecture can be refined or distilled for varied performance and resource needs.

5.2.3. Real-World Uses in Search & Classification

Search and Information Retrieval (IR)
Large-scale search engines—like Bing or Google—incorporate BERT-like encoders to interpret queries more contextually (Nayak, 2019). Instead of matching keywords superficially, these models grasp user intent, synonyms, and phrase relationships. In enterprise contexts, **semantic search** leverages BERT or RoBERTa to rank internal documents, product catalogs, or helpdesk articles with improved accuracy:

- **Query Expansion**: Rewriting user queries based on synonyms or conceptual matches.

- **Passage Ranking**: Identifying the most relevant section in a long document.

- **FAQ Assistants**: Matching user questions to known solutions.

Content Moderation and Classification
BERT-based classifiers handle tasks such as **hate speech detection**, **fake news identification**, or **spam filtering**, surpassing older rule-based or shallow machine learning methods (Georgakopoulos et al., 2020). Fine-tuning on labeled data from social media or news platforms helps them learn complex linguistic cues indicating harassment or misinformation. Real-time moderation systems can triage flagged content for human review, maintaining community standards at scale.

Domain-Specific Verticalization

Organizations often fine-tune BERT for specialized text:

- **Legal**: Contract analysis, case law retrieval, or regulatory compliance checks (Chalkidis et al., 2020).

- **Healthcare**: Medical entity extraction, patient triage, summarizing clinical notes.

- **Finance**: Earnings call sentiment, risk factor classification in annual reports, or fraud detection in transaction logs.

Performance Metrics and Monitoring

Typical evaluation uses accuracy, F1 scores, or AUC-ROC for classification tasks. In IR settings, metrics like **Mean Reciprocal Rank (MRR)**, **Normalized Discounted Cumulative Gain (nDCG)**, or **Recall@k** gauge retrieval quality (Manning, Raghavan and Schütze, 2008). Once deployed, real-time monitoring is crucial to catch model drift, especially if user language or data distributions shift over time.

Implementation Practices

- **Preprocessing**: Tokenization (WordPiece), careful management of out-of-vocabulary tokens.

- **Fine-Tuning**: Minimally change BERT's weights; typical tasks require only a simple classification head on top (Devlin et al., 2019).

- **Inference Optimization**: Techniques like quantization or knowledge distillation reduce latency in production environments (Sanh et al., 2020).

Key Insight

BERT and its variants power a new generation of search and classification systems that interpret text contextually. Their adaptability to domain-specific tasks has reshaped workflows across industries, from content moderation to legal document analysis.

5.2.4. Fine-Tuning Strategies

End-to-End Fine-Tuning

The most straightforward method is adding a small **fully connected classification head** atop BERT, then training the entire model on the downstream task. This approach works well for moderate datasets (tens of thousands of examples). However, it can be prone to overfitting if data is scarce, especially for large BERT variants:

1. **Learning Rate Scheduling**: Typically starts low (e.g., 2e-5) due to the sensitivity of pretrained weights (Devlin et al., 2019).

2. **Batch Size**: Balanced with available GPU memory.

3. **Early Stopping**: Frequent checks on validation sets to avoid catastrophic forgetting of general language knowledge.

Feature   Extraction

For tasks with extremely limited data, one may freeze most of BERT's layers and only train a few top layers or an added head. This is akin to using BERT as a feature extractor (Lee et al., 2019). While less flexible, it reduces overfitting risks and cuts training time.

Layer-Freezing and Adapter Modules

- **Layer-Freezing**: Freezes lower transformer layers to preserve fundamental linguistic patterns, fine-tuning only the higher layers.

- **Adapters**: Small "bottleneck" networks inserted between transformer layers, trained for a particular task while core parameters stay frozen (Houlsby et al., 2019). This approach is parameter-efficient, allowing multiple tasks to share the same base model with different adapters.

Hyperparameter   Tuning

BERT fine-tuning can be sensitive to:

- **Epoch Count**: Often 2–4 epochs suffice; more can lead to overfitting.

- **Warm-Up Steps**: Gradually increasing the learning rate over 10% of training steps helps stability.

- **Weight Decay**: Typically set around 0.01 to avoid large parameter drifts.

Domain   Adaption   with   Further   Pre-Training

When domain mismatch is severe (e.g., biomedical text vs. general Wikipedia), additional pre-training on in-domain corpora can significantly boost performance (Lee et al., 2020). This technique, sometimes called **domain-adaptive pre-training**, effectively re-teaches BERT the specialized jargon or style of the new corpus before fine-tuning on the target task.

Key   Insight

BERT fine-tuning strategies must be tailored to data availability, domain overlap, and computational constraints. Techniques like layer-freezing, adapters, or domain-adaptive pre-training ensure a balanced approach between performance gains and resource efficiency.

5.3. Other Notable Models

5.3.1. T5: Text-to-Text Transfer Transformer

Unified   Text-to-Text   Paradigm

Released by Google Research, **T5** (Text-To-Text Transfer Transformer) reimagines NLP tasks—classification, summarization, translation, question answering—under a **single text-to-text format** (Raffel et al., 2020). Inputs are always text strings, and outputs are also text. This unification simplifies the training pipeline and fosters multi-task learning.

Pre-Training **Objectives**

T5 is pre-trained on a **"span corruption"** objective, a variant of masked language modeling where spans of text are replaced by a special mask token, and the model learns to reconstruct them. This approach is somewhat akin to BERT's MLM but reframed in a full text-to-text manner. T5's largest version, "T5-11B," contains 11 billion parameters.

Multi-Tasking & Flexibility

- **Multi-Task Pre-Training**: T5 is also trained on multiple tasks simultaneously, labeling each input with a task prefix (e.g., "translate English to German:" or "summarize:").

- **Scalable Performance**: Larger T5 models demonstrate strong results across diverse benchmarks like GLUE, SuperGLUE, CNN/Daily Mail summarization, and SQuAD QA.

Practical Considerations

- **Resource Heavy**: Even T5-Base or T5-Large can be computationally demanding for real-time usage.

- **Prompt Format**: Because everything is cast into text, success often hinges on carefully designed prompts for each task.

- **Factual Consistency**: Like other transformers, T5 can generate plausible-sounding but erroneous answers, requiring verification or external knowledge sources (Maynez et al., 2020).

Influence **on** **Future** **Models**

T5's text-to-text philosophy inspired subsequent approaches— like **UnifiedQA** and **FLAN**—which unify task prompts and demonstrate emergent cross-task generalization. This has propelled broader interest in instruction tuning and multi-task training as ways to create more robust, adaptive language models.

Key **Insight**

T5's "one model fits all" text-to-text paradigm streamlined NLP pipelines, demonstrating how a single model can handle diverse tasks when properly prompted. Its versatility set a precedent for unified, instruction-driven architectures.

5.3.2. XLNet & ALBERT: Enhancing Architectures

XLNet: **Permutation** **Language** **Modeling**

XLNet challenged BERT by introducing a **permutation-based** language modeling objective that captures bidirectional context without relying on masked tokens (Yang et al., 2019). Key ideas:

- **Autoregressive + Autoregressive**: Instead of masking, XLNet aggregates probabilities over all possible factorization orders, effectively capturing contextual signals from both directions.

- **Transformer-XL Foundation**: XLNet built upon Transformer-XL's ability to handle longer contexts by caching hidden states across segments (Dai et al., 2019).

- **Boosted Performance**: XLNet achieved state-of-the-art results on GLUE, text classification, and question answering at release, though its complexity sometimes made it slower or less stable to train compared to BERT.

ALBERT: Parameter Sharing

ALBERT (A Lite BERT) tackled the massive memory footprint of BERT by sharing parameters across layers (Lan et al., 2020):

- **Factorized Embedding**: Splits the embedding dimension from the hidden dimension, reducing redundancy.

- **Cross-Layer Parameter Sharing**: The same weights are used for transformer layers, drastically reducing the total parameter count.

- **Two-Parameter Pools**: One for token embeddings, one for hidden transformations.

- **Impact**: ALBERT retained near state-of-the-art performance on GLUE while cutting parameters significantly, easing deployment.

Trade-Offs and Adoption

- **Complexity vs. Gains**: XLNet's permutation objective introduced overhead, whereas ALBERT's parameter sharing changed the usual "one layer per set of parameters" assumption.

- **Usage Patterns**: While overshadowed by BERT's widespread adoption, specialized tasks or resource-limited environments may favor ALBERT. XLNet remains an interesting alternative for certain generative or QA scenarios where its training objective can shine.

Community Reception

Both models contributed to the broader exploration of **architectural tweaks** beyond standard MLM. Their techniques—permutation modeling, parameter sharing, and memory-extended transformers—inform the design of subsequent LLMs, either as direct incorporation or conceptual influence.

Key Insight

XLNet and ALBERT exemplify how incremental innovations—like permutation objectives or parameter sharing—can yield noteworthy performance and efficiency improvements over baseline BERT, further diversifying the NLP model landscape.

5.3.3. Open-Source vs. Proprietary Models

Open-Source **Renaissance**

The NLP community has seen a surge in open-source releases of large language models. **Hugging Face Transformers**spearheads a repository where researchers and practitioners freely contribute or download pre-trained models, from BERT to GPT-2 and beyond (Wolf et al., 2020). This collaborative spirit fosters:

- **Transparency**: Developers can examine training scripts, hyperparameters, and architecture details.

- **Reproducibility**: Researchers replicate and extend results, accelerating progress.

- **Customization**: Organizations can adapt open-source models to proprietary data with fewer vendor constraints.

Proprietary **Giants**

Conversely, some state-of-the-art models—like GPT-3, GPT-4, and certain large offerings from Microsoft, Google, or Anthropic—remain closed-source. Companies cite concerns around:

- **Compute Costs**: Sharing enormous models is expensive and sometimes logistically impractical.

- **Misinformation & Misuse**: Advanced generative models could facilitate malicious purposes.

- **Competitive Advantage**: Exclusivity maintains a business moat, with revenue from API usage or licensing.

Hybrid **Approaches**

Meta's LLaMA release in 2023 illustrated a nuanced approach: releasing weights under restricted licenses to the research community. This "semi-open" strategy tries to balance academic collaboration with control over misuse. Some corporations adopt "open model cards" or documentation of known risks while retaining partial control over distribution (Raji et al., 2021).

Considerations for Stakeholders

- **Cost vs. Control**: Proprietary APIs may save initial R&D costs but risk vendor lock-in.

- **Security & Compliance**: On-premise open-source deployment ensures data governance but demands in-house expertise to manage large-scale training.

- **Long-Term Viability**: An open model can be extended or fine-tuned as needed, while closed APIs can discontinue or change pricing unpredictably.

Key   Insight

The tension between open-source collaboration and proprietary advantage defines the current LLM landscape. Users must weigh transparency, cost, and the potential for misuse when selecting between open or closed models.

5.3.4. Multilingual & Domain-Specific Variants

Multilingual   Models

Models like **mBERT**, **XLM-R**, and **mT5** aim to bridge language gaps by training on large corpora across dozens of languages (Conneau et al., 2020). Benefits include:

- **Cross-Lingual Transfer**: Gains in low-resource languages by sharing learned representations from high-resource counterparts.

- **Unified Deployments**: One model can handle multiple languages without separate pipelines.

- **Challenges**: Vocabulary overlaps, balancing varied script complexities, and ensuring even performance across languages.

Domain-Specific Models

- **BioBERT, ClinicalBERT**: Tailored to biomedical or clinical text, improving performance in tasks like named entity recognition for diseases or treatments (Lee et al., 2020).

- **FinBERT**: Trained on financial documents for specialized sentiment analysis or risk classification (Araci, 2019).

- **LegalBERT**: Fine-tuned on legal corpora, aiding in contract analysis, case law retrieval, or statute classification (Chalkidis et al., 2020).

Fine-Tuning   vs.   Pre-Training

For many domains, further **pre-training** on specialized corpora yields bigger boosts than simple fine-tuning alone. The model internalizes domain-specific language patterns—technical jargon, abbreviations, formal structures—reducing reliance on limited labeled data. However, domain datasets must be large enough to make additional pre-training effective.

Usage in Industry and Research

- **Healthcare**: Summarizing electronic health records, extracting patient data for clinical decision support.

- **Legal**: Automating contract drafting or compliance checks, analyzing case documents in litigation.
- **Scientific**: Literature reviews and knowledge extraction in specialized fields (chemistry, physics).

Open Challenges

- **Data Privacy**: Domain data might be confidential (medical records, financial statements), complicating large-scale pre-training.
- **Low-Resource Domains**: Some technical fields or languages have scarce corpora, restricting model coverage.
- **Continuous Updates**: Domain knowledge evolves (e.g., new medical research); models risk obsolescence without incremental training or retrieval-based methods (Gururangan et al., 2020).

Key   **Insight**

Multilingual and domain-specific LLMs broaden NLP's applicability, tackling global languages and specialized jargon. While these variants excel where general-purpose models fall short, they introduce unique challenges of data availability, privacy, and model maintenance.

References (Harvard Style)

- Araci, D. (2019) 'FinBERT: Financial Sentiment Analysis with Pre-trained Language Models', *arXiv preprint*arXiv:1908.10063.
- Beltagy, I., Peters, M.E. and Cohan, A. (2020) 'Longformer: The Long-Document Transformer', *arXiv preprint*arXiv:2004.05150.
- Bender, E.M. and Friedman, B. (2018) 'Data Statements for NLP: Toward Mitigating System Bias and Enabling Better Science', *Transactions of the Association for Computational Linguistics*, 6, pp. 587–604.
- Brown, T. et al. (2020) 'Language Models Are Few-Shot Learners', in *Advances in Neural Information Processing Systems* (NeurIPS). Red Hook, NY: Curran Associates, pp. 1877–1901.
- Chalkidis, I. et al. (2020) 'Legal-BERT: The Muppets Straight Out of Law School', in *Findings of the Association for Computational Linguistics: EMNLP 2020*. Stroudsburg, PA: ACL, pp. 2898–2904.
- Chen, M. et al. (2021) 'Evaluating Large Language Models Trained on Code', *arXiv preprint* arXiv:2107.03374.

- Conneau, A. et al. (2020) 'Unsupervised Cross-lingual Representation Learning at Scale', in *Proceedings of the 58th Annual Meeting of the Association for Computational Linguistics (ACL)*, pp. 8440–8451.

- Dai, Z. et al. (2019) 'Transformer-XL: Attentive Language Models Beyond a Fixed-Length Context', in *Proceedings of the 57th Annual Meeting of the Association for Computational Linguistics (ACL)*. Stroudsburg, PA: ACL, pp. 2978–2988.

- Devlin, J. et al. (2019) 'BERT: Pre-training of Deep Bidirectional Transformers for Language Understanding', in *Proceedings of the 2019 Conference of the North American Chapter of the ACL (NAACL)*, pp. 4171–4186.

- European Commission (2021) *Proposal for a Regulation Laying Down Harmonised Rules on Artificial Intelligence (Artificial Intelligence Act)*. Available at: https://digital-strategy.ec.europa.eu (Accessed: 10 February 2025).

- Georgakopoulos, S.V. et al. (2020) 'Hate Speech Detection: A Solved Problem? The Challenging Case of Long Tail on Twitter', *AI Communications*, 33(1), pp. 23–35.

- Gururangan, S. et al. (2020) 'Don't Stop Pretraining: Adapt Language Models to Domains and Tasks', in *Proceedings of the 58th Annual Meeting of the ACL*. Stroudsburg, PA: ACL, pp. 8342–8360.

- Houlsby, N. et al. (2019) 'Parameter-Efficient Transfer Learning for NLP', in *Proceedings of the 36th International Conference on Machine Learning (ICML)*. PMLR, pp. 2790–2799.

- Lan, Z. et al. (2020) 'ALBERT: A Lite BERT for Self-Supervised Learning of Language Representations', in *International Conference on Learning Representations (ICLR)*. Available at: https://openreview.net (Accessed: 10 February 2025).

- Lee, J. et al. (2019) 'A Comparative Study on Fine-tuning Neural Network Models for Medical Question Answering', in *Proceedings of the 18th BioNLP Workshop and Shared Task*. Stroudsburg, PA: ACL, pp. 270–279.

- Lee, J. et al. (2020) 'BioBERT: a Pre-trained Biomedical Language Representation Model for Biomedical Text Mining', *Bioinformatics*, 36(4), pp. 1234–1240.

- Liu, Y. et al. (2019) 'RoBERTa: A Robustly Optimized BERT Pretraining Approach', *arXiv preprint* arXiv:1907.11692.

- Manning, C.D., Raghavan, P. and Schütze, H. (2008) *Introduction to Information Retrieval*. Cambridge: Cambridge University Press.

- Marcus, G. and Davis, E. (2019) *Rebooting AI: Building Artificial Intelligence We Can Trust*. New York: Pantheon Books.

- Maynez, J. et al. (2020) 'On Faithfulness and Factuality in Abstractive Summarization', in *Proceedings of the 58th Annual Meeting of the Association for Computational Linguistics (ACL)*, pp. 1906–1919.

- Nayak, P. (2019) 'Understanding Searches Better than Ever Before', *Google AI Blog*. Available at: https://ai.googleblog.com (Accessed: 10 February 2025).

- OpenAI (2023) 'GPT-4 Technical Report', *OpenAI*. Available at: https://openai.com (Accessed: 10 February 2025).

- Ouyang, X. et al. (2022) 'Training Language Models to Follow Instructions with Human Feedback', *arXiv preprint* arXiv:2203.02155.

- Peters, M.E. et al. (2018) 'Deep Contextualized Word Representations', in *Proceedings of the 2018 Conference of the North American Chapter of the ACL (NAACL)*, pp. 2227–2237.

- Radford, A. et al. (2018) 'Improving Language Understanding by Generative Pre-Training', *OpenAI Blog*. Available at: https://openai.com (Accessed: 10 February 2025).

- Radford, A. et al. (2019) 'Language Models are Unsupervised Multitask Learners', *OpenAI Blog*. Available at: https://openai.com (Accessed: 10 February 2025).

- Raffel, C. et al. (2020) 'Exploring the Limits of Transfer Learning with a Unified Text-to-Text Transformer', *Journal of Machine Learning Research*, 21(140), pp. 1–67.

- Raji, I.D. et al. (2021) 'AI Model Cards: A Framework for Accountability in AI Development', *Communications of the ACM*, 64(12), pp. 42–48.

- Sajjad, H. et al. (2022) 'Performance-Efficient Language Models: A Survey on Receptive Field and Sparsity Techniques', in *Proceedings of the 60th Annual Meeting of the Association for Computational Linguistics (ACL)*. Stroudsburg, PA: ACL, pp. 1121–1135.

- Sanh, V. et al. (2020) 'DistilBERT, a Distilled Version of BERT: Smaller, Faster, Cheaper and Lighter', in *Proceedings of the 5th Workshop on Energy Efficient Machine Learning and Cognitive Computing (NeurIPS)*. Vancouver, BC: NeurIPS.

- Solaiman, I. et al. (2019) 'Release Strategies and the Social Impacts of Language Models', *arXiv preprint* arXiv:1908.09203.

- Wolf, T. et al. (2020) 'Transformers: State-of-the-Art Natural Language Processing', in *Proceedings of the 2020 Conference on Empirical Methods in Natural Language Processing: System Demonstrations*. Stroudsburg, PA: ACL, pp. 38–45.

- Yang, Z. et al. (2019) 'XLNet: Generalized Autoregressive Pretraining for Language Understanding', in *Advances in Neural Information Processing Systems* (NeurIPS). Red Hook, NY: Curran Associates, pp. 5753–5763.

- Ziegler, D. et al. (2021) 'Codex: A GPT Model for Code Generation', *arXiv preprint* arXiv:2107.03374.

- Zhang, H. et al. (2020a) 'MiniLM: Deep Self-Attention Distillation for Task-Agnostic Compression of Pre-Trained Transformers', in *Advances in Neural Information Processing Systems* (NeurIPS). Red Hook, NY: Curran Associates, pp. 5776–5788.

- Zhang, J. et al. (2022) 'GPT-3 Applications: A Comprehensive Survey', in *arXiv preprint* arXiv:2204.03862.

Chapter 6: Training a Language Model from Scratch

6.1. Data Collection & Curation

6.1.1. Public Datasets & Web Scraping

Importance **of** **Diverse** **Data**

Training a language model from scratch requires **large, varied corpora** to capture a wide range of linguistic features—vocabulary, syntax, semantics. Broader data coverage leads to better generalization across downstream tasks (Goodfellow, Bengio and Courville, 2016). Researchers often start with **public datasets** and **web-scraped text** to assemble the needed quantity of textual material.

Common Public Datasets

- **Common Crawl**: A massive, publicly available web archive. Researchers filter and deduplicate this raw HTML data to form large-scale text corpora (Raffel et al., 2020).

- **Wikipedia Dumps**: Periodic snapshots of Wikipedia (in multiple languages). While relatively clean and standardized, articles can still contain incomplete or outdated entries.

- **BookCorpus**: A dataset of free e-books, popularized by early language models such as GPT-1/2 (Zhu et al., 2015).

- **News Corpora**: For instance, **Gigaword** (Parker et al., 2011) or real-time news aggregator APIs for capturing more contemporary events.

Web Scraping Techniques

1. **Automated Crawlers**: Tools like scrapy in Python systematically traverse pages within given domains or based on certain rules.

2. **Focused Crawling**: Targets domain-specific sites—e.g., scientific repositories, legal archives—to gather specialized corpora.

3. **API-Based Collection**: Many sites or data providers offer formal APIs, reducing the noise of raw HTML scraping.

Legal & Ethical Constraints

- **Copyright & Terms of Service**: Some websites disallow large-scale scraping.

- **robots.txt**: Websites often specify scraping allowances or restrictions.

- **Privacy and PII**: Large web text collections can inadvertently include personal data. Compliance with rules like **GDPR** is crucial (European Commission, 2021).

Preprocessing   **Pipeline**

Regardless of source, raw text is usually full of HTML artifacts, duplicates, or boilerplate. A consistent, well-logged pipeline is essential for reproducible filtering—removing non-text content, normalizing text, and discarding corrupted entries.

Key   **Insight**

Robust training starts with **high-quality, diverse data**. Public datasets and web scraping jumpstart this process, but require careful attention to legal constraints and preprocessing.

6.1.2. Data Cleaning & Normalization

Why   **Cleaning**   **Matters**

Real-world text is noisy: HTML tags, repeated lines, random user posts, and so forth. Without rigorous cleaning, a model risks learning irrelevant tokens or patterns (Radford et al., 2019). A thorough **preprocessing pipeline** eliminates inconsistencies and ensures the model focuses on valid language signals.

Common Cleaning Steps

1. **HTML & Script Removal**: Stripping tags, scripts, styles.

2. **Deduplication**: Identifying near-duplicate entries, often via hashing or approximate matching (Lee et al., 2020).

3. **Normalization**: Lowercasing, standardizing punctuation, removing unusual control characters.

4. **Token Filtering**: Excluding extremely rare or non-alphabetic symbols—although for technical or domain-specific data, it may be beneficial to keep them.

Language   **Identification**

Large web corpora often mix multiple languages—sometimes even machine-generated text. Language ID tools or classifiers help isolate or label these segments. A typical classifier might compute:

$$\text{lang}(s) = \arg\max_{l \in L} P(l \mid s)$$

where s is the text sample, l is a candidate language from the set L. Such filtering ensures the corpus contains only the languages you intend to model (Conneau et al., 2020).

Handling   **Profanity**   **&**   **Sensitive**   **Content**

Massive text collections can include hate speech or other offensive language (Bender and Friedman, 2018). Some pipelines remove these strings outright; others mark them for specialized modeling or alignment. The decision depends on project goals and ethical considerations (Solaiman et al., 2019).

Maintaining data version control (e.g., DVC) ensures each cleaning pass yields a reproducible snapshot. Detailed logs describing removed items or deduplication thresholds are essential for future retraining or audits.

Key   Insight

Garbage in, garbage out: No matter how advanced the model, poor-quality input degrades performance. Meticulous cleaning is foundational to successful language model training.

6.1.3. Handling Bias & Offensive Content

The   Bias   Problem

Language corpora naturally contain societal biases—e.g., stereotypes around gender, race, or religion. Models trained on such data may internalize and perpetuate these biases (Bolukbasi et al., 2016), associating certain professions or attributes with specific demographics.

Identifying Bias

- **Statistical Checks**: Observing token co-occurrences in embeddings.

- **Intrinsic Tests**: **WEAT** (Word Embedding Association Test) reveals how word sets cluster. A simplified WEAT measure is:

$$\text{WEAT} = \sum_{w \in W^+} \sum_{w' \in W^-} (\cos(\mathbf{e_w}, \mathbf{e_A}) - \cos(\mathbf{e_w}, \mathbf{e_B})) - (\cos(\mathbf{e_{w'}}, \mathbf{e_A}) - \cos(\mathbf{e_{w'}}, \mathbf{e_B}))$$

where $\mathbf{e_w}$ is the embedding of word w, and A, B are different attribute sets.

Mitigation Strategies

1. **Data Filtering / Rebalancing**: Culling or balancing data to reduce skew.

2. **Annotation & Debiasing**: Labeling offensive or biased segments and either removing or re-weighting them.

3. **Fine-Tuning with Debiasing Objectives**: Training with custom loss functions to penalize biased outputs (Zhao et al., 2018).

4. **Post-Processing Filters**: Checking generated text at inference time for toxicity or bias.

Trade-Offs

Fully excluding harmful content may hamper a model's ability to handle real-world discourse. Conversely, leaving offensive data unfiltered risks a system that replicates or normalizes hateful patterns (Bender et al., 2021). Curating data to manage bias is thus an iterative, conscientious process.

Addressing bias starts at the **data curation** stage, before it becomes deeply embedded in the model. Ongoing evaluation and refinement are crucial to maintain fair and responsibly trained systems.

6.2. Model Architecture & Configuration

6.2.1. Setting Model Depth & Width

Depth   vs.   Width   in   Neural   Networks
A language model's architecture—particularly in Transformers—involves deciding how many layers (depth L) and how wide each layer is (d_{model}). Depth fosters hierarchical feature extraction; width increases the representational capacity at each layer (Kaplan et al., 2020).

Param   Scaling
For Transformers, approximate parameter count often scales like:

$$\text{Params} \sim L \times (d_{model})^2$$

(ignoring minor terms). Larger L or d_{model} inflates GPU memory, training time, and the risk of overfitting if data is insufficient (Carlini et al., 2021).

Practical Tiers

- **1–100M Params**: Useful for specialized or on-device scenarios, e.g., DistilBERT.

- **100M–10B**: Mainstream large models for broad NLP tasks.

- **10B+**: Cutting-edge, requiring advanced distributed setups and massive training data (Brown et al., 2020).

Trade-Offs

- **Memory & Compute**: Larger models demand more resources for both training and inference.

- **Performance Gains**: Gains typically follow a "scaling law," improving with size, but diminishing returns appear without parallel growth in dataset scale (Kaplan et al., 2020).

- **Real-Time Constraints**: Deeper/wider models may be too slow or expensive for certain production pipelines.

Key   Insight
Determine **depth and width** based on your resource limits, dataset scope, and the tasks you aim to tackle. Bigger is often better—but only if you can afford and effectively utilize the required scale.

6.2.2. Vocabulary & Tokenization Strategies

Why   **Tokenization**   **Matters**

Transformers operate on discrete tokens. A robust tokenization scheme affects vocabulary size, model capacity, and ability to handle rare words (Sennrich, Haddow and Birch, 2016). An ineffective tokenizer can balloon sequence lengths or hamper the model's ability to parse text properly.

Main Tokenization Approaches

1. **Word-Level**: Now less common for large LMs—vocab is huge, and rare words are poorly handled.

2. **Subword: Byte-Pair Encoding (BPE), WordPiece, SentencePiece**. Strikes a balance between purely word-level and character-level approaches.

3. **Character-Level**: Potentially handles any text but can explode sequence length, slowing training.

$$\mathrm{BPE}(w) = \arg\min_{S} \sum_{s \in S} \mathrm{cost}(s)$$

where S is a set of subword symbols. The "cost" might refer to how many merges or subword units are needed to represent w.

Vocabulary   Size

Common vocab sizes range from about 30k to 100k subword tokens. Larger vocabularies reduce sequence length but inflate the embedding matrix. For multilingual or domain-specific corpora, vocab can be even higher (Conneau et al., 2020).

Special Tokens

- <PAD>: Padding for uniform batch shapes.
- <MASK>: Masked language modeling tasks.
- [CLS], [SEP]: BERT-style classification and sequence separation.
- <BOS>, <EOS>: Begin/end of sequence for generative decoders.

Domain Considerations

- **Scientific**: E.g., math symbols, chemical formulas.
- **Social Media**: Emojis, hashtags, user handles.
- **Medical**: ICD codes, drug abbreviations, specialized jargon.

Key   Insight

Choosing the right tokenization strategy—a subword approach with an appropriate vocabulary size—can make or break a language model's ability to handle varied input efficiently.

6.2.3. Optimizers & Learning Schedules

Choosing **an** **Optimizer**

Most modern LMs rely on **Adam** or its derivatives, which adapt the learning rate per parameter. Popular variants include **AdamW** (decoupled weight decay) and **LAMB** (large-batch optimization). A typical Adam update is:

$$m_t = \beta_1 m_{t-1} + (1 - \beta_1)\nabla_\theta \mathcal{L}(\theta), \quad v_t = \beta_2 v_{t-1} + (1 - \beta_2)\left(\nabla_\theta \mathcal{L}(\theta)\right)^2, \quad \theta_{t+1}$$
$$= \theta_t - \alpha\,\frac{m_t/(1 - \beta_1^t)}{\sqrt{v_t/(1 - \beta_2^t)} + \epsilon}.$$

(See Kingma and Ba, 2015.)

Warm-Up

Transformers typically start with a low learning rate and **linearly ramp it up** over the first N_{warmup} steps, preventing divergence early in training (Vaswani et al., 2017).

Learning Rate Schedules

- **Inverse Square Root**: Early Transformer examples.

- **Cosine Decay**: Smoothly reduces α to near zero (Loshchilov and Hutter, 2019).

- **Polynomial**: A flexible approach that can mimic linear or other decays.

Batch **Size** **&** **Gradient** **Accumulation**

Large batch sizes leverage hardware parallelism but need more memory. **Gradient accumulation** simulates large batches by accumulating gradients over multiple mini-batches before updating weights (Shah et al., 2020).

Performance **Monitoring**

Key metrics: training loss, validation loss, perplexity, or classification accuracy. If these plateau or diverge, adjusting α, dropout, or warm-up steps is often the first fix.

Key **Insight**

Adam-based optimizers plus a well-chosen schedule (warm-up, decay) remain the de facto standard for Transformer LMs. Small changes in learning rate scheduling can drastically affect convergence stability.

6.3. Training Pipeline

6.3.1. Single-GPU vs. Multi-GPU Setup

Single-GPU   **Training**

For small or medium models—under a few hundred million parameters—single-GPU training can suffice (Sanh et al., 2020). This setup is simpler to debug but can be slow for large datasets, possibly spanning weeks for completion.

Data   **Parallelism**

When scaling beyond single-GPU capabilities, **data parallel** training is common:

1. **Replicate Model**: Each GPU holds identical model weights.

2. **Split Batch**: Input is divided among the GPUs.

3. **Synchronize Gradients**: Gradients from each GPU are averaged to update shared weights.

$$\nabla_\theta^{\text{global}} = \frac{1}{N} \sum_{i=1}^{N} \square \ \nabla_\theta^{(i)}$$

where N is the number of GPUs, and $\nabla_\theta^{(i)}$ is the local gradient for GPU i.

Model   **Parallelism**

For extremely large LMs (billions of parameters), even data parallelism might be insufficient: a single GPU can't store the entire model. **Model parallel** approaches split the layers or parameters across multiple devices (Shoeybi et al., 2019). Pipeline parallelism is one example—assigning consecutive layers to different GPUs.

Mixed   **Precision**

Employing half-precision or bfloat16 can significantly reduce memory usage and speed up matrix multiplications (Micikevicius et al., 2018). Modern GPUs (e.g., NVIDIA Ampere) have specialized cores for mixed-precision operations.

Key   **Insight**

Scaling from single-GPU to multi-GPU is essential for large language model training in a reasonable timeframe. Data parallel setups handle moderate models; model parallel or pipeline parallel strategies address extreme scales.

6.3.2. Logging & Validation

Tracking   **Training**   **Progress**

Logging frameworks—**TensorBoard**, **Weights & Biases**, **MLflow**—help you visualize training curves, compare experiments, and debug anomalies (Zaharia et al., 2018). Typical metrics include training/validation loss, accuracy (for classification tasks), or perplexity (for language modeling).

Perplexity

A common measure for language modeling is:

$$\text{Perplexity} = \exp\left(\frac{1}{N}\sum_{n=1}^{N}\square\;\mathcal{L}(x_n)\right)$$

where $\mathcal{L}(x_n)$ is the cross-entropy loss for sample x_n. Lower perplexity indicates better predictive capabilities.

Validation   Sets

Regularly evaluating on a **validation set** (withheld from training updates) reveals whether the model generalizes or overfits:

- **Hyperparameter Tuning**: e.g., stopping if validation loss fails to improve.

- **Overfitting Indicators**: A widening gap between training and validation performance.

- **Domain Consistency**: Ensuring the validation text matches the domain of interest.

Qualitative   Checks

Apart from numeric metrics, checking generated samples or classification outputs can spot issues like repetitive output, hallucinations, or ignoring key input segments (Maynez et al., 2020). Such checks guide further data or hyperparameter adjustments.

Key   Insight

Comprehensive logging and routine validation are vital. Metrics like perplexity quantify progress, but **qualitative sampling** offers additional insight into the model's linguistic fluency or coherence.

6.3.3. Early Stopping & Checkpointing

Early   Stopping   Rationale

Training large LMs is expensive. If the validation metric (e.g., perplexity) stalls or worsens for several epochs, continuing can waste resources and risk overfitting (Prechelt, 2012). **Early stopping** halts at the approximate "peak" of validation performance.

Checkpointing   Mechanics

Most frameworks allow frequent **checkpointing** of the model's weights, optimizer states, and training progress:

- **Periodic**: E.g., every 5k or 10k steps.

- **Best Checkpoint**: Save a separate copy whenever a new validation best is achieved.

- **Recovery**: If training crashes or you wish to resume, load from the latest stable checkpoint.

$$\theta^{(k)}_{\text{checkpoint}} = \theta^{(t_k)}_{\text{train}}$$

where t_k is the global step at checkpoint k.

Practical Considerations

- **Storage**: Each checkpoint can be large (especially for multi-billion parameter models), so a retention policy is often needed.

- **Evaluation**: Evaluate each checkpoint to track trends.

- **Fine-Tuning**: Well-managed checkpoints facilitate future domain adaptation or fine-tuning.

Key **Insight**

Early stopping avoids wasted training cycles and overfitting, while checkpointing safeguards progress from crashes and enables further adaptation. Manage both carefully to keep overhead at a practical level.

6.4. Overcoming Common Roadblocks

6.4.1. Memory Constraints & Gradient Accumulation

GPU **Memory** **Bottlenecks**

Transformers are memory-intensive, especially at large batch sizes and high parameter counts. Even advanced GPUs can exceed memory limits. Techniques to mitigate this include:

1. **Gradient Accumulation**: Summing gradients over several mini-batches before an update, simulating a larger effective batch.

2. **Mixed-Precision**: Using half-precision floats (fp16) drastically reduces memory usage (Micikevicius et al., 2018).

3. **Activation Checkpointing**: Recomputing forward activations in the backward pass instead of storing them (Chen et al., 2016).

4. **Sharded Optimizers**: Distributing optimizer states across multiple devices (Rajbhandari et al., 2021).

$$\Delta\theta = \frac{1}{k}\sum_{j=1}^{k} \nabla_{\theta}\mathcal{L}\big(\mathbf{x}_{(j)}\big)$$

where k is the number of mini-batches accumulated.

Trade-Offs

These methods often increase computation overhead or complexity in code. For instance, gradient accumulation means more forward passes per weight update. Nonetheless, they can be essential for training large models on limited GPU memory.

Key **Insight**

Memory optimization techniques (gradient accumulation, checkpointing) are crucial for training large language models without purchasing extremely high-memory hardware.

6.4.2. Debugging Nan Losses & Divergence

Common Symptoms

- **NaN Loss**: Training suddenly outputs "not a number."

- **Exploding Gradients**: Loss or parameters blow up after a few updates.

- **Inf Outputs**: Predictions or internal activations become infinite.

Potential Causes

1. **High Learning Rate**: A prime suspect for instability (He et al., 2016).

2. **Initialization Problems**: Inconsistent or custom layers might break stable initialization.

3. **Overflow in Half-Precision**: Mixed-precision can cause rounding or overflow errors if not managed (Micikevicius et al., 2018).

4. **Data Issues**: E.g., extremely large or malformed tokens.

Debugging Techniques

- **Gradient Clipping**: Restricts updates to avoid huge parameter steps. For norm threshold clip,

$$\hat{g} = \frac{g}{\max\left(1, \frac{|g|}{\text{clip}}\right)}.$$

- **Lower Learning Rate**: Halve or quarter the rate to stabilize.

- **Examine Data**: Check for outlier samples.

- **Enable Automatic Loss Scaling**: For half-precision, frameworks like PyTorch Apex handle dynamic scaling.

Logging

Detailed logs (loss after each batch) and anomaly detection (e.g., torch.autograd.set_detect_anomaly(True)) narrow down which operation triggers NaNs or infinities.

Instabilities are common when pushing model or batch size limits. Gradual debugging—checking the learning rate, gradient clipping, or data anomalies—typically resolves NaN or divergence issues.

6.4.3. Fine-Tuning vs. Full Retraining

Full   **Retraining**

Training **from scratch** is sometimes necessary—especially when developing new architectures or if no suitable pre-trained model exists. However, it requires huge data volumes and compute resources. Benefits include:

- **Total Control**: Tailor every aspect (tokenization, architecture, domain).

- **Novelty**: Potentially achieving new state-of-the-art or domain specialization.

Yet it can be prohibitively **expensive** in time, money, and environmental impact (Strubell, Ganesh and McCallum, 2019).

Fine-Tuning

Most practitioners instead adopt a **pre-trained base model** (GPT, BERT, T5, etc.) and fine-tune on domain-specific data. This cuts down required data and compute by orders of magnitude (Devlin et al., 2019). Even partial updates—freezing most layers—can yield strong performance if the domain is not drastically different.

$$\theta_{\text{fine-tune}} = \theta_{\text{pre-train}} - \eta\, \nabla_{\theta \mathcal{L}_{ts}}.$$

Hybrid Approaches

- **Further Pre-Training**: If your domain is specialized (biomedical, legal), you can continue pre-training on domain data before task fine-tuning (Lee et al., 2020).

- **Parameter-Efficient Tuning**: Methods like LoRA, adapters, or prompt tuning update only a fraction of parameters, preserving the original model mostly intact (Hu et al., 2022).

Decision Factors

- **Resources**: Full retraining may take weeks on multi-GPU clusters. Fine-tuning might finish in hours.

- **Data Coverage**: If your domain differs significantly from general corpora, additional pre-training or more thorough fine-tuning is key.

- **Business & Research Goals**: Researchers might prefer full control; product teams typically rely on stable, proven backbones.

Key   **Insight**

While from-scratch training can yield innovative architectures, **fine-tuning** a pre-trained model is vastly more efficient and commonly enough for top-tier results. Balancing these approaches depends on domain needs and resource constraints.

References (Harvard Style)

- Bender, E.M. and Friedman, B. (2018) 'Data Statements for NLP: Toward Mitigating System Bias and Enabling Better Science', *Transactions of the Association for Computational Linguistics*, 6, pp. 587–604.

- Bender, E.M. et al. (2021) 'On the Dangers of Stochastic Parrots: Can Language Models Be Too Big?', in *Proceedings of the 2021 ACM Conference on Fairness, Accountability, and Transparency (FAccT '21)*. New York: ACM, pp. 610–623.

- Bolukbasi, T. et al. (2016) 'Man is to Computer Programmer as Woman is to Homemaker? Debiasing Word Embeddings', in *Advances in Neural Information Processing Systems* (NeurIPS). Red Hook, NY: Curran Associates, pp. 4349–4357.

- Brown, T. et al. (2020) 'Language Models Are Few-Shot Learners', in *Advances in Neural Information Processing Systems* (NeurIPS). Red Hook, NY: Curran Associates, pp. 1877–1901.

- Carlini, N. et al. (2021) 'Extracting Training Data from Large Language Models', in *30th USENIX Security Symposium*. Berkeley, CA: USENIX Association, pp. 2633–2650.

- Chen, J. et al. (2016) 'Training Deep Nets with Sublinear Memory Cost', *arXiv preprint* arXiv:1604.06174.

- Conneau, A. et al. (2020) 'Unsupervised Cross-lingual Representation Learning at Scale', in *Proceedings of the 58th Annual Meeting of the Association for Computational Linguistics (ACL)*. Stroudsburg, PA: ACL, pp. 8440–8451.

- Devlin, J. et al. (2019) 'BERT: Pre-training of Deep Bidirectional Transformers for Language Understanding', in *Proceedings of the 2019 Conference of the North American Chapter of the ACL (NAACL)*. Stroudsburg, PA: ACL, pp. 4171–4186.

- European Commission (2021) *Proposal for a Regulation Laying Down Harmonised Rules on Artificial Intelligence (Artificial Intelligence Act)*. Available at: https://digital-strategy.ec.europa.eu (Accessed: 10 February 2025).

- Goodfellow, I., Bengio, Y. and Courville, A. (2016) *Deep Learning*. Cambridge, MA: MIT Press.

- Hu, E.J. et al. (2022) 'LoRA: Low-Rank Adaptation of Large Language Models', in *International Conference on Learning Representations (ICLR)*. Available at: https://openreview.net (Accessed: 10 February 2025).

- Kaplan, J. et al. (2020) 'Scaling Laws for Neural Language Models', *arXiv preprint* arXiv:2001.08361.

- Kingma, D.P. and Ba, J. (2015) 'Adam: A Method for Stochastic Optimization', in *3rd International Conference on Learning Representations (ICLR)*. San Diego, CA: ICLR.

- Lee, J. et al. (2020) 'BioBERT: A Pre-trained Biomedical Language Representation Model for Biomedical Text Mining', *Bioinformatics*, 36(4), pp. 1234–1240.

- Loshchilov, I. and Hutter, F. (2019) 'Decoupled Weight Decay Regularization', in *International Conference on Learning Representations (ICLR)*. Available at: https://openreview.net (Accessed: 10 February 2025).

- Maynez, J. et al. (2020) 'On Faithfulness and Factuality in Abstractive Summarization', in *Proceedings of the 58th Annual Meeting of the Association for Computational Linguistics (ACL)*. Stroudsburg, PA: ACL, pp. 1906–1919.

- Micikevicius, P. et al. (2018) 'Mixed Precision Training', in *International Conference on Learning Representations (ICLR)*. Available at: https://openreview.net (Accessed: 10 February 2025).

- Parker, R. et al. (2011) 'The English Gigaword Fifth Edition', *Linguistic Data Consortium*, University of Pennsylvania.

- Prechelt, L. (2012) 'Early Stopping — But When?', in Montavon, G., Orr, G.B. and Müller, K.-R. (eds.) *Neural Networks: Tricks of the Trade*. 2nd edn. Berlin, Heidelberg: Springer, pp. 53–67.

- Radford, A. et al. (2019) 'Language Models are Unsupervised Multitask Learners', *OpenAI Blog*. Available at: https://openai.com (Accessed: 10 February 2025).

- Raffel, C. et al. (2020) 'Exploring the Limits of Transfer Learning with a Unified Text-to-Text Transformer', *Journal of Machine Learning Research*, 21(140), pp. 1–67.

- Rajbhandari, S. et al. (2021) 'Zero-Infinity: Breaking the GPU Memory Wall for Extreme Scale Deep Learning', in *Proceedings of the International Conference for High Performance Computing, Networking, Storage and Analysis (SC)*. IEEE, pp. 1–15.

- Sanh, V. et al. (2020) 'DistilBERT, a Distilled Version of BERT: Smaller, Faster, Cheaper and Lighter', in *Proceedings of the 5th Workshop on Energy Efficient Machine Learning and Cognitive Computing (NeurIPS)*. Vancouver, BC: NeurIPS.

- Sennrich, R., Haddow, B. and Birch, A. (2016) 'Neural Machine Translation of Rare Words with Subword Units', in *Proceedings of the 54th Annual Meeting of the Association for Computational Linguistics (ACL)*. Stroudsburg, PA: ACL, pp. 1715–1725.

- Shah, S.A.A. et al. (2020) 'Predictable, Reliable and Resource-Efficient Deep Learning via Small-Batch SGD', in *International Conference on Learning Representations (ICLR)*. Available at: https://openreview.net (Accessed: 10 February 2025).

- Shoeybi, M. et al. (2019) 'Megatron-LM: Training Multi-Billion Parameter Language Models Using Model Parallelism', *arXiv preprint* arXiv:1909.08053.

- Solaiman, I. et al. (2019) 'Release Strategies and the Social Impacts of Language Models', *arXiv preprint* arXiv:1908.09203.

- Strubell, E., Ganesh, A. and McCallum, A. (2019) 'Energy and Policy Considerations for Deep Learning in NLP', in *Proceedings of the 57th Annual Meeting of the Association for Computational Linguistics (ACL)*. Florence, Italy: ACL, pp. 3645–3650.

- Vaswani, A. et al. (2017) 'Attention Is All You Need', in *Advances in Neural Information Processing Systems* (NeurIPS). Red Hook, NY: Curran Associates, pp. 5998–6008.

- Zaharia, M. et al. (2018) 'Accelerating the Machine Learning Lifecycle with MLflow', *Data-Driven Intelligence Workshop at NeurIPS*. Montréal, Canada: NeurIPS.

- Zhu, Y. et al. (2015) 'Aligning Books and Movies: Towards Story-Like Visual Explanations by Watching Movies and Reading Books', in *Proceedings of the IEEE International Conference on Computer Vision (ICCV)*. Santiago, Chile: IEEE, pp. 19–27.

- Zhao, J. et al. (2018) 'Gender Bias in Coreference Resolution: Evaluation and Debiasing Methods', in *Proceedings of the 2018 Conference of the North American Chapter of the ACL (NAACL)*. Stroudsburg, PA: ACL, pp. 15–20.

Chapter 7: Fine-Tuning and Customization

7.1. Tailoring for Specific Tasks

7.1.1. Sentiment Analysis & Classification

From General LM to Specific Classifier

While large pre-trained language models (LMs) capture broad linguistic knowledge, they need **task-specific adaptation**—known as **fine-tuning**—to excel at classification tasks like **sentiment analysis**. Typically, one appends a fully connected classification layer on top of the LM's hidden states and updates all parameters with respect to the classification objective (Devlin et al., 2019).

Common Procedure

1. **Add a Classification Head**: For example, a linear layer $W \in R^{d \times K}$ for K classes.

2. **Extract Representation**: Use the [CLS] token's final-layer embedding or an average of the last layer's token embeddings.

3. **Fine-Tune**: Minimize cross-entropy on labeled sentiment data. Typical learning rates are small (e.g., 2×10^{-5}) with a short warm-up.

$$\theta_{\text{fine-tune}} = \theta_{\text{pre-train}} - \eta \ \nabla_\theta \mathcal{L}_{sniet}$$

Handling Class Imbalance

Many real-world sentiment datasets are imbalanced (e.g., more neutral than negative). Techniques such as **weighted loss** or **oversampling** help. Alternatively, one might gather more negative samples to balance the data distribution (Chawla, 2009).

Generalization Concerns

If the domain is dissimilar from general web text (e.g., specialized product reviews, medical opinions), additional domain adaptation might be necessary (Lee et al., 2020). However, for many standard sentiment tasks (movies, tweets), a simple final-layer fine-tuning suffices.

Key Insight

Large LMs dramatically reduce the data needed for classification tasks. Fine-tuning transforms a generic text encoder into a specialized sentiment classifier with minimal modifications.

7.1.2. Question Answering & Chatbots

Reading Comprehension QA

Modern question answering (QA) tasks often revolve around **extractive** or **abstractive** approaches. For **extractive** QA (e.g., SQuAD), the model highlights a span in the context passage. Fine-tuning typically involves:

- **Start/End Head**: Two classification heads over the final layer output to predict the start and end token of the answer.

- **Loss Function**: A sum of cross-entropy losses for start/end predictions (Rajpurkar et al., 2016).

$$\mathcal{L}_Q = \left(-\sum \log P_{\text{start}}(i)\right) + \left(-\sum \log P_{\text{end}}(j)\right).$$

Chatbot   **Fine-Tuning**

For open-domain chatbots, one might fine-tune a decoder-only model (GPT-like) on dialogue data. The main difference is how you structure inputs (system prompts, dialogue context) and whether you impose constraints to avoid repetition or toxicity (Zhang et al., 2020).

- **Response Generation**: A sample-based decoding (e.g., temperature sampling) or beam search.

- **Safety Measures**: Additional filtering or specialized "safe mode" fine-tuning to reduce harmful outputs.

Domain-Specific Considerations

- **Task-Oriented Bots**: Fine-tuned to handle structured queries (flight booking, scheduling). Often combine language model outputs with a database or knowledge base.

- **Multi-Turn Context**: Maintaining conversation history requires model prompts that include previous dialogue turns. Large LMs, if not carefully truncated, can balloon in input length.

Key   **Insight**

QA systems and chatbots fine-tune LMs on specialized data with domain-specific heads or generation constraints. This allows them to handle real-world tasks like reading comprehension or interactive conversations more effectively than generic LMs.

7.1.3. Summarization & Paraphrasing

Abstractive   **Summarization**

For summarization, a **Seq2Seq** style approach often suits best—e.g., T5 or BART. The model is fine-tuned on document-summary pairs, learning to produce **abstractive** outputs:

$$\text{Decoder Output} = f_\theta\left(\text{Encoder}(document)\right)$$

Minimizing a sequence-to-sequence loss (commonly cross-entropy over tokens):

$$\mathcal{L}_{sm} = -\sum \log P\left(y_t \mid y_{<t}, x\right)$$

where x is the source text, y_t is the target summary token at time t.

Paraphrasing

Paraphrasing tasks can adopt similar methods. One approach is to treat it as a "translate English to English" scenario, labeling pairs of original text and rephrased output (Prakash et al., 2016). With large LMs, few-shot prompting or fine-tuning can yield robust paraphrases.

Evaluating   **Summaries**

Metrics like **ROUGE** measure n-gram overlap with reference summaries (Lin, 2004). However, they don't always capture factual consistency. Additional checks might use **BERTScore** or QA-based metrics for faithfulness (Maynez et al., 2020).

Challenges

- **Factual Drift**: Abstractive systems sometimes introduce incorrect facts.

- **Long Contexts**: Summarizing very long texts (research papers) can exceed the standard 512- or 1024-token limit. Strategies like chunking or using extended context models (Beltagy, Peters and Cohan, 2020) help.

Key   **Insight**

Summarization and paraphrasing fine-tune a Seq2Seq LM on (document, summary/paraphrase) pairs. Abstractive approaches can yield more human-like results than extractive or rule-based methods—but require careful evaluation for accuracy.

7.1.4. Domain-Specific Language Models

Why   **Specialize?**

A generic LM—trained mostly on web text—may not excel in specific domains like **medical**, **legal**, or **financial**. Domain-specific LMs (e.g., BioBERT, ClinicalBERT) incorporate specialized vocabulary and more relevant training examples (Lee et al., 2020). This can drastically boost performance on niche tasks (entity recognition, classification, etc.).

Additional   **Pre-Training**

One approach is **further pre-training** on in-domain corpora:

$$\theta_{\text{domain}} = \theta_{\text{general}} - \eta \nabla_{\theta \mathcal{L}_{\mathcal{L}}}(\text{domain data})$$

before fine-tuning on the final supervised task (Lee et al., 2020).

Vocabulary   **Adjustments**

In highly specialized fields, subword tokenizers might split domain terms awkwardly. Custom tokenizers or vocabulary expansions ensure minimal fragmentation of domain jargon (Sennrich, Haddow and Birch, 2016).

Domain data can be confidential (e.g., patient records, financial statements). Strict privacy or compliance guidelines (HIPAA, GDPR) might hamper large-scale data usage. Techniques like **federated learning** or **differential privacy** are sometimes employed to maintain confidentiality while training (Konečný et al., 2016).

Key Insight

Domains with unique terminology and structure benefit from specialized fine-tuning or additional LM pre-training. Tailoring data, vocabulary, and training schemes can yield significant performance gains.

7.2. Parameter-Efficient Techniques

7.2.1. LoRA (Low-Rank Adaptation)

Motivation

Fine-tuning all parameters of a large LM can be costly. **LoRA** (Low-Rank Adaptation) introduces trainable low-rank matrices inserted into specific layers (Hu et al., 2022). The original model parameters remain mostly frozen, reducing memory usage and speeding training.

Core Idea

Consider a weight update matrix ΔW of rank r, with $r \ll d_{\text{model}}$. Instead of storing a full ΔW, LoRA factors it as $A\,B$:

$$\Delta W \approx A\,B$$

where $A \in R^{d_{\text{model}} \times r}$ and $B \in R^{r \times d_{\text{model}}}$. Only A and B are trained; the rest of W remains fixed.

Benefits

- **Memory Savings**: Training fewer parameters.

- **Comparable Accuracy**: LoRA often matches full fine-tuning results if r is sufficiently large.

- **Modular**: One can store multiple ΔW for different tasks, switching them quickly without reloading the base model.

Trade-Offs

LoRA's performance hinges on the chosen rank r. Too low may degrade accuracy; too high approaches full fine-tuning cost. Additionally, some tasks might require more extensive changes than a low-rank decomposition can capture.

Key   **Insight**

LoRA offers a **parameter-efficient** route to adapt large LMs for multiple tasks, drastically cutting memory overhead while preserving strong performance.

7.2.2. Prompt Engineering & Prefix Tuning

Prompt   **Engineering**

Large LMs can sometimes perform tasks **in context** without weight updates, only by carefully crafting input prompts (Brown et al., 2020). For instance, providing a few examples within the prompt can yield near fine-tuned results—"few-shot learning." However, designing effective prompts can be tricky and reliant on trial-and-error or domain heuristics.

Prefix   **Tuning**

Instead of adjusting the entire model, **prefix tuning** prepends trainable "prefix embeddings" to each layer's input (Li and Liang, 2021). The base weights remain frozen, and the prefix acts as a "soft prompt" that guides the model toward the task.

$$\text{Layer Input}' = [\text{prefix; Layer Input}] \longrightarrow \text{Transformer Layer}$$

(Concatenating prefix embeddings with the original token embeddings.)

Advantages

- **Task-Specific**: Each prefix is small, storing custom knowledge.

- **Efficiency**: Only the prefix parameters (tens of thousands vs. billions) need updating.

- **Comparable Performance**: For many tasks, prefix tuning rivals or nearly matches full fine-tuning results.

Challenges

- **Complexity**: Prompt design or prefix length selection can be non-trivial.

- **Mixed Results**: Some tasks respond well to prompting, others require more direct gradient-based updates.

Key   **Insight**

Prompt-based methods harness the LM's vast knowledge by adjusting minimal parameters or input text. They're memory-friendly and fast to train, making them attractive for multi-task or low-resource scenarios.

7.2.3. Adapters & Other Modular Approaches

Adapter **Modules**

Adapters are lightweight feed-forward layers inserted between a Transformer's existing sub-layers (Houlsby et al., 2019). During fine-tuning, only adapter parameters update—everything else is frozen. Typically:

$$\text{AdapterBlock}(h) = W_{\text{down}}\,\sigma\!\left(W_{\text{up}}\,h\right) + h$$

where $W_{\text{up}} \in R^{d \times k}$ and $W_{\text{down}} \in R^{k \times d}$ with $k \ll d$. $\sigma(\cdot)$ is a nonlinearity like ReLU.

Benefits

- **Parameter Efficiency**: Adapters only add a small fraction of trainable weights.

- **Task Modularity**: Each task gets its own adapters, allowing quick switching.

- **Performance**: On tasks like sentence classification or NER, adapter-based fine-tuning often rivals full fine-tuning while saving memory.

Continual   **&**   **Multi-Task**   **Learning**

By training separate adapters for each task or domain, one can manage multi-task scenarios without catastrophic forgetting. The base model is consistent, and the domain/task adapter is swapped in as needed (Pfeiffer et al., 2021).

Limitations

- **Inference Overhead**: Each layer now includes an additional feed-forward.

- **Complex Integration**: For multi-lingual or multi-domain models, a proliferation of adapters can arise.

Key **Insight**

Adapters blend **fine-tuning** and **frozen-model** paradigms, updating only small modules in each layer. This approach allows memory-efficient customization for multiple tasks or domains without retraining billions of parameters.

7.2.4. Balancing Performance vs. Latency

The   **Resource**   **Dilemma**

While a fully fine-tuned large model might yield the best performance, it can be prohibitively big for edge deployments or real-time settings. Approaches like **distillation** (Sanh et al., 2020) and quantization reduce model size, but risk accuracy drops. Parameter-efficient tuning helps keep the base model intact while focusing on small layers.

Latency Considerations

- **Batch Inference**: High throughput in offline or batch scenarios can accommodate bigger models.

- **Real-Time Applications**: Chatbots, personal assistants, mobile apps demand fast response. Techniques like partial weighting or low-rank updates can reduce overhead.

- **Dynamic Model Selection**: Systems may store multiple versions—like a large server model for high-accuracy tasks and a smaller on-device variant for quick user interactions.

$$\text{Latency} \approx \frac{\text{FLOPs} \times \text{batch size}}{\text{GPU throughput}}$$

(where FLOPs per forward pass scale with model size, and GPU throughput depends on hardware generation.)

User   Experience   vs.   Accuracy
Practical systems balance quality with responsiveness. For instance, a GPT-based chatbot might run full-size inference on the cloud for paying enterprise customers but a smaller, distilled variant for free-tier or on-device usage (Ziegler et al., 2021).

Key   Insight
Achieving the "best of both worlds" entails combining parameter-efficient fine-tuning or model compression with a robust base LM, ensuring minimal latency hits while retaining strong performance.

7.3. Transfer Learning Strategies

7.3.1. When (and When Not) to Fine-Tune

Pros of Fine-Tuning

- **Domain Adaptation**: Gains in specialized fields (medical, legal).

- **Task Specialization**: Classification, QA, summarization.

- **Performance Boost**: Fine-tuning often outperforms zero-/few-shot prompting for complex tasks.

Cons of Fine-Tuning

- **Compute & Memory**: Updating billions of parameters is expensive.

- **Risk of Overfitting**: If the new dataset is small or not carefully curated.

- **Maintenance Overhead**: Each new task might require a separate fine-tuned model copy.

Zero-Shot   **or**   **Few-Shot**

Large LMs sometimes handle tasks without direct fine-tuning (Brown et al., 2020). For instance, GPT can solve basic QAs from a well-engineered prompt. This is ideal when you:

- **Lack Enough Labels**: Sparse or no labeled training data.

- **Need Quick Prototype**: Minimal overhead.

- **Are Willing to Accept**: Possibly lower or inconsistent accuracy.

Key   **Insight**

Fine-tuning is typically favored for mission-critical or domain-centric tasks. But zero-/few-shot strategies can suffice if label data is scarce or if you need to rapidly prototype.

7.3.2. Handling Out-of-Vocabulary Words & Noisy Data

Vocabulary   **Mismatches**

Subword tokenization helps, but in specialized domains, new or rare terms may still appear. If the base vocabulary splits domain words too aggressively, model performance can suffer. Solutions:

- **Further Pre-Training**: Expose the model to domain text with new tokens.

- **Dynamic Vocab Extensions**: Tools like SentencePiece or BPE can be updated with domain tokens (Kudo and Richardson, 2018).

$$w_{\text{domain}} \mapsto \{\text{subword}_1, \dots, \text{subword}_n\},$$

ensuring minimal subword splits for domain terms.

Noisy   **Labels**

In some tasks, labeled data might come from user feedback or automated processes, introducing noise. Approaches like **confidence weighting**, **teacher-student filtering**, or **robust loss functions** (e.g., Label Smoothing) can mitigate the effect (Szegedy et al., 2016).

Unstructured,   **Noisy**   **Text**

Social media or OCR-scanned documents often contain typos, emoticons, or special characters. The model's tokenization pipeline must handle or preserve them where relevant. Domain-specific normalization—like removing diacritics in some languages—may help but must be carefully tested.

Key   **Insight**

Even with advanced subword tokenizers, domain mismatch and data noise can degrade results. Adjusting the tokenizer or employing robust training methods ensures better outcomes with real-world, messy data.

7.3.3. Cross-Lingual Transfer

Multilingual   **Pre-Training**

Multilingual LMs (XLM-R, mBERT) ingest text from many languages, sharing parameters. Fine-tuning on one language can transfer partially to others (Conneau et al., 2020). For instance, training sentiment classification in Spanish might help related tasks in Portuguese.

Zero-Shot   **Transfer**

A model fine-tuned on a high-resource language can produce decent performance in a low-resource language if the underlying multilingual representation is robust (Pires, Schlinger and Garrette, 2019). This is especially effective for related language families with similar scripts.

Domain   **vs.**   **Language**

Cross-lingual transfer extends to domain adaptation as well. If you have labeled data for a domain in one language, you might still glean benefits in another language domain subset. Strategies like domain+language adapters can combine these axes (Pfeiffer et al., 2021).

Challenges

- **Vocabulary Overlaps**: For languages with distinct scripts, the subword units might be less shared.

- **Data Balance**: High-resource languages can dominate training.

- **Evaluation**: Some tasks (e.g., QA) have different cultural or domain references across languages, complicating direct transfer.

Key   **Insight**

Multilingual models enable cross-lingual fine-tuning, leveraging labeled data from resource-rich languages to improve performance in resource-scarce ones. This approach can mitigate data scarcity and foster more global NLP solutions.

7.3.4. Maintaining Model Integrity

Avoiding   **Overfitting**

Fine-tuning can accidentally overwrite the general knowledge gleaned from pre-training—a phenomenon akin to **catastrophic forgetting** (McCloskey and Cohen, 1989). Techniques like small learning rates, early stopping, or layer-freezing help preserve broader language ability.

Gradual   **Unfreezing**

One approach is to **incrementally unfreeze** layers from top to bottom (Howard and Ruder, 2018). Early layers remain frozen initially, focusing training on the final layers. Over time, more layers are unfrozen if needed:

$$\text{Unfreeze Schedule:} \quad [(\text{Layer } L), (\text{Layer } L - 1), \dots]$$

Regularization

- **Weight Decay**: Typically 0.01, preventing extreme parameter updates.

- **LayerNorm**: Already in Transformers but remains crucial for stable updates.

- **Dropout**: Usually 0.1 in attention and feed-forward blocks (Srivastava et al., 2014).

Validation   Checks

Monitoring general tasks (e.g., masked language modeling perplexity on a hold-out set) ensures the model still retains broad language understanding. If perplexity spikes, you might be overspecializing to the new data (Sun et al., 2019).

Key   Insight

Fine-tuning shapes a model to specific tasks but can erode general knowledge. Gradual unfreezing and careful hyperparameter control preserve general capabilities while achieving domain or task gains.

7.4. Case Studies in Fine-Tuning

7.4.1. E-Commerce: Product Descriptions & Chat Support

Overview

E-commerce platforms often rely on text generation (product descriptions) or classification (reviews, queries) to enhance user experience. Fine-tuned LMs can speed up content creation, detect spam/fraud in listings, or power chat support bots.

Product Description Generation

- **Data Source**: Existing product listings, user reviews, brand guidelines.

- **Fine-Tuning**: A GPT-like model on an in-house dataset of (product specs,marketing text)pairs.

- **Post-Processing**: Additional rule-based or brand-style constraints ensure factual correctness and consistent tone.

Chat   Support

Customers often ask about returns, shipping, or product info. A fine-tuned LM (e.g., BERT or T5) can classify the query and generate a short answer or route it to the correct knowledge base. Hybrid approaches combine retrieval (FAQ database) with generative expansions (doc2text summarization).

Challenges

- **Scalability**: Thousands of new products daily require constant updates.

- **Brand Voice**: The model's tone must match brand guidelines.

- **Quality Assurance**: Must avoid generating inaccurate or legally risky statements.

Key   **Insight**

E-commerce use cases benefit from fine-tuned LMs for descriptive text and customer support, boosting productivity while requiring brand alignment checks to maintain trust and correctness.

7.4.2. Healthcare: Language Models for Medical Text

Clinical   **Note**   **Summaries**

Doctors' notes and discharge summaries are typically unstructured. Fine-tuning a summarization model on real or synthetic note-summary pairs can reduce physician workload and enhance patient care (Jing et al., 2020). Data privacy is a major concern, so anonymization or on-premise training is standard (HIPAA compliance).

Entity   **Extraction**   **&**   **Coding**

Medical coding or named entity recognition (NER) identifies diagnoses, procedures, or medications. Domain-specific LMs (BioBERT, ClinicalBERT) can be fine-tuned to label these entities:

$$\mathcal{L}\,\mathcal{N}\mathcal{R} = -\sum_{t} \log P\,(\text{label}_t \mid \text{embedding}_t).$$

where each token embedding is derived from the final layer, and classification occurs per token (Lee et al., 2020).

Diagnostic   **Assistance**

A fine-tuned model might propose differential diagnoses from free-text clinical descriptions. However, real deployment demands high reliability, external verification by professionals, and disclaimers about automation's limits (Chen et al., 2020).

Ethical & Regulatory Issues

- **PHI Protection**: Models can inadvertently memorize personal data (Carlini et al., 2021).

- **Bias & Fairness**: Certain demographic groups might be underrepresented in training data, leading to worse outcomes for them.

- **Explainability**: Health professionals demand interpretable or evidence-based outputs.

Key   **Insight**

In healthcare, carefully fine-tuned LMs can revolutionize summarization, coding, and diagnostic support. Nevertheless, patient privacy and clinical reliability must be rigorously upheld.

7.4.3. Education & Tutoring Systems

Intelligent **Tutors**

Virtual tutors can deliver educational content and personalized feedback. Fine-tuning a model on educational dialogues or curated problem sets helps the system understand student queries and generate supportive responses (Piech et al., 2015).

Adaptive **Question** **Generation**

When fine-tuned on QA pairs or curated question banks, an LM can propose practice questions. This fosters interactive learning. Additional constraints ensure question difficulty aligns with the student's proficiency.

Challenges

- **Curriculum Alignment**: Ensuring the system follows standard curricula.

- **Academic Integrity**: Overly powerful systems might inadvertently provide direct solutions, hindering learning.

- **Bias & Offensive Content**: Even in educational contexts, the model may produce insensitive or culturally biased hints.

Future **Directions**

Ongoing research explores dynamic **student modeling**: a fine-tuned LM that personalizes tasks based on predicted knowledge gaps. This might require RL-based fine-tuning or specialized scaffolding prompts.

Key **Insight**

Education-based fine-tuning can yield engaging, adaptive tutoring systems. Yet ensuring academic alignment, promoting actual learning, and preventing misuse remain key concerns.

7.4.4. Creative Writing & Content Generation

Story **Generation**

Models like GPT can produce short stories or creative narratives when fine-tuned on fiction corpora (Fan, Lewis and Dauphin, 2018). The user or writer can specify prompts, controlling genre or style:

$$\text{Prompt} = Onceuponatimeinagalaxyfaraway, \quad \longrightarrow \quad \text{Autoregressive decoding.}$$

Style **Transfer**

By training on examples of text with a certain "style" (e.g., Shakespearean), a model can shift plain input into that style. This might involve a "tag" token or prefix specifying the style to be generated.

Ethical & Intellectual Property

- **Plagiarism**: The model might replicate training samples if the corpus is too small or the fine-tuning is heavy-handed.

- **Originality**: Public reception of AI-generated literature can be polarized—some find it novel, others see it as lacking true creativity or emotional depth.

Hybrid   Human-AI   Collaboration

Writers may adopt the model as a brainstorming partner—fine-tuning specialized modules for comedic tone, historical language, or specific brand voice. The AI suggests text; humans refine it for final publication.

Key   Insight

Fine-tuning for creative tasks demonstrates the model's flexibility, but raises questions about authorship, originality, and ethical reuse of data. Effective usage often pairs the model's generative power with human oversight and polishing.

References (Harvard Style)

- Beltagy, I., Peters, M.E. and Cohan, A. (2020) 'Longformer: The Long-Document Transformer', *arXiv preprint* arXiv:2004.05150.

- Brown, T. et al. (2020) 'Language Models Are Few-Shot Learners', in *Advances in Neural Information Processing Systems* (NeurIPS). Red Hook, NY: Curran Associates, pp. 1877–1901.

- Carlini, N. et al. (2021) 'Extracting Training Data from Large Language Models', in *30th USENIX Security Symposium*. Berkeley, CA: USENIX Association, pp. 2633–2650.

- Chawla, N.V. (2009) 'Data Mining for Imbalanced Datasets: An Overview', in *Data Mining and Knowledge Discovery Handbook*. 2nd edn. Boston, MA: Springer, pp. 875–886.

- Chen, T. et al. (2020) 'ClinicalBERT: Modeling Clinical Notes and Predicting Hospital Readmission', *ACM BCB*. New York: ACM, pp. 1–10.

- Devlin, J. et al. (2019) 'BERT: Pre-training of Deep Bidirectional Transformers for Language Understanding', in *Proceedings of the 2019 Conference of the North American Chapter of the ACL (NAACL)*. Stroudsburg, PA: ACL, pp. 4171–4186.

- Fan, A., Lewis, M. and Dauphin, Y. (2018) 'Hierarchical Neural Story Generation', in *Proceedings of the 56th Annual Meeting of the Association for Computational Linguistics (ACL)*. Stroudsburg, PA: ACL, pp. 889–898.

- Goodfellow, I., Bengio, Y. and Courville, A. (2016) *Deep Learning*. Cambridge, MA: MIT Press.

- HIPAA (1996) *Health Insurance Portability and Accountability Act*. Available at: https://www.hhs.gov/hipaa(Accessed: 10 February 2025).

- Howard, J. and Ruder, S. (2018) 'Universal Language Model Fine-tuning for Text Classification', in *Proceedings of the 56th Annual Meeting of the ACL (ACL)*. Stroudsburg, PA: ACL, pp. 328–339.

- Hu, E.J. et al. (2022) 'LoRA: Low-Rank Adaptation of Large Language Models', in *International Conference on Learning Representations (ICLR)*. Available at: https://openreview.net (Accessed: 10 February 2025).

- Jing, B. et al. (2020) 'On the Automatic Generation of Medical Discharge Summaries', in *Proceedings of the 2020 Conference on Empirical Methods in Natural Language Processing (EMNLP)*. Stroudsburg, PA: ACL, pp. 5462–5474.

- Konečný, J. et al. (2016) 'Federated Learning: Strategies for Improving Communication Efficiency', *arXiv preprint*arXiv:1610.05492.

- Kudo, T. and Richardson, J. (2018) 'SentencePiece: A Simple and Language Independent Subword Tokenizer and Detokenizer for Neural Text Processing', in *Proceedings of the 2018 Conference on Empirical Methods in Natural Language Processing (EMNLP): System Demonstrations*. Stroudsburg, PA: ACL, pp. 66–71.

- Lee, J. et al. (2020) 'BioBERT: A Pre-trained Biomedical Language Representation Model for Biomedical Text Mining', *Bioinformatics*, 36(4), pp. 1234–1240.

- Li, X.L. and Liang, P. (2021) 'Prefix-Tuning: Optimizing Continuous Prompts for Generation', in *Proceedings of the 59th Annual Meeting of the Association for Computational Linguistics (ACL)*. Stroudsburg, PA: ACL, pp. 4582–4597.

- Lin, C.Y. (2004) 'ROUGE: A Package for Automatic Evaluation of Summaries', in *Text Summarization Branches Out: Proceedings of the ACL-04 Workshop*. Stroudsburg, PA: ACL, pp. 74–81.

- Maynez, J. et al. (2020) 'On Faithfulness and Factuality in Abstractive Summarization', in *Proceedings of the 58th Annual Meeting of the Association for Computational Linguistics (ACL)*. Stroudsburg, PA: ACL, pp. 1906–1919.

- McCloskey, M. and Cohen, N.J. (1989) 'Catastrophic Interference in Connectionist Networks: The Sequential Learning Problem', in *The Psychology of Learning and Motivation*, 24, pp. 109–165.

- Pires, T., Schlinger, E. and Garrette, D. (2019) 'How Multilingual is Multilingual BERT?', in *Proceedings of the 57th Annual Meeting of the Association for Computational Linguistics (ACL)*. Stroudsburg, PA: ACL, pp. 4996–5001.

- Pfeiffer, J. et al. (2021) 'AdapterFusion: Non-Destructive Task Composition for Transfer Learning', in *Proceedings of the 2021 Conference on Empirical Methods in Natural Language Processing (EMNLP)*. Stroudsburg, PA: ACL, pp. 3631–3646.

- Piech, C. et al. (2015) 'Deep Knowledge Tracing', in *Proceedings of the 28th International Conference on Neural Information Processing Systems (NIPS)*. Red Hook, NY: Curran Associates, pp. 505–513.

- Prakash, A. et al. (2016) 'Neural Paraphrase Generation with Stacked Residual LSTM Networks', in *Proceedings of the 26th International Conference on Computational Linguistics (COLING)*. Stroudsburg, PA: ACL, pp. 2923–2934.

- Rajpurkar, P. et al. (2016) 'SQuAD: 100,000+ Questions for Machine Comprehension of Text', in *Proceedings of the 2016 Conference on Empirical Methods in Natural Language Processing (EMNLP)*. Stroudsburg, PA: ACL, pp. 2383–2392.

- Sanh, V. et al. (2020) 'DistilBERT, a Distilled Version of BERT: Smaller, Faster, Cheaper and Lighter', in *Proceedings of the 5th Workshop on Energy Efficient Machine Learning and Cognitive Computing (NeurIPS)*. Vancouver, BC: NeurIPS.

- Sennrich, R., Haddow, B. and Birch, A. (2016) 'Neural Machine Translation of Rare Words with Subword Units', in *Proceedings of the 54th Annual Meeting of the Association for Computational Linguistics (ACL)*. Stroudsburg, PA: ACL, pp. 1715–1725.

- Srivastava, N. et al. (2014) 'Dropout: A Simple Way to Prevent Neural Networks from Overfitting', *Journal of Machine Learning Research*, 15(1), pp. 1929–1958.

- Sun, C. et al. (2019) 'How to Fine-Tune BERT for Text Classification?', in *Proceedings of the 12th Asian Conference on Machine Learning (ACML)*. PMLR, pp. 1–11.

- Szegedy, C. et al. (2016) 'Rethinking the Inception Architecture for Computer Vision', in *Proceedings of the IEEE Conference on Computer Vision and Pattern Recognition (CVPR)*. Las Vegas, NV: IEEE, pp. 2818–2826.

- Ziegler, D. et al. (2021) 'Codex: A GPT Model for Code Generation', *arXiv preprint* arXiv:2107.03374.

- Zhang, J. et al. (2020) 'DIALOGPT: Large-Scale Generative Pre-training for Conversational Response Generation', in *Proceedings of the 58th Annual Meeting of the Association for Computational Linguistics (ACL): System Demonstrations*. Stroudsburg, PA: ACL, pp. 270–278.

- Zhao, J. et al. (2018) 'Gender Bias in Coreference Resolution: Evaluation and Debiasing Methods', in *Proceedings of the 2018 Conference of the North American Chapter of the ACL (NAACL)*. Stroudsburg, PA: ACL, pp. 15–20.

Chapter 8: Evaluating Language Models

8.1. Metrics & Benchmarks

8.1.1. Perplexity & Cross-Entropy

Defining **Perplexity**

Perplexity is a standard metric for language modeling that measures how well a model predicts a sample of text. Lower perplexity indicates better predictive ability. Formally, for a dataset D of size N, the perplexity (PPL) is:

$$\text{PPL}(D) = \exp\!\left(\frac{1}{N}\sum_{i=1}^{N}\mathcal{L}(x_i)\right)$$

where $\mathcal{L}(x_i)$ is the cross-entropy loss (negative log-likelihood) of sample x_i.

Cross-Entropy **Loss**

Cross-entropy for predicting next token y given context x is:

$$\mathcal{L}(y \mid x) = -\log P_\theta(y \mid x).$$

Summing (or averaging) across all tokens in the dataset yields a measure of how well the model assigns probabilities to observed sequences.

Interpretation

- **Perplexity = 1**: Perfect prediction.

- **Perplexity = 2**: The model is as uncertain as flipping a fair coin.

- **Large PPL**: The model struggles to predict tokens accurately.

Limitations

- **Vocabulary & Tokenization**: Different subword or word-based vocabularies can shift perplexity. Comparisons across models require consistent tokenization (Sennrich, Haddow and Birch, 2016).

- **Absolute Scale**: There is no universal "good" or "bad" perplexity. Domains differ in complexity (Radford et al., 2019).

Key **Insight**

Perplexity and cross-entropy provide a **foundational** measure of language model quality. Though widely used, they do not fully capture higher-level textual properties like coherence or factual correctness.

8.1.2. BLEU, ROUGE & Other NLP Metrics

BLEU: Machine Translation

The **BLEU** metric (Bilingual Evaluation Understudy) measures overlap of n-grams between a model's translation and reference translations (Papineni et al., 2002). Formally, BLEU can be approximated by:

$$\text{BLEU} = \exp\left(\sum_{n=1}^{4} w_n \log p_n\right) \times \exp\left(-\max\{0, \frac{r}{c} - 1\}\right),$$

where p_n is the n-gram precision, w_n are weights (often uniform), r is reference length, and c is candidate length. BLEU excels at comparing machine vs. human translations but can underrate paraphrastic flexibility.

ROUGE: Summarization

ROUGE (Recall-Oriented Understudy for Gisting Evaluation) focuses on recall of overlapping n-grams or sub-sequences (Lin, 2004). Common variants: ROUGE-N (n-grams), ROUGE-L (longest common subsequence). Despite popularity in summarization tasks, ROUGE doesn't fully address factual correctness (Maynez et al., 2020).

Other Metrics

- **METEOR**: Evaluates alignment between candidate and reference translations using synonyms, stemming (Banerjee and Lavie, 2005).

- **CIDEr**: Often used for image captioning, weighting n-grams by their tf-idf in reference sets (Vedantam, Zitnick and Parikh, 2015).

- **BERTScore**: Compares embeddings from a trained LM to gauge semantic similarity (Zhang et al., 2020b).

Choosing the Right Metric

Different tasks demand different metrics:

- **Machine Translation**: BLEU or METEOR.

- **Summarization**: ROUGE, possibly combined with factuality checks.

- **Captioning**: CIDEr or BERTScore.

Key Insight

Traditional n-gram metrics (BLEU, ROUGE) have guided NLP progress. But each has **blind spots**—particularly regarding semantics, fluency, or factual correctness. Model selection should consider complementary or more advanced metrics where possible.

8.1.3. Human Evaluation & Crowd-Sourced Feedback

Why **Human** **Evaluation?**

No single automated metric captures all aspects of language quality—coherence, style, creativity, factual consistency. **Human judgments** remain a gold standard for tasks like dialog generation, summarization, or creative writing (Callison-Burch, 2009).

Methods

1. **Likert Scales**: Raters judge text on a scale (1–5) for fluency, relevance, etc.

2. **Pairwise Comparison**: Raters see two outputs and select the better one.

3. **Error Annotation**: Mark specific issues (factual errors, grammar mistakes, offensive content).

$$\text{score}_{\text{human}} \in \{1,2,3,4,5\} \quad \text{or} \quad \text{ranking approach.}$$

Crowdsourcing **Platforms**

Amazon Mechanical Turk or Figure Eight (Appen) allow quick feedback from many users, but quality must be monitored—crowd workers vary in expertise (Snow et al., 2008). Strategies to ensure reliability include:

- **Qualification Tests**

- **Gold Standard Traps**

- **Redundancy**: Multiple raters per item.

Challenges

- **Cost & Time**: Manual evaluation can be slow and expensive for large datasets.

- **Inter-Rater Agreement**: Language tasks can be subjective. Using metrics like Cohen's kappa or Krippendorff's alpha helps gauge consistency (Artstein and Poesio, 2008).

- **Cultural & Domain Expertise**: Evaluators must match the domain or language variety.

Key **Insight**

Human judgments provide **nuanced** evaluations that automated metrics miss, especially for open-ended tasks. Well-designed crowd-sourced or expert evaluations remain indispensable for truly measuring model quality.

8.2. Stress Testing & Robustness

8.2.1. Adversarial Inputs & Prompt Manipulation

Adversarial **Attacks**

Models can be brittle if malicious inputs trick them into wrong or harmful outputs. Examples include:

- **Text Perturbations**: Minor spelling manipulations or synonyms that confuse classification (Ebrahimi et al., 2018).

- **Prompt Twisting**: For large language models, carefully crafted prompts might reveal undesired or policy-violating content.

$x' = \text{Perturb}(x)$,$\text{Perturb}(\cdot)$ is a small textual transformation designed to confuse the model.

Testing Strategies

- **White-Box Attacks**: Attackers have partial knowledge of the model internals.

- **Black-Box Attacks**: Attackers only see model inputs/outputs.

Mitigation

- **Adversarial Training**: Incorporate adversarial examples into fine-tuning (Goodfellow, Shlens and Szegedy, 2015).

- **Prompt Filtering**: For generative LMs, post-process or block suspicious user prompts.

- **Regularization**: Helps reduce over-sensitivity to small input shifts.

Key **Insight**

Language models face adversarial text manipulations, prompting specialized testing. By exposing models to deliberate perturbations, developers can bolster robustness and lessen vulnerabilities.

8.2.2. Handling Rare & Ambiguous Cases

Rare **Words** **&** **Long-Tail** **Phenomena**

Large LMs generally handle frequent expressions well but might fail for uncommon tokens or domain-specific terms (Sato et al., 2020). Rare or newly coined words (e.g., brand names, trending slang) may remain out of the model's subword lexicon.

Ambiguity

Natural language frequently contains ambiguous references—e.g., polysemous words, pronouns with multiple possible antecedents. If a model lacks sufficient context or training examples, it may produce incorrect or unclear predictions.

Evaluation Approaches

1. **Stress Tests**: Curated sets of ambiguous or rare inputs (Naik et al., 2018).

2. **Disambiguation Tasks**: Specialized benchmarks (Winograd Schema Challenge) that check pronoun resolution.

3. **OOV or Unseen Terms**: Checking how the model handles newly introduced tokens or subwords.

$\text{TestSet}_{\text{rare}} = \{x \mid \text{freq}(x) < \delta\}$, focusing on low-frequency items in training.

Mitigation

- **Augmentation**: Synthetic expansions of rare examples.

- **Further Fine-Tuning**: Specifically targeting ambiguous constructs or domain expansions.

- **Retrieval-Based**: For especially unusual queries, some systems retrieve external references, bridging knowledge gaps (Lewis et al., 2020).

Key   **Insight**

Rare words and ambiguous sentences expose LMs' limitations. Testing with specialized sets or domain expansions highlights these weaknesses, guiding additional fine-tuning or data augmentation.

8.2.3. Sensitivity to Domain Shifts

Domain   **Shift**

Models trained on certain distributions (e.g., general web text) might degrade when facing data from a different domain—technical manuals, legal filings, social media slang. This "domain shift" can significantly drop performance (Ben-David et al., 2010).

$$\Delta\text{Performance} = \mathcal{M}\text{\textcrightcurve}tandm - \mathcal{M}\text{\textcrightcurve}ts\text{-}dm.$$

Tests for Robustness

- **Cross-Domain Evaluation**: Train on domain A, test on domain B.

- **Temporal Shift**: Check model performance on older vs. newer data (time-based drift).

- **Style Shift**: E.g., from formal news to casual tweets.

Mitigating Domain Shift

- **Unsupervised Domain Adaptation**: E.g., further pre-train on unlabeled target-domain text.

- **Few-Shot Fine-Tuning**: With small labeled sets in the target domain, bridging distribution gaps.

- **Hybrid & Multi-Domain**: If feasible, train or fine-tune on multiple domains simultaneously, encouraging generalization (Sun et al., 2019).

Continuous   **Adaptation**

In real-world systems, domain shift is ongoing. Solutions like **online learning** or **periodic re-training** keep the model fresh. Monitoring performance changes in production helps trigger such updates (Section 8.4.1).

Key   **Insight**

Domain shifts can cripple a model trained on mismatched data. Systematic cross-domain testing and targeted adaptation strategies ensure more stable performance across diverse or evolving data sources.

8.3. Comparing Models

8.3.1. Baseline vs. State-of-the-Art

Role   **of**   **Baselines**

A strong **baseline** clarifies whether new model improvements are genuinely meaningful (Bowman et al., 2015). For instance, on a text classification task, a logistic regression with bag-of-words can serve as a minimal baseline. Alternatively, an established neural architecture from prior papers can be used to anchor improvements.

State-of-the-Art   **Benchmarks**

Many tasks have leaderboards—e.g., GLUE for general language understanding, WMT for translation. Models near the top are labeled "state-of-the-art (SOTA)." However, chasing leaderboard gains can lead to minimal incremental improvements without broader utility (Marcus and Davis, 2019).

Reproducibility   **&**   **Fair**   **Comparison**

Comparisons must control for:

- **Same Tokenization**: Different subword splits can skew perplexity or BLEU.

- **Training Data Size**: Extra unlabeled data can yield bigger gains than architectural tweaks.

- **Hardware & Hyperparameters**: Large-batch training or different learning rates can confound direct comparisons (Bergstra and Bengio, 2012).

Key   **Insight**

Baselines anchor model performance and reveal incremental gains. Quoting "SOTA" results carries weight only if accompanied by transparent, reproducible protocols that confirm genuine advancement over prior baselines.

8.3.2. Interpreting Leaderboards & Papers

Leaderboards

Sites like **Papers With Code** or official competition portals (e.g., Kaggle, Codalab) host leaderboards, showing top-performer metrics on tasks like sentiment classification, summarization, or question answering. While valuable, there are caveats:

1. **Inconsistent Preprocessing**: Some participants use different cleaning or tokenization steps.

2. **Private Test Sets**: Overfitting can occur if participants repeatedly tweak models to rank higher.

3. **Hidden Constraints**: Some teams might use large external data or ensembles, overshadowing simpler solutions.

Conference & Journal Papers

Academic publications detail new architectures, training regimes, or data expansions. Interpretation challenges include:

- **Selective Reporting**: Negative or neutral results might be omitted (publication bias).

- **Lack of Ablations**: Papers that skip ablations on essential hyperparameters or data usage hamper comparisons.

- **Complex Codebases**: Implementation details matter. If code is not released or is incomplete, reproducing results can be tough (Pineau et al., 2020).

Guidelines

- **Read the Experimental Section Carefully**: Check data splits, hyperparameters, version of the LM used.

- **Look for Confidence Intervals**: Minor metric changes (e.g., 0.1 on BLEU) may not be statistically significant.

- **Community Efforts**: Reproducibility challenges, open-source releases, and replication studies bolster trust in claimed improvements.

Key Insight

Leaderboards and research papers offer valuable benchmarks but require **critical evaluation**. Subtle differences in data, code, or experimental setup can inflate claims, so thorough replication and transparency are vital for genuine progress.

8.3.3. Choosing the Right Metric for the Task

Task   **Diversity**

Language modeling, classification, summarization, translation, QA—each involves different success criteria:

- **LM**: Perplexity or cross-entropy.

- **Classification**: Accuracy, F1, AUC.

- **Summarization**: ROUGE, factual consistency metrics.

- **Dialogue**: Human preference scores, context coherence.

Quantitative   **vs.**   **Qualitative**

No single metric can capture **all** aspects of language quality. For creative text generation, style or emotional resonance might matter more than raw overlap. Automated metrics can be combined with targeted human checks:

$$\text{Score}_{\text{total}} = \alpha \, \text{Metric}_{\text{auto}} + \beta \, \text{Rating}_{\text{human}}.$$

Context   **&**   **Application**

In business contexts, the chosen metric must reflect real-world objectives, e.g., user satisfaction or improved conversion rates in e-commerce. In research contexts, a widely recognized metric or a standard benchmark fosters comparability.

Evolution   **of**   **Metrics**

As language models grow more sophisticated, new metrics—like **BERTScore** or **BLEURT**—attempt to incorporate **semantic** or **contextual** matching (Sellam, Das and Parikh, 2020). Ongoing exploration aims to measure factual correctness or logical consistency in generative outputs.

Key   **Insight**

Align evaluation with the **task's end goals**. While perplexity or BLEU remain useful, specialized or hybrid metrics are essential for capturing nuances like factual accuracy, style, or user satisfaction.

8.4. Continuous Improvement

8.4.1. Online Learning & Incremental Updates

Motivation

Real-world data distributions shift over time: new slang, events, or product lines appear. A static model may degrade if it never updates. **Online learning** or **incremental training** addresses this drift (Al-Shedivat et al., 2021).

$$\theta_{t+1} = \theta_t - \alpha \, \nabla_\theta \mathcal{L}(\theta_t; x_{\text{new}}).$$

(Incremental step on new data x_{new}.)

Implementation

1. **Streaming**: Continuously gather new data; update model periodically.

2. **Mini-Batch Online**: Accumulate batches, train briefly each day/week.

3. **Model Checkpointing**: Save stable versions in case of performance regression.

Pros & Cons

- **Up-to-Date**: The model quickly adapts to emerging terms or patterns.

- **Forgetting**: Overemphasizing new data can degrade old knowledge. Strategies like replay buffers or weighted sampling maintain historical contexts (Sun et al., 2019).

Key   **Insight**

Incremental or online updates keep language models fresh but require careful management of catastrophic forgetting and a robust pipeline for newly ingested data.

8.4.2. Monitoring Model Drift

Model   **Drift**

A model might perform well initially but degrade when input data changes or user behavior evolves. **Drift** can be **data drift** (feature distribution shift) or **concept drift** (label definitions shift) (Gama et al., 2014).

Detection Methods

- **Performance Metrics**: Monitoring validation error or user feedback changes over time.

- **Statistical Tests**: Checking distribution differences between new data vs. training data.

- **Trigger Thresholds**: If a performance metric drops below δ, retraining or adaptation is triggered.

$$\Delta\text{metric} = \text{metric}_{\text{current}} - \text{metric}_{\text{previous}}.$$

If ` Δmetric $< -$, drift might be significant.

Infrastructure

Setting up **continuous integration** for ML (MLOps) ensures the model is regularly tested on fresh data. Alerts can be automated if drift surpasses a threshold. This approach also fosters stable deployments, reducing unexpected failures in production (Lwakatare et al., 2020).

Key   **Insight**

Detecting drift early avoids severe performance drops or embarrassing user experiences.

Systematic logging and threshold-based alerts support timely interventions like retraining or domain adaptation.

8.4.3. Setting Up a Feedback Loop

User **Feedback**

Deployed models often receive implicit (clicks, dwell time) or explicit (thumbs up/down, star ratings) user feedback. Integrating these signals can refine the model—especially for dialogue, recommendation, or search tasks (Amatriain and Basilico, 2015).

1. **Collect**: Log user interactions, error reports, or success metrics.

2. **Analyze**: Identify patterns of failure or dissatisfaction.

3. **Retrain/Refine**: Incorporate high-quality feedback points into the training pipeline.

Active **Learning**

In some scenarios, the system queries users for labels on uncertain cases (Settles, 2009). This can expedite data collection for tricky, high-value inputs:

$$\text{Query}(x) = \arg\max_x \text{Uncertainty}\left(P_\theta(y \mid x)\right).$$

Human-in-the-Loop

Important in areas like medical text analysis or contract review, where model suggestions are validated by domain experts. Gradually, the model improves from these corrections or confirmations.

Sustained **Improvements**

By continually ingesting real-world feedback and iterating fine-tuning cycles, LMs evolve with user needs. This requires robust architecture for ingesting labeled or unlabeled feedback, updating models, and validating improvements in production.

Key **Insight**

A well-designed **feedback loop** aligns model updates with real user interactions, creating a virtuous cycle of continuous improvement. Active learning or user instrumentation helps gather the most impactful data.

References (Harvard Style)

- Al-Shedivat, M. et al. (2021) 'Continuously Learning Neural Networks for Search Applications', *arXiv preprint*arXiv:2106.00870.

- Amatriain, X. and Basilico, J. (2015) 'Recommender Systems in Industry: A Netflix Case Study', in *Recommender Systems Handbook*. 2nd edn. Boston, MA: Springer, pp. 385–419.

- Artstein, R. and Poesio, M. (2008) 'Inter-Coder Agreement for Computational Linguistics', *Computational Linguistics*, 34(4), pp. 555–596.

- Banerjee, S. and Lavie, A. (2005) 'METEOR: An Automatic Metric for MT Evaluation with Improved Correlation with Human Judgments', in *Proceedings of the ACL Workshop on Intrinsic and Extrinsic Evaluation Measures for Machine Translation and/or Summarization*. Stroudsburg, PA: ACL, pp. 65–72.

- Ben-David, S. et al. (2010) 'A Theory of Learning from Different Domains', *Machine Learning*, 79(1–2), pp. 151–175.

- Bergstra, J. and Bengio, Y. (2012) 'Random Search for Hyper-Parameter Optimization', *Journal of Machine Learning Research*, 13(Feb), pp. 281–305.

- Bowman, S.R. et al. (2015) 'A Large Annotated Corpus for Learning Natural Language Inference', in *Proceedings of the 2015 Conference on Empirical Methods in Natural Language Processing (EMNLP)*. Stroudsburg, PA: ACL, pp. 632–642.

- Callison-Burch, C. (2009) 'Fast, Cheap, and Creative: Evaluating Translation Quality Using Amazon's Mechanical Turk', in *Proceedings of the 2009 Conference on Empirical Methods in Natural Language Processing (EMNLP)*. Stroudsburg, PA: ACL, pp. 286–295.

- Ebrahimi, J. et al. (2018) 'HotFlip: White-Box Adversarial Examples for NLP', in *Proceedings of the 56th Annual Meeting of the Association for Computational Linguistics (ACL)*. Stroudsburg, PA: ACL, pp. 31–36.

- Goodfellow, I.J., Shlens, J. and Szegedy, C. (2015) 'Explaining and Harnessing Adversarial Examples', in *3rd International Conference on Learning Representations (ICLR)*. San Diego, CA: ICLR.

- Lewis, P. et al. (2020) 'Retrieval-Augmented Generation for Knowledge-Intensive NLP Tasks', in *Advances in Neural Information Processing Systems* (NeurIPS). Red Hook, NY: Curran Associates.

- Lin, C.-Y. (2004) 'ROUGE: A Package for Automatic Evaluation of Summaries', in *Text Summarization Branches Out: Proceedings of the ACL-04 Workshop*. Stroudsburg, PA: ACL, pp. 74–81.

- Lwakatare, L.E. et al. (2020) 'DevOps and MLOps in Practice: A Case Study on Software Development for Machine Learning', in *International Conference on Product-Focused Software Process Improvement (PROFES)*. Cham: Springer, pp. 422–437.

- Marcus, G. and Davis, E. (2019) *Rebooting AI: Building Artificial Intelligence We Can Trust*. New York: Pantheon Books.

- Maynez, J. et al. (2020) 'On Faithfulness and Factuality in Abstractive Summarization', in *Proceedings of the 58th Annual Meeting of the Association for Computational Linguistics (ACL)*. Stroudsburg, PA: ACL, pp. 1906–1919.

- Naik, A. et al. (2018) 'Stress Test Evaluation for Natural Language Inference', in *Proceedings of the 27th International Conference on Computational Linguistics (COLING)*. Stroudsburg, PA: ACL, pp. 2340–2353.

- Papineni, K. et al. (2002) 'BLEU: A Method for Automatic Evaluation of Machine Translation', in *Proceedings of the 40th Annual Meeting of the Association for Computational Linguistics (ACL)*. Stroudsburg, PA: ACL, pp. 311–318.

- Pineau, J. et al. (2020) 'Improving Reproducibility in Machine Learning Research', *Journal of Machine Learning Research*, 21(219), pp. 1–20.

- Radford, A. et al. (2019) 'Language Models are Unsupervised Multitask Learners', *OpenAI Blog*. Available at: https://openai.com (Accessed: 10 February 2025).

- Sellam, T., Das, D. and Parikh, A. (2020) 'BLEURT: Learning Robust Metrics for Text Generation', in *Proceedings of the 58th Annual Meeting of the Association for Computational Linguistics (ACL)*. Stroudsburg, PA: ACL, pp. 7881–7892.

- Sato, M. et al. (2020) 'Evaluating Subword Embeddings for Low-Resource Languages', *arXiv preprint* arXiv:2011.04563.

- Sennrich, R., Haddow, B. and Birch, A. (2016) 'Neural Machine Translation of Rare Words with Subword Units', in *Proceedings of the 54th Annual Meeting of the Association for Computational Linguistics (ACL)*. Stroudsburg, PA: ACL, pp. 1715–1725.

- Snow, R. et al. (2008) 'Cheaper and Faster? Using Mechanical Turk to Translate a Language Model', in *Proceedings of the 2008 Conference on Empirical Methods in Natural Language Processing (EMNLP)*. Stroudsburg, PA: ACL, pp. 286–295.

- Srivastava, A. et al. (2022) 'Beyond the Imitation Game: Quantifying and Extrapolating the Capabilities of Language Models', *arXiv preprint* arXiv:2206.04615.

- Sun, C. et al. (2019) 'How to Fine-Tune BERT for Text Classification?', in *Proceedings of the 12th Asian Conference on Machine Learning (ACML)*. PMLR, pp. 1–11.

- Vedantam, R., Zitnick, C.L. and Parikh, D. (2015) 'CIDEr: Consensus-based Image Description Evaluation', in *Proceedings of the IEEE Conference on Computer Vision and Pattern Recognition (CVPR)*, pp. 4566–4575.

- Zhang, T. et al. (2020b) 'BERTScore: Evaluating Text Generation with BERT', in *International Conference on Learning Representations (ICLR)*. Available at: https://openreview.net (Accessed: 10 February 2025).

Chapter 9: Real-World Applications

9.1. Conversational Agents & Chatbots

9.1.1. Use Cases in Customer Service

Proliferation of Chatbots

Modern businesses increasingly rely on chatbots for **first-line customer support**, tackling issues like account information, refunds, or frequently asked questions. Compared to older rule-based systems, **Transformer-based** chatbots understand nuanced queries and produce more coherent responses (Zhang et al., 2020). This lowers support costs and speeds up response times.

Advantages

- **24/7 Availability**: No downtime, consistent service.

- **Scalability**: High volumes of queries can be handled in parallel with minimal marginal cost.

- **Data Insights**: Logs reveal common user issues, informing product improvements.

Architectural Approaches

1. **Encoder-Decoder**: E.g., T5 or BART fine-tuned on dialogue corpora.

2. **Decoder-Only**: GPT-based, possibly with a retrieval module to incorporate knowledge.

3. **Hybrid**: Task-oriented chatbots that combine structured slot-filling with generative subcomponents for open-ended questions (Chen et al., 2017).

$$\text{Response} = \arg\max_{y} \text{LM}\left(y \mid \text{context, user query}\right).$$

Challenges

- **Domain Context**: E.g., banking specifics or e-commerce processes. Fine-tuning on domain data is crucial.

- **Error Recovery**: Incomplete or ambiguous user inputs. A fallback strategy (handover to a human agent) is typical.

- **Brand Voice**: Chatbots must maintain a consistent, on-brand tone.

Key Insight

Chatbots in customer service highlight the synergy of domain fine-tuning, robust language understanding, and scalable deployment—transforming support operations with consistent, always-on service.

9.1.2. Designing Dialogue Flows

Structured　　　　　vs.　　　　　Free-Form　　　　　Dialogue

Traditional chatbots follow structured decision trees or state machines. Large language models (LLMs), by contrast, handle **free-form** user inputs, generating flexible responses. However, many real-world solutions blend both approaches:

- **Rule-based** for well-defined actions (like ID verification).

- **Generative** for chit-chat or broad queries.

$$"\{Flow\}("\{user\ input\})$$
$$\rightarrow \ [\{cases\}\ "\{Rule$$
$$- based\ route\}, \& "\{if\ recognized\ pattern\}\backslash$$
$$\backslash "\{LLM\ generation\}, \& "\{otherwise\}\ ]\ \{cases\}$$

Context　　　　　　　　　　　　　　Management

Conversations can span multiple turns. The model must keep track of user history—**conversation context**—to avoid repetitive or contradictory answers (Wolf et al., 2020). Techniques include storing conversation embeddings or appending previous turns as text prompts.

Dialog　　　　　　　　　State　　　　　　　　　Tracking

For **task-oriented** scenarios, the system maintains a **dialogue state**—slots representing user needs (destination, date, preferences). A BERT-based tracker can update these slots after each turn (Henderson et al., 2020), feeding them to a policy module that decides next actions or responses.

Testing　　　　　　　　　&　　　　　　　　　Iteration

Designing robust flows requires iterative prototyping and user testing:

1. **Wizard-of-Oz Studies**: Simulate the chatbot with a human operator.

2. **Beta Deployments**: Real users with disclaimers or fallback to humans.

3. **Logging & Analysis**: Identify user confusion or high-abandonment points.

Key　　　　　　　　　　　　　　　Insight

Successful dialogue systems mix **structured flows** for known tasks with **generative flexibility** for open-ended queries. Thorough design of state tracking, context handling, and iterative testing fosters user-friendly, coherent interactions.

9.1.3. Hybrid (Rule-Based + NLP) Approaches

Why　　　　　　　　　　　　　　　Hybrid?

Purely generative models can be unpredictable in critical tasks—exposing brand or compliance risks (Roller et al., 2021). **Hybrid** designs combine best-of-breed: rule-based logic for validated steps and an NLP model for interpretive or free-form segments.

Architecture

1. **Intent Classification**: BERT-based classifier detects user intent.

2. **Rule Engine**: If intent = "Check Balance," forward to a rule-based function.

3. **Generative NLP**: For fallback or open-ended queries not covered by rules.

$$\{System\}(x) = \llbracket\{cases\} \text{ "}\{rule - based\}(x), \& \text{ "}\{if \} \text{ "}\{intent\ recognized\}\backslash\backslash \text{ "}\{gen - model\}(x), \& \text{ "}\{otherwise\}\rrbracket \{cases\}$$

Benefits

- **Reliability**: High-stakes tasks (e.g., account changes) rely on tested, deterministic logic.

- **Flexibility**: The model can handle unexpected user input or chit-chat.

- **Maintainability**: Domain experts can easily update rules without retraining the entire model.

Case   Example

A banking chatbot:

- Rule-based flow handles secure login or funds transfer.

- GPT or T5 segments handle general queries: "What's the best way to save money?"

- System logs user satisfaction metrics for continuous iteration.

Key   Insight

Hybrid systems mitigate generative unpredictability by directing well-defined tasks to rules. Meanwhile, LLM components tackle unstructured conversation, achieving a pragmatic balance for real-world deployment.

9.2. Content Generation & Summarization

9.2.1. Automated Reporting in Journalism

News   Summaries   &   Bulletins

Media outlets produce daily or real-time updates on financial markets, sports, or weather. **Automatic summarization** or template-based generation historically used simple fill-in methods. Modern LMs can create more varied, fluent texts (Fan, Lewis and Dauphin, 2018).

Workflow

- **Data Ingestion**: E.g., sports scores, company earnings.

- **Text Generation**: A fine-tuned GPT or T5 processes structured data to produce a short article.

- **Post-Processing**: Add standard disclaimers, ensure no factual hallucinations (Maynez et al., 2020).

- **Editor Review**: Journalists or editors might finalize the draft.

$$\text{Report} = \text{LM}(\text{structured data} \mid \text{template prompt}).$$

Benefits

- **Speed**: Rapid generation of short articles for routine events (weather, stock updates).

- **Cost-Effectiveness**: Freed journalists can focus on investigative or high-value reporting.

- **Consistency**: Minimizes style or grammatical errors (once well-tuned).

Ethical & Quality Concerns

- **Accuracy**: Data drift or wrong feeds can propagate factual errors.

- **Editorial Oversight**: Vital for controversial or sensitive topics.

- **Uniqueness**: Risk of repetitive "boilerplate" style if not carefully diversified.

Key   **Insight**

Automated reporting expedites large volumes of routine news coverage. However, editorial guardrails remain crucial to ensure factual integrity and maintain brand reputation.

9.2.2. Email & Document Summaries

Email   **Summaries**

Busy professionals may get hundreds of emails daily. Summarization can yield quick previews, highlighting major points, deadlines, or calls to action (Shapira et al., 2021). One approach: an encoder-decoder model trained on real or synthetic (email, summary) pairs. Alternatively, an unsupervised extractive method might select key sentences.

Document   **Summaries**

Law firms or researchers face massive document sets. Summaries help filter relevant content:

1. **Extraction**: Identify important sentences or bullet points.

2. **Abstraction**: Transform them into a concise narrative, removing redundancies.

3. **Validation**: Potentially verify references or citations, ensuring no fabricated facts.

Challenges

- **Privacy**: Emails or legal documents often contain sensitive info. On-premises solutions or encryption help maintain confidentiality.

- **Context Preservation**: Summaries risk losing subtle but crucial details.

- **Customization**: Different users might want different summary styles (e.g., bullet points vs. short paragraphs).

$$\text{Summary}(d) \approx \arg\max_{y} P(y \mid d) \quad \text{subject to length/style constraints.}$$

Key   **Insight**

Automated summaries in emails or lengthy documents streamline information intake. However, domain specificity, user preference, and data confidentiality must be carefully managed to produce accurate, relevant results.

9.2.3. Creative Writing Tools

AI-Assisted   **Creativity**

From brainstorming plot ideas to drafting marketing copy, LMs can function as "writing partners." For instance, GPT-based systems can generate or rewrite text in a user-specified style (Clark et al., 2018).

Human-in-the-Loop

Professionals typically use an **interactive** approach:

- **Model Prompting**: "Write a short sci-fi paragraph about space explorers."

- **Editing & Polishing**: The user refines or discards suggestions, ensuring final copy meets their standards.

Genre-Specific   **Fine-Tuning**

Writers can compile domain text (e.g., romance novels, fantasy lore) to fine-tune a base LM for:

$$\text{CreativeLM} = \text{FineTune}(\text{BaseLM}, \text{genre corpora}).$$

This yields a specialized model attuned to certain themes, archetypes, or language styles (Elsahar, Vougiouklis and Gravier, 2021).

Ethical & Artistic Debates

- **Originality**: Some argue AI "lacks true creativity," merely remixing training data.

- **Plagiarism Risks**: Overfitting or echoing source text can raise IP concerns.

- **Authorial Ownership**: If the system produces substantial content, do you credit the AI as co-author?

Generative LMs provide powerful writing aids, though final creative oversight typically remains human-driven. The synergy between AI suggestions and human curation can accelerate ideation while preserving artistic intentionality.

9.3. Language Models in Healthcare

9.3.1. Assisting Medical Coding & Billing

Coding   **Complexity**

Healthcare providers must convert diagnoses, procedures, and prescriptions into standardized codes (ICD, CPT) for billing and record-keeping. Manual coding is tedious and error-prone. Large LMs can help parse clinical notes or discharge summaries, suggesting relevant codes:

1. **NER**: Identifying medical entities.

2. **Classification**: Mapping entities to standard codes.

3. **Confidence Scores**: Indicating uncertain predictions for human review.

$$\hat{c} = \arg\max_{c \in \mathcal{C}} P_\theta\left(c \mid \text{note}\right).$$

Benefits

- **Improved Accuracy & Speed**: Automating routine parts of the coding workflow.

- **Cost Savings**: Reducing coder burden, accelerating claims processing.

- **Focus on Edge Cases**: Skilled coders handle complex or ambiguous charts.

Data   **Privacy**

Healthcare data is heavily regulated (HIPAA in the US, GDPR in Europe). LMs typically train on anonymized text or carefully controlled environments, minimizing risk of patient identity leaks (Strubell, Ganesh and McCallum, 2019).

Limitations

- **Ambiguous Notes**: Some clinical notes lack clarity, requiring domain expertise.

- **Adversarial Audits**: Mistakes can lead to insurance rejections or compliance issues.

- **Continuous Updates**: Medical coding standards evolve regularly (ICD expansions).

Key   **Insight**

Automating medical coding with LMs yields efficiency gains, but the system must handle domain-specific complexities, privacy constraints, and evolving code sets. Human coders remain crucial for QA and intricate cases.

9.3.2. Analyzing Patient Records & Clinical Notes

Clinical **Text** **Processing**

Physicians generate extensive unstructured notes capturing diagnoses, lab results, and observations. NLP-based analysis can reveal patterns or biomarkers for disease progression (Lee et al., 2020). Tasks include:

- **NER** for diseases, medications, or symptoms.
- **Relation Extraction** for linking symptoms to diagnoses.
- **Summarization** to produce concise discharge reports.

Transformer-Based **Tools**

Domain-specific models like BioBERT or ClinicalBERT incorporate medical literature, capturing specialized terminology. Fine-tuning on EHR data or local hospital corpora further refines performance:

$$\text{FineTune}(\text{BioBERT}, \text{Hospital EHR Corpus}) \rightarrow \text{ClinicalNER}.$$

Challenges

- **Data Quality**: Notes often contain abbreviations or incomplete statements.
- **Interpretability**: Doctors prefer explainable predictions (which note segments led to a diagnosis?).
- **Ethical Boundaries**: Automated suggestions must not override physician judgment.

Key **Insight**

Transformer LMs can unlock insights buried in clinical text, from extracting key signals to summarizing visits. Yet careful oversight, domain adaptation, and ethical guardrails remain paramount.

9.3.3. Ethical Considerations & Data Privacy

Regulatory **Compliance**

Healthcare data is sensitive—violation of privacy laws risks severe penalties. Datasets for LM training must be **de-identified** (removing names, SSNs, etc.) or processed behind secure firewalls (HIPAA, GDPR) (European Commission, 2021).

Data **Leakage** **Risks**

Large LMs can inadvertently memorize training samples (Carlini et al., 2021). If unredacted text included personal details, malicious prompts might retrieve them. Mitigations:

- **Differential Privacy**: Adding noise to gradients (Abadi et al., 2016).

- **Prompt Filters**: Blocking suspicious queries that might probe for private info.

Bias & Equity

Healthcare data can reflect historical disparities—e.g., fewer resources in certain demographics. The model might yield suboptimal recommendations for underrepresented groups (Bender et al., 2021). Continuous bias monitoring and dataset balancing help mitigate these issues.

Key Insight

In healthcare, strong privacy protections and domain scrutiny are non-negotiable. A well-designed pipeline for anonymized data usage, alongside robust security and bias oversight, fosters responsible LM deployment in clinical contexts.

9.4. Finance, Marketing & Beyond

9.4.1. Sentiment Analysis for Stock Movements

News & Social Media Impact

Market sentiment can shift rapidly based on breaking news or social media trends. **Sentiment analysis** can glean signals about potential stock movements (Bollen, Mao and Zeng, 2011):

1. **Data Streams**: Financial news outlets, Twitter feeds, forums (e.g., Reddit).

2. **LM Fine-Tuning**: Tailored for financial language—tickers, jargon, abbreviations.

3. **Signal Extraction**: Aggregating sentiment scores for certain companies or sectors.

$$\text{sentiment}(x) = \text{LM}_{\text{fin}}(x) \to [-1, +1] \quad \text{(negative to positive)}.$$

Trading Strategies

Model outputs feed into quant or algorithmic trading signals. Some hedge funds or proprietary traders factor sentiment in buy/sell decisions. However, correlation does not guarantee causation—sentiment spikes can mislead if not combined with fundamental analysis.

Caution

- **Overfitting**: Market data is volatile and can produce spurious correlations.

- **Latency**: Real-time processing demands low-latency solutions.

- **Regulatory Boundaries**: Insider info or compliance with financial laws.

LMs for sentiment-driven stock predictions show promise, but success requires robust domain adaptation, real-time pipelines, and complementary analysis to avoid chasing false signals.

9.4.2. Personalized Marketing Campaigns

Hyper-Personalized **Messaging**

Businesses want to engage customers with tailored product recommendations or promotional texts. Fine-tuned LMs can craft messages that match user profiles (age, location, preferences). For instance:

$$Message = LM(\text{user data} \mid \text{marketing prompt}).$$

Dynamic **Content**

Email marketing or in-app notifications can vary by user segments. LMs interpret user histories:

- **Past Purchases**: Indicate relevant product categories.

- **Browsing Behavior**: Identify top interests or repeated search queries.

- **Demographics**: Adjust language style or tone.

Ethical & Privacy

- **Data Minimization**: Only use essential user data. Transparent user consent is crucial (European Commission, 2021).

- **Avoid Manipulation**: Persuasion or borderline "dark patterns" risk reputational harm.

- **Evaluation**: A/B testing helps refine message efficacy without creeping over privacy lines.

Key **Insight**

Personalized marketing campaigns see significant lifts in engagement by fusing user data with fine-tuned text generation. Nonetheless, user privacy and ethical messaging stand as critical guardrails.

9.4.3. Automated Report Generation

Enterprise **Reporting**

Large enterprises produce recurring reports—sales summaries, performance metrics, compliance documents. Relying on an LLM can automate templated text, interpret structured data, and provide a polished narrative:

- **Extract**: Pull data from internal databases or spreadsheets.

- **Generate**: "One-pager" summaries or detailed departmental overviews.

- **Review**: Optionally, a human manager checks final outputs for sign-off.

Technical Setup

- **Data Fusion**: The LM is fed a structured input representation, e.g., JSON from a database.

- **Natural Language Output**: GPT-like generation with constraints or placeholders.

- **Customizable Templates**: Mark certain fields as mandatory (like disclaimers or standard paragraphs).

$$\text{Report}(D) = \text{LM}(\text{ structured embeddings} \mid \text{company style prompt}).$$

Advantages

- **Efficiency**: Replaces repetitive writing tasks.

- **Consistency**: Uniform style across multiple departments or months.

- **Scalability**: Rapidly adapt to new data sets or more frequent reporting cycles.

Risks

- **Error Propagation**: Wrong data ingestion leads to confidently stated incorrect facts.

- **Unclear Accountability**: If an automated report misstates figures, which part of the pipeline is at fault?

- **Template Overfitting**: Too-rigid or too-liberal generation can hamper clarity or accuracy.

Key   **Insight**

Automated report generation harnesses LMs to transform structured data into textual summaries. Well-designed templates and QA steps ensure business reliability and reduce repetitive manual reporting overhead.

9.5. Case Studies & Success Stories

9.5.1. Small Startups Leveraging NLP

Scenario

Imagine a **bootstrapped startup** building a specialized chatbot for mental health support. They can't afford from-scratch training but can **fine-tune** an open-source model (e.g., GPT-2 or BERT) with ~10,000 conversation examples from volunteer counselors.

Outcome

- **Rapid Prototype**: Deployed a minimum viable product (MVP) in weeks.

- **User Feedback**: Iteratively refined model responses, focusing on empathetic yet non-diagnostic phrasing.

- **Community Impact**: Provided 24/7 support, bridging care gaps or offering immediate resources.

Lessons Learned

- **Ethical Boundaries**: Clear disclaimers that the system is not a certified therapist.

- **Scalability**: Cloud-based GPU hosting handles peak times.

- **Continuous Improvement**: Logging user interactions to train subsequent versions.

Key   **Insight**

Startups lacking large budgets can exploit open-source LMs plus small-scale domain data to carve out valuable niche products, as long as they carefully manage the system's reliability and limitations.

9.5.2. Large Tech Giants & Their Proprietary Models

Major   **Players**

Companies like Google, Microsoft, Meta, and OpenAI invest heavily in **mega-scale** LMs (10B+ parameters). They train these on vast web corpora plus proprietary data, fueling products from search to cloud APIs (Brown et al., 2020).

Example: OpenAI GPT Series

- **GPT-2** release spurred interest in generative NLP.

- **GPT-3** with 175B parameters offered strong few-shot learning (Brown et al., 2020).

- **GPT-4** introduced multi-modal capabilities and improved reasoning (OpenAI, 2023).

$$\theta_{GPT4} \sim \text{Train(billions docs,massive HPC cluster)}.$$

Advantages

- **Resource Depth**: HPC clusters accelerate large-scale experiments.

- **Talent**: Leading NLP researchers refine architectures, training pipelines, or scaling.

- **Commercial APIs**: Monetizing advanced LMs by offering them as pay-per-query services.

Debates

- **Closed Source**: Full model weights or training details might be withheld.

- **Ethical & Societal Impacts**: Potential for misinformation or job displacement.

- **Competition**: Smaller labs struggle to match the scale, but open-source communities (e.g., EleutherAI) attempt to replicate with resource pooling.

Key   **Insight**

Tech giants push LLM boundaries, offering powerful but often proprietary systems. Their breakthroughs drive the field forward, yet raise questions about openness, competition, and governance.

9.5.3. Open-Source Projects Making Waves

Community-Driven   **Innovation**

Groups like **Hugging Face, EleutherAI**, or academia-led consortia develop open-source LMs. Examples include GPT-Neo, GPT-J, BLOOM—trained on public HPC resources with collaborative efforts (Black et al., 2022). Their significance:

- **Transparency**: Publicly released code, model weights, data splits.

- **Democratized Research**: Smaller teams can replicate or build on large LMs without forging everything in-house.

- **Ethical Oversight**: Some projects apply community-led governance or "model cards" disclaimers (Mitchell et al., 2019).

Notable Achievements

- **GPT-Neo**: Showed it's possible for non-corporate volunteers to train multi-billion parameter models.

- **BLOOM**: A large multilingual model from BigScience, a year-long collaborative effort.

- **Continued Community**: Open forums for sharing fine-tuning tips, prompt engineering hacks, or specialized domain expansions.

Trade-Offs

- **Resource Limitations**: Even large open-source groups can't always match the HPC scale of big tech.

- **Fragmentation**: Many forks or variants can cause user confusion.

- **Sustainability**: Funding volunteer HPC is challenging; corporate or philanthropic support often needed.

Key   **Insight**

Open-source LLM projects broaden access and foster transparency, enabling widespread experimentation and adaptation. This collaborative environment drives innovation parallel to (and sometimes beyond) proprietary solutions.

References (Harvard Style)

- Black, S. et al. (2022) 'GPT-NeoX-20B: An Open-Source Autoregressive Language Model', *arXiv preprint* arXiv:2204.06745.

- Brown, T. et al. (2020) 'Language Models Are Few-Shot Learners', in *Advances in Neural Information Processing Systems* (NeurIPS). Red Hook, NY: Curran Associates, pp. 1877–1901.

- Chen, W. et al. (2017) 'Agent-Aware Dropout DQN for Safe and Collaborative Multi-Agent Reinforcement Learning', *arXiv preprint* arXiv:1709.05468.

- Clark, E. et al. (2018) 'Creative Writing with a Machine in the Loop: Case Studies on Slogans and Stories', in *Proceedings of the 23rd International Conference on Intelligent User Interfaces (IUI)*. New York: ACM, pp. 329–340.

- Elsahar, H., Vougiouklis, P. and Gravier, C. (2021) 'Stylized Story Generation with Style-GPT', *arXiv preprint* arXiv:2106.00314.

- Fan, A., Lewis, M. and Dauphin, Y. (2018) 'Hierarchical Neural Story Generation', in *Proceedings of the 56th Annual Meeting of the Association for Computational Linguistics (ACL)*. Stroudsburg, PA: ACL, pp. 889–898.

- Henderson, M. et al. (2020) 'Conventional Sequence to Sequence Models Can Be Strong Dialogue State Trackers', in *Proceedings of the 58th Annual Meeting of the Association for Computational Linguistics (ACL)*. Stroudsburg, PA: ACL, pp. 1592–1604.

- Lee, J. et al. (2020) 'BioBERT: A Pre-trained Biomedical Language Representation Model for Biomedical Text Mining', *Bioinformatics*, 36(4), pp. 1234–1240.

- Maynez, J. et al. (2020) 'On Faithfulness and Factuality in Abstractive Summarization', in *Proceedings of the 58th Annual Meeting of the Association for Computational Linguistics (ACL)*. Stroudsburg, PA: ACL, pp. 1906–1919.

- Mitchell, M. et al. (2019) 'Model Cards for Model Reporting', in *Proceedings of the Conference on Fairness, Accountability, and Transparency (FAT)**. New York: ACM, pp. 220–229.

- OpenAI (2023) 'GPT-4 Technical Report', *OpenAI Blog*. Available at: https://openai.com (Accessed: 10 February 2025).

- Roller, S. et al. (2021) 'Recipes for Building an Open-Domain Chatbot', in *Proceedings of the 16th Conference of the European Chapter of the Association for Computational Linguistics (EACL)*. Stroudsburg, PA: ACL, pp. 300–325.

- Sennrich, R., Haddow, B. and Birch, A. (2016) 'Neural Machine Translation of Rare Words with Subword Units', in *Proceedings of the 54th Annual Meeting of the Association for Computational Linguistics (ACL)*. Stroudsburg, PA: ACL, pp. 1715–1725.

- Strubell, E., Ganesh, A. and McCallum, A. (2019) 'Energy and Policy Considerations for Deep Learning in NLP', in *Proceedings of the 57th Annual Meeting of the Association for Computational Linguistics (ACL)*. Florence, Italy: ACL, pp. 3645–3650.

- Wolf, T. et al. (2020) 'Transformers: State-of-the-Art Natural Language Processing', in *Proceedings of the 2020 Conference on Empirical Methods in Natural Language Processing: System Demonstrations*. Stroudsburg, PA: ACL, pp. 38–45.

- Zhang, J. et al. (2020) 'DIALOGPT: Large-Scale Generative Pre-training for Conversational Response Generation', in *Proceedings of the 58th Annual Meeting of the Association for Computational Linguistics (ACL): System Demonstrations*. Stroudsburg, PA: ACL, pp. 270–278.

Chapter 10: Ethical and Societal Implications

10.1. Bias in AI

10.1.1. Sources of Bias: Data & Algorithms

Data-Driven   **Bias**

Machine learning models learn patterns from training corpora. If these corpora reflect societal stereotypes or skewed distributions, the resulting model may replicate or even amplify such biases (Bolukbasi et al., 2016). Common issues:

- **Gender Bias**: Examples like associating "doctor" with male pronouns and "nurse" with female pronouns.

- **Racial & Ethnic Bias**: Underrepresentation or negative portrayal of certain ethnic groups.

- **Cultural or Linguistic Bias**: Sparse data for lesser-spoken languages, leading to poorer performance.

$$D \tan \mapsto \theta \quad \text{(bias if distribution } D \text{ } i \text{ } see\text{)}.$$

Algorithmic   **Amplification**

Even if data is somewhat balanced, certain algorithms can introduce or aggravate biases. For instance, sampling-based training might under-weight minority groups, or objective functions might inadvertently optimize for majority-class performance (Barocas, Hardt and Narayanan, 2018).

Feedback   **Loops**

In deployed systems (e.g., recommendation engines), user interactions form part of the next training dataset—reinforcing existing biases in a vicious cycle (Sun et al., 2019). Breaking this requires careful monitoring or active counter-bias interventions.

Key   **Insight**

Bias often originates from **training data**, which can be unrepresentative or culturally biased. Algorithmic choices then magnify these imbalances. Recognizing where bias enters is the first step toward mitigation.

10.1.2. High-Profile Bias Controversies

Facial   **Recognition**

High-profile cases revealed that facial recognition systems performed poorly on darker-skinned individuals, leading to misidentification (Buolamwini and Gebru, 2018). Although not strictly language-based, the parallels hold: biased training data caused disproportionate errors for certain demographics.

Word Embeddings & Stereotypes

Early word embedding models like word2vec exhibited stark stereotypes—e.g., linking "female" to "homemaker" and "male" to "programmer" (Caliskan, Bryson and Narayanan, 2017). Transformers pre-trained on large web text can carry similar or deeper biases (Bender et al., 2021).

Misinformation & Toxicity

Models generating hateful or offensive text reflect the presence of such content in training corpora (Gehman et al., 2020). When large LMs are integrated into chatbots or creative writing tools, the potential for generating harmful text in user interactions becomes high-profile.

$$\text{Toxic Output} \sim P_\theta(\text{offensive} \mid \text{prompt}).$$

Impact on Public Trust

These controversies highlight the **real-world consequences** of AI bias—ranging from reputational damage to discriminatory outcomes. They drove calls for fairness guidelines, stricter audits, and more transparent data governance.

Key Insight

High-profile incidents spotlight the tangible harm from biased AI. Public scrutiny and stakeholder pressure often accelerate corporate or governmental reforms for more equitable systems.

10.1.3. Mitigation Strategies

Data-Level Approaches

- **Balanced Datasets**: Oversample minority categories or gather targeted data to reduce skew.

- **Filtering Offensive Content**: Removing or down-weighting hateful segments before training.

- **Annotation & Debiasing Corpora**: Label and correct stereotypes or negative portrayals (Dixon et al., 2018).

Model-Level Techniques

1. **Bias-Conscious Objectives**: Add terms penalizing biased predictions or embeddings.

2. **Adversarial Debiasing**: Train a discriminator to detect protected attributes from embeddings and discourage it.

3. **Post-Processing**: Adjust final layer outputs or embedding spaces post-hoc (Bolukbasi et al., 2016).

Organizational Policies

Companies adopt **fairness guidelines**—like Microsoft's Responsible AI or Google's AI Principles (Google, 2022)—to systematically check and mitigate biases. This includes internal audits, external reviews, and cross-functional "fairness committees."

$$\text{FairnessLoss}(\theta) = \mathcal{L}_{ts} + \lambda \, \mathcal{L}_{fi}(\theta).$$

Limitations

No single method permanently "fixes" bias—ongoing vigilance, updated data, and iterative re-checking remain essential. Cultural, linguistic, or domain shifts can reintroduce bias if not continuously monitored.

Key Insight

Bias mitigation requires a **multi-pronged strategy**: data audits, algorithmic debiasing, and organizational commitment. Sustained efforts ensure models remain fair under evolving contexts.

10.2. Privacy & Data Protection

10.2.1. GDPR, CCPA & Regulatory Frameworks

Global Privacy Regulations

- **GDPR** (EU): The General Data Protection Regulation imposes strict rules on data collection, processing consent, and user rights (European Commission, 2021).

- **CCPA** (California): The California Consumer Privacy Act grants residents rights to know how personal data is collected and used, including the right to opt out of sales.

- **Other Jurisdictions**: Similar or variant frameworks (e.g., Brazil's LGPD, Japan's APPI) reflect a global trend toward privacy enforcement.

Implications for AI

1. **Consent & Transparency**: ML systems must clarify data usage, potentially requiring explicit user opt-in.

2. **Right to Be Forgotten**: Users can request data deletion—complicating model retraining or inference if personal data is embedded.

3. **Data Minimization**: Only essential data should be collected. Large-scale "collect everything" approaches risk compliance breaches.

$$\mathcal{D}raw \rightarrow \text{Anonymize} \rightarrow \mathcal{D}tan.$$

Fines & Enforcement

Non-compliance can incur heavy fines (up to 4% of annual global turnover under GDPR). This incentivizes robust privacy checks and dedicated compliance teams in AI projects.

Key Insight

Large language models must navigate **privacy regulations** that restrict data usage. Building anonymized or consent-based pipelines, plus legal guidance, is essential to avoid hefty penalties and loss of public trust.

10.2.2. Federated Learning Approaches

Why Federated Learning?

Some industries (healthcare, finance) have stringent data-localization or privacy rules preventing central data aggregation. **Federated learning** (FL) trains models across distributed nodes, only exchanging model updates rather than raw data (Konečný et al., 2016).

Federated Workflow

1. **Local Training**: Each client (hospital, bank branch) trains a model on local data.

2. **Model Aggregation**: A server aggregates parameters or gradients into a global model.

3. **Iterative Rounds**: Clients receive the updated global model, continuing the process.

$$\theta_{t+1} = \sum_{k=1}^{K} \omega_k \theta_{t+1}^{(k)},$$

where $\theta_{t+1}^{(k)}$ is the locally trained model at client k, and ω_k is a weighting factor (e.g., dataset size).

Challenges

- **Heterogeneous Data**: Different nodes have different distributions or label definitions.

- **Communication Overhead**: Frequent parameter exchanges can be costly.

- **Security**: Although data stays local, malicious nodes could leak information via updates.

LMs in FL

Adapting large LMs to FL scenarios is non-trivial, given massive parameter counts and complex multi-head attention structures. Innovations like parameter-efficient fine-tuning or partial updates can reduce communication burdens (Liang et al., 2020).

Key   **Insight**
Federated learning enables collaborative model building without pooling sensitive data. While beneficial in privacy-constrained environments, it requires careful design to handle model size, communication overhead, and node heterogeneity.

10.2.3. Data Anonymization & Encryption

Anonymization   **Techniques**
To meet privacy standards, personal identifiers (names, addresses, IDs) must be stripped from training text. Automated approaches use named entity recognition or hashing. However, re-identification can occur if context remains too specific (Narayanan and Shmatikov, 2008).

1. **Masking**: Replace names with generic tokens (e.g., <NAME>).

2. **Generalization**: Replace exact birthdays with year or age range.

3. **Perturbation**: Inject small random changes to further obfuscate identity details.

$$\text{AnonymizedDoc}(x) = \text{Doc}(x) - \{\text{PII fields}\}.$$

Differential   **Privacy**
Adds controlled noise to model updates, bounding the influence of any single training example. The model can't precisely recall unique or identifying examples. Solutions like **DP-SGD** ensure a quantifiable privacy budget ϵ (Abadi et al., 2016).

Encryption   at   Rest   &   in   Transit
To protect data during training or inference, modern MLOps pipelines adopt:

- **AES-256** or similar for database encryption.

- **TLS** for all network communications.

- **Secure enclaves** or homomorphic encryption for advanced scenarios (Gentry, 2009).

Trade-Offs

- **Utility vs. Privacy**: Over-anonymizing can hamper language quality, losing subtle context.

- **Compute Overheads**: DP or encryption methods raise computational costs.

- **Legal & Ethical**: Even anonymized data can pose re-identification risks for highly unique records.

Key   **Insight**
Effective anonymization and encryption ensure compliance and trustworthiness.

Balancing data utility against privacy overheads remains a core tension in large-scale LM training and deployment.

10.3. The Deepfake Dilemma

10.3.1. Generated Text vs. Authentic Human Content

Rise **of** **Deepfakes**

Generative adversarial networks and LLMs can synthesize human-like text, images, or speech—coined "deepfakes." While many applications are benign (creative writing, marketing), malicious uses include misinformation campaigns or impersonations (Zellers et al., 2019).

Textual Deepfakes

- **Fake News**: Auto-generated articles that appear authoritative.

- **Impersonation**: Chatbots or emails mimicking a real person's style.

- **Phishing**: Tailored messages that fool recipients by replicating personal details gleaned from public data.

$$\text{FakeArticle} = \text{LM}(\text{prompt,malicious style}).$$

Detection **Challenges**

High-quality generative text can be indistinguishable from genuine prose, especially when fine-tuned or carefully prompted. Automated detection tools rely on subtle stylistic discrepancies or metadata signals (OpenAI, 2023). However, arms races are ongoing, with new generation models outpacing existing detectors.

Key **Insight**

Textual deepfakes threaten to blur the lines between human-generated and machine-generated content, stoking misinformation risks. Vigilance—through detection research and robust content verification—remains essential.

10.3.2. Detecting Synthetic Media

Automated **Classifiers**

Efforts include training CNN or Transformer-based classifiers on real vs. generated text examples. Such classifiers learn statistical patterns that deepfakes often share—e.g., unusual repetition or improbable collocations (Zellers et al., 2019).

$$\hat{y} = \text{Detect}(\text{document}) \in \{\text{real,fake}\}.$$

Signature **Watermarking**

Developers of generative LMs may embed watermarks—cryptographic or subtle changes in token distributions—into outputs. A verifying script checks whether the sequence aligns with the watermark (Kirchenbauer et al., 2023). This approach requires cooperation from model publishers.

Human   Fact-Checking

In sensitive or high-stakes contexts (e.g., political statements, legal documents), manual or specialized fact-checking is indispensable. Tools like *ClaimReview* or reference-based cross-checking help, but scaling to global content streams is challenging (Vosoughi, Roy and Aral, 2018).

Arms   Race

As detection methods improve, adversaries refine deepfake techniques. A cat-and-mouse cycle emerges—reminiscent of spam filters vs. spam authors. Ongoing research invests in generative detection arms races, spurring open dialogues about regulation and responsible usage.

Key   Insight

Synthetic text detection leverages classifiers, watermarking, and human oversight, but no single solution is foolproof. Cooperation and transparency from AI developers can facilitate robust detection and accountability.

10.3.3. Societal Impacts & Misinformation

Influencing   Public   Opinion

Advanced text generation can churn out floods of misleading articles or social media posts, swaying opinions or echoing propaganda (Allcott and Gentzkow, 2017). Rapid, large-scale generation lowers the barrier to orchestrating disinformation.

Erosion   of   Trust

As more content can be faked with high fidelity, public skepticism might rise—people doubt authentic news or personal communications, undermining confidence in digital media (Zellers et al., 2019).

Regulatory & Policy Responses

- **Labeling Requirements**: Proposed rules that synthetic content must be flagged with disclaimers.

- **Platform Oversight**: Social media sites actively detect and remove large-scale bot or deepfake campaigns.

- **Legal Measures**: Some jurisdictions criminalize malicious deepfake usage targeting defamation or election tampering (Maras and Alexandrou, 2019).

Balancing   Innovation   &   Harm

Generative LMs have constructive uses: data augmentation, creative expression, corporate communications. Overly strict regulations may stifle legitimate research.

Policymakers and technologists must walk a fine line—supporting beneficial applications while mitigating risks of manipulated media.

Key   **Insight**
The deepfake dilemma challenges society's ability to trust digital content. Ethical AI development, detection tools, and balanced regulation can help safeguard against mass misinformation while preserving legitimate innovation.

10.4. Building Responsible AI

10.4.1. Fairness & Transparency

Fairness   **Principles**
An AI system is fair if it treats individuals or groups equitably according to context-specific definitions (Hardt et al., 2016). Common fairness measures:

- **Demographic Parity**: Similar outcomes across demographic groups.

- **Equalized Odds**: Equal true/false positive rates among groups.

- **Calibration**: Predicted probabilities reflect real outcome likelihood equally across groups.

$$\text{FairLoss}(\theta) = \mathcal{L}_{ts} + \alpha\,\mathcal{L}_{ba}(\theta).$$

Transparency
Releasing model documentation or "model cards" clarifies training data sources, intended use cases, and limitations (Mitchell et al., 2019). Some organizations open-source or partially share code, but confidentiality or competitive edges may limit full transparency.

Institutionalizing   **Responsible**   **AI**
Internal committees, external audits, or third-party certifications can embed fairness and transparency in an AI pipeline. Tools like IBM's AI Fairness 360 or Microsoft Fairlearn systematically check for bias or disparate impact (Bellamy et al., 2019).

Key   **Insight**
Fairness demands carefully defined metrics, thorough data audits, and design choices to reduce harm. Transparency fosters user and stakeholder trust, clarifying how decisions are reached and which constraints or biases may remain.

10.4.2. AI Governance & Policy

Self-Regulation   **vs.**   **Government**   **Oversight**
Some major tech companies propose **internal** guidelines or ethics boards. However,

critics argue external oversight remains crucial, given potential conflicts of interest (Floridi, 2019). Governments explore AI-specific regulations:

- **EU AI Act**: Proposes risk-based categorization and compliance for AI systems (European Commission, 2021).

- **Algorithmic Accountability**: Legislations requiring impact assessments, akin to environmental reviews.

Standards & Certification

Professional bodies or global consortia (ISO, IEEE) might define standardized best practices, akin to ISO 27001 for information security. For instance, an **AI Safety** certification could require tested bias mitigation, robust data privacy, and logging for traceability (Jobin, Ienca and Vayena, 2019).

International Coordination

AI tools and data cross borders easily—coordinated efforts help ensure common baseline rules. However, national interests, cultural values, and economic priorities create patchworks of regulatory regimes.

Key Insight

AI governance stands at the intersection of corporate self-regulation, national laws, and international standards. Enforceable frameworks must balance innovation with the public good, ensuring AI deployments remain safe, fair, and transparent.

10.4.3. Collaborative Efforts Toward Better Standards

Research Consortia

Groups like **Partnership on AI** or **BigScience** convene academia, industry, and civil society to share knowledge. They develop guidelines or open-source tooling for responsible AI, fostering synergy rather than secretive competition (Raji et al., 2020).

Data & Benchmark Collaboration

Shared datasets with diverse demographics or robust annotations help reduce bias in standard training sets. Collaborative benchmark expansions highlight fairness concerns or domain-specific complexities (Stanford, 2022).

Public-Private Partnerships

Governments sponsor research labs or HPC resources for open AI development, bridging the resource gap that otherwise entrenches corporate dominance. E.g., certain EU-funded HPC centers provide compute grants for ethical AI initiatives (European Commission, 2021).

Future Outlook

As LMs permeate more sectors, inclusive governance frameworks that combine technical best practices, legal oversight, and communal knowledge-sharing will shape responsible

AI evolution. Initiatives bridging corporate interests, regulators, and nonprofit advocacy can bolster trust and accountability.

Key   **Insight**

Sustainable, ethical AI requires **collaborative efforts** spanning academia, industry, and policy spheres. By uniting diverse stakeholders, we can create robust standards and effectively safeguard against AI misuse or inequities.

References (Harvard Style)

- Abadi, M. et al. (2016) 'Deep Learning with Differential Privacy', in *Proceedings of the 2016 ACM SIGSAC Conference on Computer and Communications Security (CCS)*. New York: ACM, pp. 308–318.

- Barocas, S., Hardt, M. and Narayanan, A. (2018) *Fairness and Machine Learning*. [Preprint]. Available at: http://fairmlbook.org (Accessed: 10 February 2025).

- Bellamy, R.K.E. et al. (2019) 'AI Fairness 360: An Extensible Toolkit for Detecting, Understanding, and Mitigating Unwanted Algorithmic Bias', *IBM Journal of Research and Development*, 63(4/5), pp. 4:1–4:15.

- Bender, E.M. et al. (2021) 'On the Dangers of Stochastic Parrots: Can Language Models Be Too Big?', in *Proceedings of the 2021 ACM Conference on Fairness, Accountability, and Transparency (FAccT '21)*. New York: ACM, pp. 610–623.

- Bolukbasi, T. et al. (2016) 'Man is to Computer Programmer as Woman is to Homemaker? Debiasing Word Embeddings', in *Advances in Neural Information Processing Systems* (NeurIPS). Red Hook, NY: Curran Associates, pp. 4349–4357.

- Buolamwini, J. and Gebru, T. (2018) 'Gender Shades: Intersectional Accuracy Disparities in Commercial Gender Classification', in *Proceedings of Machine Learning Research* (FAT* 2018). New York: PMLR, pp. 77–91.

- Caliskan, A., Bryson, J. and Narayanan, A. (2017) 'Semantics Derived Automatically from Language Corpora Contain Human-Like Biases', *Science*, 356(6334), pp. 183–186.

- Dixon, L. et al. (2018) 'Measuring and Mitigating Unintended Bias in Text Classification', in *Proceedings of the 2018 AAAI/ACM Conference on AI, Ethics, and Society*. New York: ACM, pp. 67–73.

- European Commission (2021) *Proposal for a Regulation Laying Down Harmonised Rules on Artificial Intelligence (Artificial Intelligence Act)*. Available at: https://digital-strategy.ec.europa.eu (Accessed: 10 February 2025).

- Floridi, L. (2019) 'Translating Principles into Practices of Digital Ethics: Contents, Contexts and Constraints', *Philosophy & Technology*, 32(4), pp. 795–823.

- Gehman, S. et al. (2020) 'RealToxicityPrompts: Evaluating Neural Toxic Degeneration in Language Models', in *Proceedings of the 2020 Conference on Empirical Methods in Natural Language Processing (EMNLP)*. Stroudsburg, PA: ACL, pp. 3357–3370.

- Gentry, C. (2009) 'Fully Homomorphic Encryption Using Ideal Lattices', in *Proceedings of the 41st Annual ACM Symposium on Theory of Computing (STOC)*. New York: ACM, pp. 169–178.

- Google (2022) 'Our AI Principles', *Google AI Blog*. Available at: https://ai.google/principles (Accessed: 10 February 2025).

- Hardt, M., Price, E. and Srebro, N. (2016) 'Equality of Opportunity in Supervised Learning', in *Advances in Neural Information Processing Systems* (NeurIPS). Red Hook, NY: Curran Associates, pp. 3315–3323.

- Konečný, J. et al. (2016) 'Federated Learning: Strategies for Improving Communication Efficiency', *arXiv preprint* arXiv:1610.05492.

- Liang, P. et al. (2020) 'Think Locally, Act Globally: Federated Learning with Local and Global Representations', in *International Conference on Learning Representations (ICLR)*. Available at: https://openreview.net (Accessed: 10 February 2025).

- Maras, M.-H. and Alexandrou, A. (2019) 'Determining Authenticity of Video Evidence in the Age of Artificial Intelligence and in the Wake of Deepfake Videos', *The International Journal of Evidence & Proof*, 23(3), pp. 255–262.

- Narayanan, A. and Shmatikov, V. (2008) 'Robust De-anonymization of Large Sparse Datasets', in *2008 IEEE Symposium on Security and Privacy (SP)*. Oakland, CA: IEEE, pp. 111–125.

- OpenAI (2023) 'GPT-4 Technical Report', *OpenAI Blog*. Available at: https://openai.com (Accessed: 10 February 2025).

- Raji, I.D. et al. (2020) 'Closing the AI Accountability Gap: Defining an End-to-End Framework for Internal Algorithmic Auditing', in *Proceedings of the 2020 Conference on Fairness, Accountability, and Transparency (FAccT)*. New York: ACM, pp. 33–44.

- Sennrich, R., Haddow, B. and Birch, A. (2016) 'Neural Machine Translation of Rare Words with Subword Units', in *Proceedings of the 54th Annual Meeting of the Association for Computational Linguistics (ACL)*. Stroudsburg, PA: ACL, pp. 1715–1725.

- Stanford (2022) 'The Stanford Center for Research on Foundation Models', *Stanford CRFM*. Available at: https://crfm.stanford.edu/ (Accessed: 10 February 2025).

- Sun, C. et al. (2019) 'How to Fine-Tune BERT for Text Classification?', in *Proceedings of the 12th Asian Conference on Machine Learning (ACML)*. PMLR, pp. 1–11.

- Vosoughi, S., Roy, D. and Aral, S. (2018) 'The Spread of True and False News Online', *Science*, 359(6380), pp. 1146–1151.

- Zellers, R. et al. (2019) 'Defending against Neural Fake News', in *Advances in Neural Information Processing Systems* (NeurIPS). Red Hook, NY: Curran Associates, pp. 9054–9065.

Chapter 11: Deployment and Scaling

11.1. Model Serving & Infrastructure

11.1.1. Cloud vs. On-Premise Deployment

Infrastructure   **Choices**

When serving large language models (LLMs) in production, teams must decide between **cloud-based** vs. **on-premise** setups. Cloud providers (AWS, Azure, GCP) offer **managed services** (e.g., auto-scaling), while on-premise environments give more **control** over hardware and data security (Lwakatare et al., 2020).

Cloud Advantages

- **Scalability**: Dynamically add or remove computing instances to match traffic.

- **Lower Capital Expenditure**: Pay only for used resources, avoiding large upfront hardware costs.

- **Integrated Ecosystems**: Managed solutions for logging, monitoring, or serverless components.

$$\text{Cost}_{\text{cloud}}(t) \approx \text{usage}(t) \times \text{pay-per-use rate}.$$

On-Premise Advantages

- **Data Sovereignty**: Critical in regulated domains (health, finance) to keep data within local servers.

- **Performance Tuning**: Direct hardware customization—GPU selection, networking optimization—can yield better throughput.

- **Stable Long-Term Costs**: If usage is consistently high, purchasing hardware might be cheaper in the long run.

Hybrid   **Clouds**

Many enterprises adopt a **hybrid model**—run sensitive workloads on internal servers while bursting to cloud for peak demands (Zhao et al., 2020). This approach balances compliance with elasticity.

Key   **Insight**

Cloud deployment suits many LLM use cases due to **elastic scaling** and reduced maintenance. On-premise remains relevant for data-sensitive or performance-critical scenarios. Hybrid solutions can combine the best of both.

11.1.2. Microservices & Serverless Functions

Microservices   **Architecture**

In a **microservices** approach, each part of an AI system—model inference, authentication, logging—runs independently, communicating via APIs (Newman, 2015). This decouples the model-serving layer from the rest of the app, facilitating updates or scaling just the ML component.

- **Service Discovery**: Tools like Kubernetes or Consul track service endpoints.
- **API Gateway**: Centralizes requests, routes them to the right microservice.
- **Load Balancing**: Ensures no single instance is overloaded.

$$API\_Gateway(x) \rightarrow ModelService(x).$$

Serverless   **Functions**

Serverless (e.g., AWS Lambda, Azure Functions) let developers run code without managing servers. For smaller or sporadic traffic, serverless inference can be economical:

- **Automatic Scaling**: New function instances spin up on demand.
- **Billing**: Pay only for execution time.
- **Cold Starts**: A drawback if containers sleep, causing a short delay on new requests (Adzic and Chatley, 2017).

Trade-Offs

- **Latency**: Serverless may introduce overhead from spin-up or ephemeral containers.
- **Model Size Limits**: Some serverless environments limit memory, restricting large LMs.
- **Complex Architecture**: Microservices require robust DevOps culture and monitoring to handle distributed complexities.

Key   **Insight**

Microservices and serverless paradigms modularize model deployment, enabling flexible scaling and simplified maintenance. However, overhead (like cold starts) and resource constraints can complicate large-model hosting.

11.1.3. Model Compression & Quantization

Why   **Compress**   **Models?**

Large LMs are resource-hungry, requiring abundant memory and compute. **Compression** techniques—pruning, quantization, knowledge distillation—shrink model size without drastically hurting accuracy (Sanh et al., 2020). This improves inference speed, lowers costs, and suits edge deployments.

Quantization

Quantization reduces parameter precision from float32 to int8 or similar. Typical forms include:

- **Post-Training Quantization**: Convert a trained model.

- **Quantization-Aware Training**: Train the model with quantization constraints.

- **Mixed Precision**: e.g., float16 for most parameters, float32 for critical layers.

$$\theta_{\text{quant}} = \text{round}(\theta \times \text{scale}).$$

Pruning & Distillation

- **Pruning**: Remove weights or entire attention heads that contribute little (Voita et al., 2019).

- **Knowledge Distillation**: A smaller "student" network learns to mimic a large "teacher" LM, retaining much of its knowledge (Hinton, Vinyals and Dean, 2015).

Trade-Offs

- **Accuracy vs. Size**: Aggressive quantization or pruning can degrade performance.

- **Hardware Compatibility**: Some inference engines or GPUs have specialized instructions for int8 or float16 but not others.

- **Complexity**: Additional training or hyperparameter tuning for optimal compression settings.

Key   Insight

Model compression speeds up inference and lowers memory usage—critical for production. Careful technique selection and validation ensure minimal performance loss.

11.1.4. Caching & Load Balancing

Caching   Inference   Results
High-traffic systems often see repeated queries (e.g., the same text prompt). **Caching** model outputs avoids recomputing them, especially if generation is deterministic or if a small change in input yields nearly identical responses.

- **Key-Based Storage**: Hash of input text or tokens $h(x)$ maps to cached output.

- **Time-to-Live (TTL)**: Limits staleness if updated model logic or context changes.

$$\text{Cache}(h(x)) = \text{LM}(x), \text{ if not present, compute and store.}$$

Load balancers distribute incoming requests among a pool of model-serving instances to ensure **high availability** and **scalability**. Common patterns:

- **Round Robin**: Even distribution.

- **Weighted**: Route more traffic to powerful GPUs or less busy nodes.

- **Least Connections**: Dynamic approach, always sending new requests to the instance with the fewest active sessions.

Performance Gains

- **Reduced Latency**: Avoid bottlenecks by parallel processing across multiple replicas.

- **Failover**: If one instance crashes, the LB reroutes traffic automatically.

- **Autoscaling**: Real-time metrics (CPU, GPU usage) can trigger new instance launches or shutdowns.

Key   **Insight**

Caching repeated results and employing robust load balancing significantly enhance user experience and resource efficiency. They form crucial components of a high-throughput, fault-tolerant model-serving system.

11.2. Edge AI & On-Device Inference

11.2.1. Constraints & Trade-Offs (Memory, Power)

Edge   **AI**   **Overview**

"Edge AI" involves running models on local devices (smartphones, IoT appliances) to minimize latency and preserve data privacy (Lane et al., 2015). This is critical for time-sensitive tasks (autonomous vehicles, industrial sensors) or where real-time connectivity is unreliable.

$$\text{Inferenceedge}(\mathbf{x}) \approx \arg\max y \, P_\theta(y \mid \mathbf{x}).$$

Resource Constraints

- **Memory**: Edge devices might have only 512MB or less for inference.

- **Compute Power**: Mobile CPUs, small GPUs, or specialized NPUs (like Apple Neural Engine).

- **Energy**: Battery life is precious; compute-heavy operations can drain power rapidly (Wang et al., 2019).

Model **Optimization**

On-device LMs require **compression** (quantization, pruning) or specialized architectures (DistilBERT, MobileBERT). Ensuring minimal accuracy loss while drastically cutting parameter sizes is an ongoing challenge (Sanh et al., 2020).

Key **Insight**

Deploying LMs on resource-constrained devices demands a careful balance between **model footprint** and **task performance**. Novel optimization techniques pave the way for near-real-time local inference.

11.2.2. Mobile & IoT Applications

Smartphones

From virtual assistants (Siri, Google Assistant) to real-time text translation (Google Translate offline mode), on-device LMs offer immediate responses without sending user data to the cloud (Wu et al., 2016). Distillation and quantization are standard to fit these constraints.

IoT **Scenarios**

Sensors or embedded controllers might interpret text logs or voice commands. For instance:

- **Smart Home**: Interpreting voice commands locally for privacy.

- **Industrial IoT**: Reading and summarizing sensor logs in remote facilities with limited internet.

Connectivity **Challenges**

Relying on the cloud introduces **latency** and **network reliability** issues. Edge LMs circumvent these by performing inference locally, though updates or additional training may still need cloud connectivity at intervals.

$$\text{LocalLM}(x) = \arg\max_y P_\theta(y \mid x).$$

Key **Insight**

Mobile and IoT devices benefit from **local** inference, ensuring low-latency interactions and data privacy. This requires substantial model compression and hardware-specific optimizations.

11.2.3. Privacy Benefits of On-Device Processing

Data **Ownership**

Processing user input (e.g., personal messages) on-device keeps raw text from leaving the phone or sensor. This approach aligns well with privacy regulations or user preferences for minimal data sharing (McMahan and Ramage, 2017).

As discussed (Section 10.2.2), training or updating the model can occur locally, with only gradient updates traveling to a central server. This drastically reduces the risk of data breaches or unauthorized data mining.

On-device LMs remain functional even without internet access—vital for rural areas, traveling, or emergencies. Tasks like translation or summarization continue uninterrupted, boosting user satisfaction.

Trade-Offs

- **Model Size Limits**: Extremely large LMs may be impractical.

- **Update Delays**: Rolling out new features or bug fixes to many edge devices can be slow.

- **Potential Quality Gap**: Due to heavier compression or smaller architectures, on-device models might lag behind cloud-based counterparts.

Key   **Insight**
On-device AI fosters privacy and offline resilience. Though capacity constraints remain, user trust in local processing can outweigh minor performance trade-offs.

11.2.4. Tools for Mobile Deployment

Frameworks & Libraries

- **TensorFlow Lite**: Optimized for Android/iOS with quantization or pruning (Abadi et al., 2016).

- **PyTorch Mobile**: Simplifies exporting PyTorch models to mobile.

- **ONNX Runtime**: Converts models from multiple frameworks into a mobile-friendly format (Bai et al., 2019).

$$\text{DeployedModel} = \text{Convert}(\theta_{\text{train}}, \text{runtime}).$$

Hardware   **Accelerators**
Many mobile SoCs include NPUs (Neural Processing Units) or DSPs. Taking advantage of these often requires specialized kernels or vendor toolchains:

- **Apple Neural Engine (ANE)**

- **Qualcomm Hexagon DSP**

- **Huawei Ascend** or **Samsung Neural** APIs

Testing   **&**   **Profiling**
Real-time profiling helps identify bottlenecks in memory or CPU usage. Tools like

Android Profiler, Xcode Instruments, or specialized GPU profiling libraries measure end-to-end latency, verifying the user experience (Tang et al., 2020).

Key **Insight**

Deploying on mobile or edge hardware demands specialized frameworks, format converters, and hardware-aware optimizations. Thorough testing ensures smooth user experiences under real-world conditions.

11.3. CI/CD for AI Projects

11.3.1. Automated Testing of Models

Why **Test** **ML** **Models?**

Traditional CI/CD (Continuous Integration / Continuous Delivery) focuses on code correctness. In ML, the model's predictive performance must also be systematically tested:

- **Sanity Checks**: Confirm no catastrophic drop in metrics after code or data updates.

- **Reproducibility**: Identical inputs yield consistent predictions.

- **Edge Cases**: Checking adversarial or boundary scenarios.

$$"\{TestResult\} = [\{cases\} "\{Pass\}, \& "\{if\ performance\} \geq "\{threshold\},\backslash\backslash "\{Fail\}, \& "\{otherwise\}.] \{cases\}$$

Integration **with** **CI**

Tools like Jenkins, GitLab CI, or GitHub Actions can run an ML pipeline—pull code, spin up a training job, evaluate on a validation set, then produce a pass/fail. Some organizations keep a "blessed baseline model" for reference, ensuring any new model does not degrade performance by more than δ.

Mock **&** **Staging** **Environments**

Before production, models are tested in staging with limited real traffic or synthetic data to catch runtime errors, memory leaks, or unexpected latencies (Fowler, 2018). This approach parallels typical software QA but includes performance metrics and confusion matrix checks.

Key **Insight**

Automated tests for data, training metrics, and inference behavior bolster confidence in ML changes. By embedding ML testing into CI/CD, teams can rapidly iterate while maintaining reliability.

11.3.2. Version Control for Data & Checkpoints

Data   **Versioning**

Unlike code, data evolves: new samples appear, labeling mistakes are corrected. Tools like **DVC (Data Version Control)** or Git LFS track dataset changes in sync with code commits (Zaharia et al., 2018).

- **Metadata**: Summaries of data shape, distribution.

- **Hashes**: Unique IDs for each data snapshot.

- **Pipelines**: Data transformations, ensuring consistent reprocessing.

$$\text{DVC } \mathcal{D}_{tan} = \text{Commit(hash,timestamp)}.$$

Model   **Checkpoints**

Checkpoints store model weights at various training stages. In CI/CD, storing them with metadata about hyperparameters and data versions ensures reproducibility. E.g., a naming scheme:

$$\theta_{\text{model\_v2.3\_data\_hashX}}.$$

Collaboration   **&**   **Rollback**

Versioned data and checkpoints let teams revert or compare performance across older runs. This fosters collaboration among data scientists, enabling them to replicate each other's experiments precisely (Kondo et al., 2019).

Security

Encrypted or access-controlled storage is crucial if data or models contain proprietary or sensitive information. Policies define who can pull or push new data versions, preventing unauthorized modifications.

Key   **Insight**

Proper version control for both **data** and **model checkpoints** is indispensable for robust CI/CD in AI. It enables reproducibility, rollback, and clear lineage of each experiment or deployment candidate.

11.3.3. Blue-Green Deployments & Canary Releases

Model   **Release**   **Strategies**

Unlike static code, model performance can shift user experience drastically. **Blue-green** and **canary** releases mitigate risk by introducing new models gradually:

1. **Blue-Green**: Two identical production environments ("blue" for old, "green" for new). Traffic swaps from blue to green once the new model is validated. Easy to roll back if issues arise (Humble and Farley, 2010).

2. **Canary**: The new model receives a small fraction of traffic initially. If metrics remain good, gradually increase. If problems emerge, revert or fix.

$$\text{Traffic}_{\text{canary}}(t) = \rho_t \times \text{Requests}.$$

Monitoring

Real-time metrics—latency, user satisfaction, error rates—guide canary progression. Tools like Prometheus or Grafana track performance and alert on anomalies. If KPI dips below θ, the canary is halted or undone.

Benefits

- **Minimized Disruption**: Users mostly see the stable model; a few see the new.

- **Safe Experimentation**: Teams can gather real user feedback on the new model in production with limited exposure.

- **Fast Rollback**: If major flaws appear, revert traffic to the old environment swiftly.

Key   **Insight**

Deploying new models gradually is standard best practice in modern MLOps. Blue-green and canary strategies reduce the blast radius of failures and let real-world data validate model improvements.

11.3.4. Monitoring Performance in Production

Runtime   **Observability**

Once deployed, LMs should be monitored for throughput (QPS), response times, GPU/CPU utilization, and memory usage. Logging frameworks capture inputs (or hashed metadata) and outputs for diagnosing anomalies (Fowler, 2018).

$$\text{Latency}(\text{time}) = \text{timeend} - \text{timestart}.$$

Model   **Drifts**

Performance metrics like accuracy, perplexity, or user satisfaction can degrade if domain distributions shift. Setting up dashboards or automated alerts ensures quick detection. For classification tasks, confusion matrices updated over time can reveal emerging error patterns (Section 8.4.2).

Error   **Handling**

Unexpected behaviors—like NaN outputs or drastically large memory usage—trigger fallback systems or graceful shutdown. For chatbots, a minimal rule-based reply might handle the conversation while the issue is resolved. This ensures user experience remains consistent.

Security   **&**   **Audit**   **Trails**

In regulated sectors, storing inference logs might be mandatory for compliance.

Encryption at rest plus secure user ID handling ensures privacy. Tools like Splunk, ELK stack, or Datadog correlate model logs with other system logs to produce end-to-end traceability.

Key **Insight**

Continuous monitoring tracks model health, detects drifts, and ensures stable performance. Observability frameworks merging logs, metrics, and alerting are key pillars of robust ML operations.

11.4. Handling Scale & Growth

11.4.1. Horizontal vs. Vertical Scaling

Vertical **Scaling** **(Scaling** **Up)**

Adding more powerful hardware—faster GPUs, more memory—on a single node. This typically simplifies architecture but hits a limit once the largest GPU is insufficient or cost-ineffective. Large LMs can exceed even high-end GPU memory capacities (Shoeybi et al., 2019).

Horizontal **Scaling** **(Scaling** **Out)**

Deploy multiple model replicas or shards across many nodes:

- **Data Parallelism**: Each GPU processes a subset of the batch.

- **Model Parallelism**: Layers or parameters are split across GPUs in a pipeline or tensor fashion.

- **Hybrid Approaches**: Combining data and model parallel for extremely large architectures.

$$\text{PipelineParallel}(\theta) = [\theta_1, \theta_2, \dots, \theta_n].$$

Cost & Complexity

- **Horizontal**: Achieves near-linear throughput gains but demands sophisticated distributed training/inference. Network overhead can hamper speed.

- **Vertical**: Lower overhead, simpler devops, but quickly outgrown by large models or traffic surges.

Key **Insight**

For massive workloads or advanced LLMs, **horizontal scaling** is the typical route. Vertical scaling remains an option for moderate sizes or prototypes but eventually hits hardware constraints.

11.4.2. Real-Time Stream Processing

Streaming **Context**

Some applications require real-time text ingestion—like social media feeds, sensor logs, or financial tick data. The model may need to classify or summarize incoming text on the fly, ensuring minimal latency.

Event-Driven **Pipelines**

Frameworks like Kafka, Flink, or Spark Streaming route incoming messages to ML inference microservices (Kreps et al., 2011). The system might:

- **Buffer** events briefly.

- **Run inference** (sentiment analysis, entity extraction).

- **Store** results in a data lake or forward to a real-time dashboard.

$$\text{MLService}\big(\text{stream}(t)\big) = \text{prediction}_t \quad \text{in near real time.}$$

Scaling **&** **Fault** **Tolerance**

Real-time pipelines scale horizontally—multiple processing nodes share the event queue. Fault tolerance is built in: if one node fails, others take over partition responsibilities. The ML container must handle ephemeral restarts gracefully (Zaharia et al., 2016).

Use Cases

- **Fraud Detection**: Flag suspicious transactions as soon as they appear.

- **Live Sentiment**: Gauge public reactions to an ongoing event or product launch.

- **Automated Moderation**: Filter hateful or spam content in near real time.

Key **Insight**

Real-time data streams require **low-latency** model serving integrated with streaming frameworks. Horizontal scaling and robust checkpointing ensure high-throughput, fault-tolerant pipelines essential for time-critical tasks.

11.4.3. Fault Tolerance & High Availability

Redundancy

Production systems typically host multiple model-serving instances behind a load balancer. If an instance fails, traffic seamlessly shifts to healthy replicas. This approach ensures minimal downtime (Humble and Farley, 2010).

$$\text{Uptime} \approx \prod_{i=1}^{n}\big(1 - p_{\text{fail}}(i)\big).$$

Auto-Recovery

Orchestrators like Kubernetes watch service health. If a pod (model container) crashes or becomes unresponsive, the orchestrator restarts it or schedules a new pod. Logging the root cause helps devs fix underlying bugs or resource constraints.

Distributed   Checkpoints

In large-scale training (Section 6.3.3), frequent **checkpointing** ensures partial progress is saved. For inference, ephemeral state is often minimal—but some systems caching user context or ephemeral embeddings must replicate or store them externally (e.g., Redis).

Disaster   Recovery

Geo-redundant backups handle scenario where an entire data center fails. The system automatically reroutes to a different region if a catastrophe occurs (Tang et al., 2017). The cost overhead is justified by the high SLAs demanded for critical enterprise services.

Key   Insight

Fault tolerance in ML deployments ensures consistent user experience and minimal downtime. Techniques like multi-instance load balancing, orchestrator auto-recovery, and distributed backups collectively sustain high availability.

11.4.4. Global Infrastructure & Regional Regulations

Multi-Region   Deployments

Large user bases span continents with distinct data privacy laws or connectivity constraints. Placing model-serving nodes geographically close to users reduces latency, while satisfying data residency rules (Kolb and Wirtz, 2020).

$$\text{Latency(continent)} \approx \text{network distance} + \text{processing time}.$$

Compliance

EU's GDPR demands data remain within EU boundaries, leading some organizations to maintain servers in European data centers. Other nations have local data laws as well. **Splitting** training or inference across regions complicates pipeline design but ensures compliance.

CDN   Integration

For simpler tasks—like caching model outputs or static embeddings—a content delivery network (CDN) can store frequently accessed items in edge locations. This boosts speed for repeated queries or standard prompts (Liu et al., 2020).

Operational   Complexity

Coordinating cross-region updates, monitoring, and failover is nontrivial:

- **Version Skew**: Different regions might run different model versions.
- **Networking**: High-latency or inconsistent bandwidth across continents.

- **Local Support**: Possibly separate DevOps or data teams per region.

Key   Insight

Serving LLMs globally involves more than just spinning up servers in multiple data centers. Latency, data sovereignty, version management, and ops overhead all factor into a robust multi-region deployment strategy.

References (Harvard Style)

- Abadi, M. et al. (2016) 'TensorFlow: A System for Large-Scale Machine Learning', in *12th USENIX Symposium on Operating Systems Design and Implementation (OSDI 16)*. Berkeley, CA: USENIX Association, pp. 265–283.

- Adzic, G. and Chatley, R. (2017) 'Serverless Computing: Economic and Architectural Impact', in *Proceedings of the 2017 11th Joint Meeting on Foundations of Software Engineering (ESEC/FSE)*. New York: ACM, pp. 884–889.

- Bai, Y. et al. (2019) 'ONNX: Open Neural Network Exchange', *arXiv preprint* arXiv:1907.04448.

- Brown, T. et al. (2020) 'Language Models Are Few-Shot Learners', in *Advances in Neural Information Processing Systems* (NeurIPS). Red Hook, NY: Curran Associates, pp. 1877–1901.

- Fowler, M. (2018) *Patterns of Enterprise Application Architecture*. Boston, MA: Addison-Wesley.

- Hinton, G., Vinyals, O. and Dean, J. (2015) 'Distilling the Knowledge in a Neural Network', *arXiv preprint* arXiv:1503.02531.

- Humble, J. and Farley, D. (2010) *Continuous Delivery: Reliable Software Releases through Build, Test, and Deployment Automation*. Boston, MA: Addison-Wesley.

- Kondo, S. et al. (2019) 'Reproducible Research with Data Version Control: A Case Study', *arXiv preprint* arXiv:1905.05362.

- Kolb, J. and Wirtz, G. (2020) 'Infrastructure As Code: Automated Provisioning of a Docker Container Cluster', in *Proceedings of the 2020 IEEE 24th International Enterprise Distributed Object Computing Conference (EDOC)*. IEEE, pp. 210–219.

- Kreps, J. et al. (2011) 'Kafka: A Distributed Messaging System for Log Processing', in *Proceedings of the NetDB Workshop*. Berkeley, CA: USENIX, pp. 1–7.

- Lane, N.D. et al. (2015) 'DeepX: A Software Accelerator for Low-Power Deep Learning Inference on Mobile Devices', in *Proceedings of the 14th International Conference on Information Processing in Sensor Networks (IPSN)*. Seattle, WA: ACM, pp. 1–12.

- Liu, Y. et al. (2020) 'Cross-Lingual Transfer via Multi-Task Learning with Multilingual Text Encoders', in *Proceedings of the 2020 Conference on Empirical Methods in Natural Language Processing (EMNLP)*. Stroudsburg, PA: ACL, pp. 7049–7060.

- Lwakatare, L.E. et al. (2020) 'DevOps and MLOps in Practice: A Case Study on Software Development for Machine Learning', in *International Conference on Product-Focused Software Process Improvement (PROFES)*. Cham: Springer, pp. 422–437.

- Newman, S. (2015) *Building Microservices*. 1st edn. Sebastopol, CA: O'Reilly Media.

- Sanh, V. et al. (2020) 'DistilBERT, a Distilled Version of BERT: Smaller, Faster, Cheaper and Lighter', in *Proceedings of the 5th Workshop on Energy Efficient Machine Learning and Cognitive Computing (NeurIPS)*. Vancouver, BC: NeurIPS.

- Shoeybi, M. et al. (2019) 'Megatron-LM: Training Multi-Billion Parameter Language Models Using Model Parallelism', *arXiv preprint* arXiv:1909.08053.

- Tang, L. et al. (2017) 'IBM's Hybrid Cloud Data Warehouse Architecture for Online Hosted Analytics Services', *Proceedings of the VLDB Endowment*, 10(12), pp. 1858–1869.

- Tang, Z. et al. (2020) 'Effective Evaluation and Testing of Deep Learning Pipelines', in *Proceedings of the 28th ACM Joint Meeting on European Software Engineering Conference and Symposium on the Foundations of Software Engineering (ESEC/FSE)*. New York: ACM, pp. 788–799.

- Voita, E. et al. (2019) 'Analyzing Multi-Head Self-Attention: Specialized Heads Do the Heavy Lifting, the Rest Can Be Pruned', in *Proceedings of the 57th Annual Meeting of the Association for Computational Linguistics (ACL)*. Stroudsburg, PA: ACL, pp. 5797–5808.

- Wang, Z. et al. (2019) 'Pushing the Limits of Mobile GPUs with Multi-Application Concurrency', in *Proceedings of the 2019 USENIX Annual Technical Conference (USENIX ATC)*. Renton, WA: USENIX, pp. 351–364.

- Wu, Y. et al. (2016) 'Google's Neural Machine Translation System: Bridging the Gap between Human and Machine Translation', *arXiv preprint* arXiv:1609.08144.

- Zaharia, M. et al. (2016) 'Apache Spark: A Unified Engine for Big Data Processing', *Communications of the ACM*, 59(11), pp. 56–65.

- Zaharia, M. et al. (2018) 'Accelerating the Machine Learning Lifecycle with MLflow', *Data-Driven Intelligence Workshop at NeurIPS*. Montréal, Canada: NeurIPS.

- Zhai, X. et al. (2020) 'Scalable Image Pretraining on Weakly Supervised Data Pulls the Performance of Large Models Closer to GPT-3 Level', *arXiv preprint* arXiv:2010.01690.

- Zhao, H. et al. (2020) 'Serverless End-to-End Fine-Grained Resource Auto-Scaling for Microservices in Cloud Environment', *arXiv preprint* arXiv:2009.12998.

Chapter 12: The Road Ahead—Future Trends and Opportunities

12.1. Emerging Research & Directions

12.1.1. Multimodal Models (Text + Image + Audio)

Beyond **Text**

While early large language models (LLMs) mostly focused on text, the current wave of **multimodal** approaches integrates images, audio, or even video streams. These models learn unified representations that can understand and generate content across different data types. Notable examples include CLIP for text-image alignment (Radford et al., 2021) and generative image models (Ramesh et al., 2021).

1. **Text + Image**: E.g., describing images or generating images from text prompts ($\text{Image} \sim \text{Model}(\text{prompt})$).

2. **Text + Audio**: Speech recognition or text-to-speech tasks integrated with large language models for richer context.

3. **Video**: Summarizing events in video frames or generating short clips from textual outlines.

Challenges

- **Data Alignment**: Large labeled corpora that pair text with images or audio remain limited.

- **Architecture Complexity**: Additional modules for vision or audio processing.

- **Compute Intensiveness**: Even bigger models and more training overhead.

Promises

These models can handle tasks like advanced question answering on images, describing scenes to visually impaired users, or real-time audiovisual translations. As computing hardware improves and datasets expand, truly multimodal LLMs may become standard in domains like robotics, AR/VR, and human-computer interaction.

Key **Insight**

Multimodal LLMs broaden the scope beyond text, fueling breakthroughs in image captioning, video summarization, or cross-sensory experiences. Ongoing research aims for truly **unified** architectures that parse and generate diverse data seamlessly.

12.1.2. Continual & Lifelong Learning

Static **vs.** **Dynamic** **World**

Classical LLMs train once on large corpora, then remain fixed. But real-world knowledge evolves—new events, scientific discoveries, or slang appear daily. **Continual**

learning addresses this by updating models without forgetting previously learned tasks (Parisi et al., 2019).

Catastrophic   **Forgetting**

A naive approach—just retrain on new data—often overwrites old knowledge:

$$\theta_{new} = \theta_{old} - \eta \nabla_\theta \mathcal{L}(\text{new data}).$$

If the new data is domain-specific, older general knowledge can degrade. Solutions involve:

- **Regularization**: Penalizing deviations from old parameters.

- **Memory Replay**: Keep samples of old data for joint training.

- **Module Expansion**: Adding new layers or "adapters" for fresh tasks.

Applications

- **News Summarizers**: Must stay up to date with daily events.

- **Customer Support**: Real-time updates to handle new products or policies.

- **Educational Tools**: Integrate newly published research findings or curricula changes.

Key   **Insight**

Continual learning lets models adapt to **ever-changing** knowledge while preserving prior abilities. Overcoming catastrophic forgetting is a prime frontier, crucial for robust long-term AI.

12.1.3. Federated & Collaborative Training

Protecting   **User**   **Data**

When training on sensitive user text (health data, private messages), conventional centralization is problematic. **Federated learning** (FL) keeps data on user devices or private servers, sharing only model updates (Konečný et al., 2016). This approach extends to large LMs if handled carefully:

1. **Local Fine-Tuning**: Each client updates a portion of the model.

2. **Global Aggregation**: A central server merges updates.

3. **Repeat**: The aggregated model is distributed back to clients.

Challenges

- **Communication Overhead**: Exchanging large parameter sets among many devices.

- **Device Heterogeneity**: Different hardware, offline times, or partial updates.

- **Privacy & Security**: Even gradient updates can leak information if not processed with differential privacy (Abadi et al., 2016).

Collaborative **Learning**

Similar paradigms exist for multi-institution data pooling (e.g., multiple hospitals training a medical LM without sharing patient records). By adopting distributed protocols, participants jointly build robust models while respecting local data regulations or competition barriers.

Key **Insight**

Federated and collaborative training expand advanced LMs to sensitive or distributed contexts. Techniques addressing communication cost, partial updates, and privacy are essential to make FL viable for large-scale language modeling.

12.1.4. Quantum AI Prospects

Quantum **Computing** **Intersection**

Quantum AI explores how quantum computers might accelerate or transform machine learning. While still experimental, potential speedups in matrix multiplications or optimization methods could reduce the massive cost of training LLMs (Biamonte et al., 2017).

$$U\_"\{quantum\}(|\psi\rangle) \ = \ \textstyle\sum\_\{i\} \alpha\_i \, |i\rangle,$$

(representing superpositions of states, presumably enabling parallel computations.)

Hybrid **Quantum-Classical** **Approaches**

One notion is a classical front-end controlling parameter updates while a quantum backend handles high-dimensional transformations. However, existing quantum hardware remains limited in qubit counts and error correction. Scalable quantum ML might be years away, though research is ongoing (Rebentrost et al., 2018).

Speculative Implications

- **Exponential Representations**: Potentially encode large parameter spaces more compactly.

- **Quantum Feature Maps**: Enhanced capacity for capturing global patterns, though still theoretical.

- **Hype vs. Reality**: Practical large-scale quantum LMs remain elusive; we must track hardware and algorithmic breakthroughs carefully.

Key **Insight**

While quantum computing in ML is currently exploratory, it could eventually revolutionize large-model training if quantum hardware matures. For now, quantum-enhanced LMs remain a promising but **long-term**research avenue.

12.2. Specialized Domains

12.2.1. Legal Tech & Contract Analysis

Rising **Need**

Law firms and corporate legal departments handle contracts, compliance documents, and case law. LLMs can extract key clauses, flag risky terms, or even suggest contract revisions automatically (Chalkidis et al., 2021).

Domain **Adaptation**

Fine-tune or further pre-train on legal corpora (cases, regulations). Special tokenization may handle legal references ($\text{Article VI, Clause (2)(b)}$) or archaic terms. Document parsing is crucial—splitting large PDFs or scanned images into structured text.

Benefits

- **Time Savings**: Routine contract reviews become partially automated.

- **Risk Reduction**: Consistent detection of missing or ambiguous clauses.

- **Scalability**: Large volumes of M&A or vendor contracts, quickly summarized or flagged for legal anomalies.

Limitations

- **Nuance**: Legal language is complex, context-laden. Mistakes can have serious financial or legal implications.

- **Regulation**: Some jurisdictions require licensed attorneys to finalize agreements. AI-based suggestions must disclaim they are not legal advice.

- **Confidentiality**: Client data and privileged communications must remain secure, often requiring on-premise deployments.

Key **Insight**

Legal tech harnessing LMs can expedite contract analysis, compliance checks, and case law research. However, the domain's complexity, confidentiality needs, and liability concerns necessitate rigorous oversight and disclaimers.

12.2.2. Education: Intelligent Tutoring Systems

Personalized **Learning**

Intelligent tutoring systems adapt to individual student progress, knowledge gaps, and preferences. LLMs can generate hints, explain concepts in simpler terms, or produce custom practice questions (Piech et al., 2015).

Dialog-Based **Tutors**

A GPT-like chatbot simulates a teacher's role, answering queries or guiding problem-solving:

- **Prompt**: Student question ("I don't understand how to factor polynomials.")

- **Response**: Model-generated explanation or step-by-step approach.

- **Adaptive Assessment**: Suggest next tasks if the student shows mastery or confusion.

Challenges

- **Ensuring Accuracy**: Hallucinated solutions or incorrect explanations can mislead students.

- **Pedagogical Strategies**: The model lacks inherent teaching strategies, requiring fine-tuning on educational corpora or human-labeled "best practice" dialogues.

- **Cheating Concerns**: Overly powerful systems might provide direct answers, undermining learning objectives.

Key **Insight**

LLM-based tutoring can scale personalized education globally. Yet the system must balance detailed help with safeguarding authentic student learning, plus verifying correctness for high-stakes educational content.

12.2.3. Creative Industries: Art, Music & Design

Generative **Arts**

Text-based models can collaborate with visual generative models. For instance:

- **AI Storyboards**: GPT develops a narrative structure, feeding a visual model for concept art.

- **Music Lyrics**: Models propose lyrics or musical themes, possibly integrated into audio generation pipelines (Dhariwal and Nichol, 2021).

- **Fashion & Product Design**: Brainstorming references for new collections or functional prototypes.

Human-AI **Co-Creation**

Artists or designers use LLMs as brainstorming partners. An "ideation prompt" might yield 10 variants of a storyline or concept pitch. The user picks promising ones to refine manually. Tools like ChatGPT or custom fine-tuned creativity models facilitate synergy rather than full automation (Clark et al., 2018).

Content   Licensing   &   Ownership

Creating IP from AI-based outputs triggers questions of authorship. Some jurisdictions do not grant copyright to purely machine-generated works. Artists or studios might credit AI as an aide but claim final creative rights.

Key   Insight

LMs empower creative workflows with rapid idea generation, from storylines to music lyrics. Artists remain central, curating, refining, or integrating these suggestions into cohesive, human-driven expressions.

12.2.4. Robotics & Human-Robot Interaction

Robust   Natural   Language   Interfaces

Robots—whether domestic assistants or factory arms—can interpret voice or text commands. LLM-based language understanding can facilitate more intuitive instructions:

- **"Bring me a glass of water from the kitchen."**

- **"Close the top drawer of the cabinet."**

Multi-Step   Reasoning

Robots often need procedural instructions. Advanced LLMs can parse user requests and break them down into discrete actions (Tellex et al., 2011). Combining this with sensor data leads to context-aware planning:

$$\text{Plan} = \arg\max_{\text{action seq}} P(\text{actions} \mid \text{goal, environment}).$$

Challenges

- **Physical World**: Noisy sensor inputs, dynamic obstacles. LLMs alone are insufficient; must integrate with classical robotics or reinforcement learning.

- **Safety & Reliability**: Misinterpretation of a user command might risk accidents or damage.

- **Ethical Concerns**: Overly human-like interactions could raise user expectations or privacy issues.

Key   Insight

LLMs unify high-level command interpretation in robotics, bridging natural language instructions with planning. However, robust real-world integration demands synergy with specialized sensor fusion, control algorithms, and safety checks.

12.3. Entrepreneurship and Careers

12.3.1. Building AI Startups

Opportunity   **Landscape**

The surge in LLM capabilities has opened countless niches—vertical chatbots, domain-specific summarizers, data analytics, creative content generation. Startups can differentiate by focusing on specialized data or unique fine-tuning approaches. Potential areas:

- **Healthcare**: Automated coding or clinical note analysis.
- **Legal**: Contract or case law solutions.
- **Finance**: Sentiment-based stock insights, compliance auditing.
- **Education**: Personalized tutoring or content creation.

Key Steps

1. **MVP**: Demonstrate domain viability with minimal training overhead, possibly using open-source or cloud LLM APIs.
2. **Data Partnerships**: Acquire or build specialized corpora.
3. **Scalability**: Plan for multi-GPU or cloud-based expansions as user base grows.
4. **Ethics & Compliance**: Address privacy laws (GDPR), model bias, disclaimers.

Key   **Insight**

Startups that innovate around **domain specialization**, data curation, or user-centric design can carve valuable niches. LLMs drastically reduce time to build advanced NLP features, but require thoughtful scaling and compliance strategies.

12.3.2. Freelancing & Consulting in NLP

Freelance   **Demand**

Small and mid-sized companies often lack in-house AI teams. They hire **freelance NLP experts** to build or deploy chatbots, text analyzers, or summarization pipelines. Platforms like Upwork or Toptal see growing demand for LLM-savvy developers.

Consulting   **Roles**

Established consulting firms also expand AI/NLP divisions. Consultants handle:

- **Discovery**: Assessing business use cases, feasibility.
- **Prototyping**: Quick PoCs or minimal-labeled data solutions.
- **Integration**: MLOps best practices, devops pipelines, and domain adaptation.

$$\text{Rate}_{\text{consultant}}(\text{hr}) \sim \text{expertise, domain skill.}$$

Skills for Success

- **Technical Mastery**: Familiarity with frameworks (PyTorch, Hugging Face, TensorFlow).

- **Domain Knowledge**: E.g., finance, legal, or healthcare for specialized tasks.

- **Communication & Client Management**: Translating client goals into feasible AI solutions, setting realistic expectations.

Key   **Insight**

Freelancing and consulting for LLM-based solutions offer flexible, high-value career paths. A strong portfolio showcasing domain insights, robust model deployment, and effective communication stands out.

12.3.3. Upskilling Pathways & Certifications

Academic   **Programs**

Universities rapidly update curricula, adding courses in deep learning, NLP, or specialized LLM labs. Some even offer dedicated Master's tracks in AI ethics or MLOps, bridging technology with policy and devops (Stanford, 2022).

Online   **Platforms**

Coursera, edX, Udacity, and others host advanced NLP or LLM courses. These can be self-paced, concluding with capstone projects. For instance:

- **Deep NLP**: Transformers, attention, sequence-to-sequence tasks.

- **Responsible AI**: Bias detection, fairness metrics, differential privacy.

Certification   **Models**

Leading cloud vendors (AWS, Azure, GCP) provide official certifications for ML pipelines, MLOps, or domain-specific AI solutions. Earning these demonstrates practical deployment skills for prospective employers.

Continuous   **Learning**

The LLM field evolves so fast that skill sets must remain agile. Reading recent papers, joining open-source communities, or attending conferences (ACL, NeurIPS) fosters ongoing growth (Pineau et al., 2020).

Key   **Insight**

Formal and informal **learning pathways** keep professionals current in LLM best practices. Continuous education across data engineering, domain adaptation, and ethical guidelines is key to thriving in AI careers.

12.3.4. The Role of Community & Open Source

Collective **Progress**

Communities like **Hugging Face Transformers, EleutherAI**, or **OpenMined** accelerate LLM innovation by sharing code, pretrained models, and best practices (Black et al., 2022). Collective problem-solving outpaces isolated efforts.

Contribution Avenues

- **Code Contributions**: Improving libraries or creating new modules for specialized tasks.

- **Documentation & Tutorials**: Guiding newcomers on usage patterns.

- **Discussion Forums**: Slack, Discord, or GitHub Issues for real-time Q&A or brainstorming.

Career **Benefits**

Participation signals skill and fosters networking. Many developers land full-time roles or consulting gigs after recognized open-source contributions or community leadership. These collaborative spaces also shape ethical standards, e.g., responsible dataset curation (Bender and Friedman, 2018).

Long-Term **Vision**

As LLMs become integral to more industries, open-source communities will keep democratizing access, bridging knowledge gaps between corporate labs and smaller players, ensuring continued momentum in research, fairness, and domain expansions.

Key **Insight**

Vibrant open-source and community ecosystems form the **backbone** of LLM innovation. By joining or contributing, professionals gain expertise, shape ethical norms, and help push the field forward.

12.4. Call to Action

12.4.1. Learning Continuously: Staying Current

Rapid **Progress**

New model releases, novel architectures (like Transformer variants), and better training methods appear monthly. Staying up to date requires:

- **Research Paper Tracking**: ArXiv, Google Scholar, or aggregator sites like Papers With Code.

- **Conferences & Workshops**: ACL, EMNLP, NeurIPS, or specialized gatherings (like EACL, ICML).

- **Community Mentorship**: Actively participating in open forums or local AI meetups fosters peer learning (Wolf et al., 2020).

$$\Delta\text{knowledge} \approx \text{reading} + \text{practice} - \text{obsolescence rate.}$$

Focus on Fundamentals

While reading state-of-the-art papers is helpful, a solid grasp of ML basics—probability, linear algebra, optimization—underpins real mastery (Goodfellow, Bengio and Courville, 2016). Build on these fundamentals to interpret new techniques effectively.

Key Insight

The LLM domain evolves swiftly. A **lifelong learner** mindset—combining foundational theory with real-time research updates—ensures you remain a valuable AI professional or researcher.

12.4.2. Ethical Innovators: Fostering Trust in AI

Responsibility in Deployment

Given LLMs' power to influence opinions or handle sensitive info, practitioners bear responsibility. Ethical innovators proactively address:

- **Bias & Fairness**: Regular audits, dataset checks (Section 10.1).

- **Privacy**: Minimizing personal data usage, employing anonymization.

- **Transparency**: Clear disclaimers about limitations and potential content errors.

Public Engagement

AI developers can educate policymakers, media, or the general public about capabilities vs. hype, bridging misunderstandings. Engaging with interdisciplinary stakeholders— ethicists, social scientists—helps align technology with societal values (Floridi, 2019).

Corporate & Government Ethics Boards

In large orgs, dedicated ethics committees can review new deployments. Government agencies consult AI experts to frame regulations. By participating, professionals help shape laws that balance innovation with public welfare (European Commission, 2021).

Key Insight

Trust in AI arises when practitioners and organizations transparently address biases, privacy, and potential misuses. Actively contributing to ethical frameworks fosters a climate of responsible innovation.

12.4.3. Engaging with Policy & Public Understanding

Bridging Tech and Policy

Complex technical details—like model interpretability, adversarial vulnerabilities, or bias metrics—can confuse policymakers. AI experts can translate these into accessible insights, shaping **evidence-based** regulations (Tutt, 2017).

Forums & Panels

Professional associations (e.g., ACM, IEEE) and public conferences often invite ML experts to discuss upcoming legislation or guidelines. Through these channels, practitioners influence or refine policy proposals before they become law (Jobin, Ienca and Vayena, 2019).

Public Outreach

Educational outreach, from blog posts to local workshops, fosters an informed public. Clarifying:

1. **Capabilities**: LLM strengths, typical tasks.

2. **Limits**: Hallucinations, biases, domain mismatches.

3. **Implications**: Personal data usage, misinformation risk.

Benefits

- **Informed Citizens**: People make better decisions about adopting or trusting AI tools.

- **Collaborative Solutions**: Shared understanding paves the way for more balanced policies or guidelines.

- **Reduced Polarization**: Substantive public discourse combats hyperbole or fear-driven narratives around AI.

Key Insight

Effective engagement with policymakers and the public is crucial for shaping **balanced** AI governance. By fostering nuanced understanding, AI experts help society harness LLM benefits while mitigating potential harms.

12.4.4. Looking Forward: The Next AI Frontier

Exponential or Steady Growth?

Debates persist about AI's trajectory—whether we'll see a continuous scaling of LLMs or a plateau soon. Some foresee quantum leaps, while others predict incremental refinement. Ultimately, research will keep exploring new paradigms, from memory-augmented models to unsupervised multi-domain techniques (Section 12.1).

Interdisciplinary Convergence

Future AI might blend insights from neuroscience, cognitive science, and symbolic reasoning, forging **hybrid** approaches that unify data-driven learning with structured knowledge bases or common-sense logic (Marcus and Davis, 2019).

Ethical   **Co-Creation**

As technology permeates more daily tasks, collaborative design—engineers working alongside ethicists, domain experts, and communities—can ensure AI systems reflect shared values, respect cultural norms, and remain accessible globally (Bender et al., 2021).

A   **Sustainable**   **Vision**

With LLM training consuming huge energy, green AI methods gain attention (Strubell, Ganesh and McCallum, 2019). Designing **energy-efficient** architectures, reusing pre-trained backbones, or adopting **distillation** for smaller specialized models might tame the ecological footprint while still unlocking AI's transformative potential.

Key   **Insight**

The future of AI depends on bridging disciplines, forging more **holistic** and **responsible** approaches to model design. Continued collaboration, innovation, and ethical reflection will shape how LLMs evolve—and how they reshape our world.

References (Harvard Style)

- Abadi, M. et al. (2016) 'Deep Learning with Differential Privacy', in *Proceedings of the 2016 ACM SIGSAC Conference on Computer and Communications Security (CCS)*. New York: ACM, pp. 308–318.

- Bender, E.M. et al. (2021) 'On the Dangers of Stochastic Parrots: Can Language Models Be Too Big?', in *Proceedings of the 2021 ACM Conference on Fairness, Accountability, and Transparency (FAccT '21)*. New York: ACM, pp. 610–623.

- Biamonte, J. et al. (2017) 'Quantum Machine Learning', *Nature*, 549(7671), pp. 195–202.

- Black, S. et al. (2022) 'GPT-NeoX-20B: An Open-Source Autoregressive Language Model', *arXiv preprint* arXiv:2204.06745.

- Chalkidis, I. et al. (2021) 'Paragraph-Level Legal Summarization with BART-Large', in *Proceedings of the 2021 Conference on Empirical Methods in Natural Language Processing (EMNLP)*. Stroudsburg, PA: ACL, pp. 8627–8636.

- Clark, E. et al. (2018) 'Creative Writing with a Machine in the Loop: Case Studies on Slogans and Stories', in *Proceedings of the 23rd International Conference on Intelligent User Interfaces (IUI)*. New York: ACM, pp. 329–340.

- Dhariwal, P. and Nichol, A. (2021) 'Diffusion Models Beat GANs on Image Synthesis', *arXiv preprint* arXiv:2105.05233.

- European Commission (2021) *Proposal for a Regulation Laying Down Harmonised Rules on Artificial Intelligence (Artificial Intelligence Act)*. Available at: https://digital-strategy.ec.europa.eu (Accessed: 10 February 2025).

- Floridi, L. (2019) 'Translating Principles into Practices of Digital Ethics: Contents, Contexts and Constraints', *Philosophy & Technology*, 32(4), pp. 795–823.

- Goodfellow, I., Bengio, Y. and Courville, A. (2016) *Deep Learning*. Cambridge, MA: MIT Press.

- Konečný, J. et al. (2016) 'Federated Learning: Strategies for Improving Communication Efficiency', *arXiv preprint* arXiv:1610.05492.

- Marcus, G. and Davis, E. (2019) *Rebooting AI: Building Artificial Intelligence We Can Trust*. New York: Pantheon Books.

- McMahan, B. and Ramage, D. (2017) 'Federated Learning: Collaborative Machine Learning without Centralized Training Data', *Google AI Blog*. Available at: https://ai.googleblog.com/2017/04/federated-learning-collaborative.html (Accessed: 10 February 2025).

- Parisi, G. et al. (2019) 'Continual Lifelong Learning with Neural Networks: A Review', *Neural Networks*, 113, pp. 54–71.

- Piech, C. et al. (2015) 'Deep Knowledge Tracing', in *Proceedings of the 28th International Conference on Neural Information Processing Systems (NeurIPS)*. Red Hook, NY: Curran Associates, pp. 505–513.

- Pineau, J. et al. (2020) 'Improving Reproducibility in Machine Learning Research', *Journal of Machine Learning Research*, 21(219), pp. 1–20.

- Radford, A. et al. (2021) 'Learning Transferable Visual Models from Natural Language Supervision', in *Proceedings of the 38th International Conference on Machine Learning (ICML)*. PMLR, pp. 8748–8763.

- Ramesh, A. et al. (2021) 'Zero-Shot Text-to-Image Generation', in *Proceedings of the 38th International Conference on Machine Learning (ICML)*. PMLR, pp. 8821–8831.

- Rebentrost, P. et al. (2018) 'Quantum Gradient Descent and Newton's Method for Constrained Polynomial Optimization', *Quantum Information & Computation*, 18(7–8), pp. 607–629.

- Sennrich, R., Haddow, B. and Birch, A. (2016) 'Neural Machine Translation of Rare Words with Subword Units', in *Proceedings of the 54th Annual Meeting of the Association for Computational Linguistics (ACL)*. Stroudsburg, PA: ACL, pp. 1715–1725.

- Stanford (2022) 'The Stanford Center for Research on Foundation Models', *Stanford CRFM*. Available at: https://crfm.stanford.edu/ (Accessed: 10 February 2025).

- Strubell, E., Ganesh, A. and McCallum, A. (2019) 'Energy and Policy Considerations for Deep Learning in NLP', in *Proceedings of the 57th Annual Meeting of the Association for Computational Linguistics (ACL)*. Florence, Italy: ACL, pp. 3645–3650.

- Tellex, S. et al. (2011) 'Understanding Natural Language Commands for Robotic Navigation and Mobile Manipulation', in *Proceedings of the 25th AAAI Conference on Artificial Intelligence*. Palo Alto, CA: AAAI Press, pp. 1–7.

- Tutt, A. (2017) 'An FDA for Algorithms', *Administrative Law Review*, 69(1), pp. 83–123.

- Wolf, T. et al. (2020) 'Transformers: State-of-the-Art Natural Language Processing', in *Proceedings of the 2020 Conference on Empirical Methods in Natural Language Processing: System Demonstrations*. Stroudsburg, PA: ACL, pp. 38–45.

Conclusion: A Journey Toward Intelligent Collaboration

From the earliest theories of computing and language to today's **large language models** capable of producing human-like text, our field has undergone a remarkable evolution. Each **chapter** in this book has charted a piece of that transformation—traversing historical roots, the mechanics of neural networks, the rise of transformers, domain-specific applications, and ethical implications. In studying these topics, we've seen not just technological advances but also the profound ways AI can shape (and be shaped by) human society.

Unprecedented Capabilities, Unfinished Work

We stand at a tipping point: language models achieve near-human performance on tasks once deemed too subtle—like creative writing, legal document analysis, or domain-based question answering. Yet challenges remain. Real-world data is messy and biased; models sometimes hallucinate or lack common-sense reasoning. Robust **model evaluation**, thorough **bias mitigation**, and continuous user feedback loops help us address these shortcomings. Building more **explainable, fair**, and **privacy-preserving** systems is a collective mission that extends beyond raw technical know-how.

Convergence of Disciplines

The next frontier likely involves **multimodal** or **embodied** intelligence, where text-based LMs integrate with vision, audio, or robotics. This will demand cross-domain expertise: data scientists collaborating with designers, linguists, ethicists, and domain experts. Similarly, **federated** or **collaborative learning** approaches will expand LLM reach into heavily regulated or distributed environments—empowering more inclusive, privacy-aware AI ecosystems.

A Call for Responsible Progress

In harnessing LMs' potential, **responsibility** stands paramount. Equitable data representation, transparent deployment, and mindful regulatory compliance ensure that we elevate human capacities rather than displacing them. By driving open discussions between AI developers, policymakers, and diverse stakeholders, we foster a balanced environment that rewards innovation without neglecting social well-being or environmental impact.

A Shared Future

The trajectory of large language models and broader AI will be shaped by our collective choices—where we invest in research, how we govern data, how we address ethical dilemmas, and how we open opportunities for a wider audience. If we do this right, LMs can become tools for bridging knowledge gaps, advancing healthcare, democratizing education, and fueling artistic creativity—ultimately enriching our societies in ways we're only beginning to imagine.

As you move forward—whether as a developer building next-generation chatbots, a researcher exploring novel transformer architectures, a policy advocate seeking fair governance, or a student just delving into these concepts—remember that **AI is a shared journey**. We each have a part in guiding large language models and other AI technologies toward outcomes that empower humanity. Let this book serve as one stepping stone in your ongoing pursuit: a foundation of knowledge, a springboard for new ideas, and an invitation to shape the future of intelligence, together.

References (Harvard Style)

- Bolukbasi, T. et al. (2016) 'Man is to Computer Programmer as Woman is to Homemaker? Debiasing Word Embeddings', in *Advances in Neural Information Processing Systems* (NeurIPS). Red Hook, NY: Curran Associates, pp. 4349–4357.

- Goodfellow, I., Bengio, Y. and Courville, A. (2016) *Deep Learning*. Cambridge, MA: MIT Press.

- Parisi, G. et al. (2019) 'Continual Lifelong Learning with Neural Networks: A Review', *Neural Networks*, 113, pp. 54–71.

- Radford, A. et al. (2021) 'Learning Transferable Visual Models from Natural Language Supervision', in *Proceedings of the 38th International Conference on Machine Learning (ICML)*. PMLR, pp. 8748–8763.

- Ramesh, A. et al. (2021) 'Zero-Shot Text-to-Image Generation', in *International Conference on Machine Learning (ICML)*. PMLR, pp. 8821–8831.

- Strubell, E., Ganesh, A. and McCallum, A. (2019) 'Energy and Policy Considerations for Deep Learning in NLP', in *Proceedings of the 57th Annual Meeting of the Association for Computational Linguistics (ACL)*. Florence, Italy: ACL, pp. 3645–3650.

- Wolf, T. et al. (2020) 'Transformers: State-of-the-Art Natural Language Processing', in *Proceedings of the 2020 Conference on Empirical Methods in Natural Language Processing: System Demonstrations*. Stroudsburg, PA: ACL, pp. 38–45.